**DO NOT REMOVE
CARDS FROM POCKET**

American Profiles

American Profiles

Somebodies and Nobodies
Who Matter

Walt Harrington

University of Missouri Press
Columbia and London

Copyright © 1985, 1986, 1987, 1988, 1989, 1990, 1992 by
The Washington Post Company
University of Missouri Press, Columbia, Missouri 65201
Printed and bound in the United States of America
All rights reserved
5   4   3   2   1   96   95   94   93   92

Library of Congress Cataloging-in-Publication Data

Harrington, Walt, 1950–
    American profiles : somebodies and nobodies who
matter / Walt Harrington.
        p.   cm.
    A collection of articles which previously appeared in the
Washington Post magazine.
    Includes bibliographical references.
    ISBN 0–8262–0839–8 (alk. paper)
    1. Biography—20th century. 2. United States—Biography.
I. Title.
CT220.H34   1992
920.073—dc20
[B]   91–42712
                                                                CIP

∞™ This paper meets the requirements of the
American National Standard for Permanence of Paper
for Printed Library Materials, Z39.48, 1984.

Designer: Rhonda Miller
Typesetter: Connell-Zeko Type & Graphics
Printer and binder: Thomson-Shore, Inc.
Typefaces: Melliza and Coronet

To my parents

Contents

viii   Contents

$\mathcal{A}$cknowledgments

$\mathcal{A}$ lot of people have contributed to the profiles in this book, but it is the institution of the *Washington Post* to which I am most indebted. From publisher Donald Graham, Executive Editor Leonard Downie, and recently retired Executive Editor Ben Bradlee, I've received much-appreciated encouragement and support. From top to bottom, the *Post* is so thick with talented people it has made me look good. In my years at the *Post Magazine*, I've had a series of chief editors who have always improved my work— Steve Petranek, Jay Lovinger, and Bob Thompson. My *Post Magazine* assignment editor for most of the articles in this book was John Cotter. He has become my indispensable critic, always forcing me to say exactly what I thought I had already said. The *Post*'s News Research Center also deserves credit for the many background articles and books its staff, especially Kim Klein, has supplied. Thanks also to the center's Jennifer Belton and Sandy Davis, who helped pull these profiles together. Former *Post* researcher Lynda Edwards also contributed helpful research to the Carl Bernstein and Lynda Robb profiles. I'd also like to thank the *Post* photo department for its help, as well as Bill Dickinson of the *Post* Writers Group, *Post* lawyer Mary Ann Werner, and *Post Magazine* photo editor Deborah Needleman for their help in putting this book together.

Over the years, my colleagues and friends Edmund Lambeth, Pete Earley, Frank Whelan, and Mike Sager have encouraged and criticized me in just the right mix. I especially want to thank my friend and colleague Steve Weinberg, the biographer of Armand Hammer, for hounding me into doing this collection. Steve also contributed valuable research to the Jack Anderson profile. My book editors, Beverly Jarrett and Jane Lago, made doing the project a pleasure. Thanks also to my agent, Amanda Urban.

Finally, a special thank you to my wife, Keran, for marrying a guy with so strange a job and to my kids, Matthew and Kyle, for just being around. And thanks to the people who let me write about them.

American Profiles

INTRODUCTION
On Intimate Journalism

$\mathcal{A}$ wise Catholic priest once told me that it is only at the end of our lives, when we are looking back, that we can see the hand of providence at work. I'm not a religious man, but I've always liked that idea, because even stripped of religion, it's a beautiful and simple notion: The "meaning" we see in the facts of our lives, rather thán the facts themselves, creates our personal life stories. Mark Twain put it this way: "What a wee little part of a person's life are his acts and words! His real life is led in his head, and is known to none but himself. All day long, and every day, the mill of his brain is grinding, and his thoughts, not those other things, are his history."

While working on the *Washington Post Magazine* profiles collected in this book, I've tried to keep the advice of both the wise priest and Mark Twain in mind. My goal: to understand people as they understand themselves. One of my profile subjects, Bucky Jenkins, a man whose son had committed suicide, described better than I ever could what I hope to discover: "Your thoughts when you say your prayers in a quiet room." Yes, exactly.

Naturally, a skeptic might say this is only my fancy way of looking back and finding meaning in what I do—a high-minded rationale for a man whose job it is to dig around in other people's lives and then announce his findings, good or bad, to the world. There's certainly some truth in that, because before I had any high-minded ideas about doing profiles, I still loved writing them, even as a young journalist when my editors expected me to spend my time covering fires and city council meetings. Long before that, as a boy, I suppose I showed an aptitude for profile writing, because my mother often complained that I was the nosiest kid she'd ever known. Later, as a young man, I drove my wife nuts with my irritating habit of eavesdropping on the conversations of strangers at nearby restaurant tables.

I plead guilty: For as long as I can remember, people and the remarkable intricacies of their lives have fascinated me. I could sit and listen to a high-school buddy talk about his mother or father for hours. I can even recall taking my first airplane ride as a teenager,

1

looking down at the thousands and thousands of houses that made up my hometown of Chicago and thinking not about the majesty or the frightfulness of flight. No, I was awestruck at the sudden realization that each of those houses contained different people leading different lives. I know it's weird, but it's true.

Flash ahead twenty-five years and I am a writer of profiles. Those presented in *American Profiles* range from pieces about famous people—George Bush, Jesse Jackson, Lynda Bird Johnson Robb, Carl Bernstein, Jerry Falwell, Jack Anderson, and Kelly McGillis—to portraits of decidedly unfamous folks—a retarded man, a fundamentalist Baptist family, a young father whose infant son was kidnapped, the founder of the Church of Satan, a teenage genius, a husband and wife whose son committed suicide, an aspiring Washington dealmaker, and my own father.

What I hope these stories share is a tone of inquiry that doesn't poke gratuitous fun at people, not even at the satanic high priest. Someone once asked me what kind of stories I enjoy doing most, and without much thought, I answered, "Those about how people live and what they value." Over the years, I've come to like that answer, because it implies that to understand people we must know something about how they live their everyday lives—with their spouses and children, friends and enemies—as well as what is going on inside their heads, what the events and choices of their lives have meant to them. My goal, however impossible to achieve, is to look at people from the inside out.

This is not everyone's journalism. If there's one criticism I've heard repeatedly from colleagues over the years it is that I'm not "hard" enough on my subjects, that I am too "soft." The implications of these words are what they seem: In journalism, to be "soft," not "hard," is to be unmanly. In that vein, one critic wrote that my profile of George Bush was "lick-spittle toadying." An editor once suggested that I analyze my need to always find something good to say about everybody. Truth is, I'm forever baffled by such criticisms, because my aim is to be tough and soft at once. I think of novelist Nelson Algren's words: "I try to write accurately from the poise of mind which lets us see that things are exactly what they seem."

My models for what I do come as much from the fields of documentary photography and writing and from the case studies of the social sciences as they do from journalism. My goal is not to criticize, but to understand. I guess it's in my blood, because I often think of two of my father's favorite truisms from my boyhood: "There are two sides to every story—then there are two sides to each of those stories." And, "Everything's beautiful if you just look at it right." Anyway, as an antidote to the "hard" versus "soft" criticism, I keep the advice of Robert Penn Warren on my desk: "As Louis Armstrong is reported to have said, 'There's some folks that if they don't know, you can't tell 'em.'"

Naturally, I bring a bag of personal assumptions to each story. First, I assume there is humanity in everybody and that everyone is a blend of better and worse. Next, I assume that nothing that has been written about my subject is necessarily correct. Then I try to suspend my biases, without agonizing over the philosophical debate about whether that's possible. In a commonsense way, it is possible. When I began to research my George Bush profile, for instance, I had little respect for the man. Being shaped by my own working-class childhood, I saw the upper-class-bred Bush as a "coaster"—someone riding on the advantages of birth. But the details of Bush's life invaded my prejudices. Let me tell you, if I had been right, I would have taken glee in saying so. But I was not right, and like the scientist who must be ready to abandon a hypothesis when the lab experiments go bust, I had to be ready to do the same.

Struggling to suspend my preconceptions was just as important when writing about, say, Gary Poe, the mentally retarded man, or the family of fundamentalist Baptists, the Websters. It was a surprise for me to find that Gary, although slow in his mind, was very smart about the way people constantly dehumanized him. It was equally eye-opening to find that the fundamentalist Websters were frightened by the same changes in American society that are feared by liberal and secular critics. The Websters simply filtered those fears through the lens of their faith.

I try to approach each subject, whether a vice president or a retarded man, from the same cast of mind—the belief that each person, famous or obscure, is at once ordinary and extraordinary in his own ways. My job is to discover those ways. Although it marks me as a hopeless optimist, I also believe that most of us spend our lives yearning to do better, to be better people—better parents and children, better gardeners, golfers, congressmen, journalists, or garbagemen. In fact, I once knew a garbageman who held his city's title as the fastest trash "runner"—the man who jogs behind the moving garbage truck picking up, dumping, and replacing trash cans as he goes. For years, my acquaintance had successfully defended his title in head-to-head competition. But he was pushing thirty and the youngsters were crowding him, and he was training harder and harder to hold on. Like the champion trash runner, most of us struggle through life seeking small redemptions, which is what many of these profiles are about: people struggling fitfully to be better people. Nearly all of the people profiled here are also struggling in their own ways to find mastery over their lives, to feel they are *in control* in the face of the conflicting demands and expectations of parents, family, and society. Perhaps this will to individual improvement and empowerment is a distinctly American trait.

Always, I begin my research looking for continuities or rifts in each subject's life that might help clarify how he or she came to be the person he or she is. I look for the social context—how a subject's sex, race, age, religion, or social class might have shaped his or her life. I look for the individual context—how family and personal experiences might have shaped a subject. Yet I'm not one who believes that everything that came before explains everything about us now. If this were so we would know which abused child would grow up to be a child abuser. Too much magic or monstrosity occurs in passage. I don't believe we are stamped out of our social backgrounds and personal experiences like letters from the mechanical imprints of a typewriter's keys. I believe it is the interplay and struggle between being and transcending our social categories and personal experiences that makes us who we are. It is called character.

Little art and much craft went into the making of these profiles. Each took between one and three months to complete. All included many hours of conversation with the subjects. Most included days of tagging along as they did whatever they usually did. With George Bush, I went on the campaign trail and visited his boyhood home in Connecticut, weaseling a tour of it from the current owners. I walked the streets of the Texas oil towns where he made his fortune, and I visited his family estate in Kennebunkport, Maine. With the teenage genius Evan Sherbrooke, I went back to high school. With the nocturnal satanist Anton LaVey, I spent most of a week arriving at his San Francisco Victorian at 10:00 P.M. and talking all night in the eerie glow of his purple living room. With actress Kelly McGillis, I spent a hot August month traipsing to daily rehearsals and then back to Kelly's apartment, where she would analyze her day on stage. Most of these profiles also included numerous interviews with the subjects' family, friends, and enemies. For the George Bush and Carl Bernstein profiles, I did about eighty interviews each. Always there are also newspaper and magazine clippings, books, and documents to read.

Sometimes the work pays off in a visible way and an article has what we journalists like to call "impact." For instance, after he was elected president, George Bush invited me to his house one Saturday morning and told me that, although his wife was angered by my profile, it had profoundly affected his campaign for the presidency. The article had appeared in the middle of Bush's second vice presidency, during the height of the "Doonesbury" cartoon caricatures of him, at a time when there was actually talk that Bush might not run for president. That morning, Bush told me that my profile had redefined the direction of press coverage about him and, he believed, contributed to a series of newspaper and magazine profiles that were far more positive than those that had come before. Bush said, "I don't think you know how important your article was." Being a good liberal I didn't—and still don't—know how to take that. But I am certain that worrying about an article's impact during its doing can only get in the way of getting it right.

Another time, my article about how a young father named Rob Thate had reacted to the kidnapping of his baby son was read by a fireman who later that day noticed a white infant in the arms of a black woman near the scene of a fire. Suspicious, the fireman edged closer to the woman, who quickly ran away. The fireman reported the incident to the police, and Rob Thate's son was soon back at home. But these small glories are rare. Usually, pieces come and go without a ripple, which is why I'm lucky I enjoy doing the work. For instance, although it didn't change the world, my profile of Kelly McGillis is one of my favorites. I found the acting methods and personal intuition through which she created the stage character of Viola in Shakespeare's *Twelfth Night* enthralling. I still do. Sometimes I'm my own best audience. I also thought my portrayal of televangelist Jerry Falwell as a raging liberal by fundamentalist measures and as a sincere champion of his mostly blue-collar, dispossessed flock was truly interesting stuff. But it didn't generate a peep.

About two-thirds of the time, I'd guess, the people I've profiled more or less like their portrayals, as did Bush. Kelly McGillis liked her profile, although she thought it made her look neurotic. The retarded man, Gary Poe, began sobbing as I read him his published profile. Afraid that I'd hurt his feelings, I stopped and asked why he was crying. He said, "I never thought anyone could understand what it's like to be me." Among the satisfied, I also include muckraking journalist Jack Anderson and the young Washington dealmaker David Carmen. Anderson wrote thanking me for the depth of the story, but added that it had been painful for him to read. Carmen also liked his profile, but said he had at first become depressed at reading the chronology of his own inexorable transformation from idealist to pragmatist.

I'm greatly relieved when subjects don't hate their profiles. I know journalists of the tough-guy breed who say, "The hell with 'em! If they don't like it, I must be doing somethin' right." But I don't agree, because I've found that if the family and friends of the people I'm writing about can't see the people they know well in my portrayals, something is probably out of whack. For instance, George Bush's mother wrote me an angry note after her son's profile, saying that I had made Prescott Bush, her husband and George Bush's father, appear far too stuffy and cold. It was years later, in an *Esquire* article by journalist Richard Ben Cramer, that I learned Mrs. Bush was right: Cramer found that Prescott was among the least stuffy of the Bush clan of his generation and that he constantly railed against the evils of social pretension. He even refused to vacation with some pompous members of the family whom he could not stand to be around. I hadn't looked deep enough, which is a lesson I must learn, and learn again. Far more often, however, a subject will dislike his or her profile, but the subject's friends will quietly say, yes, that is the person I know.

I'd guess a good third of the time people don't like their profiles at all, although I'm never able to predict who those people will be. For instance, the wife of the man whose kidnapped baby was re-covered after my article appeared told me her husband still didn't like the story, because he thought it made him look strange. The teenage genius Evan Sherbrooke hated his portrayal, believing it put far too much emphasis on his efforts to fit in. Through the grape-vine I heard that Carl Bernstein, famous for his Watergate investiga-tion at the *Washington Post* and immortalized by Dustin Hoffman in *All the President's Men*, and Lynda Bird Johnson Robb, the daughter of former president Lyndon Johnson and the wife of Virginia sen-ator Chuck Robb, both disliked their profiles. Yet before they ap-peared, I was convinced each was a redemptive, if painful, portrayal.

I can never predict. I was so afraid that my story about the suicide of Ruth and Bucky Jenkins's son would devastate the couple that I skirted a *Washington Post* rule that says subjects can never read a story in advance of publication. I sat down in the Jenkinses' living room and read the story to them out loud, knowing that as non-public figures they could still withdraw their permission for me to tell their stories. My editors wouldn't have been happy to see six weeks of my work lost. But several psychiatrists had warned me my article could trigger another suicide in the family, and I figured no article was worth that. So for half an hour, Ruth and Bucky Jenkins listened quietly. Then they cried, hugged each other, and hugged me. Then we all cried. They didn't want a word changed.

In American journalism today, the "personality profile" has become epidemic—politicians, athletes, authors, intellectuals, and ordinary folks made suddenly famous by events are profiled. A lot of good journalists are doing good work. The character reporting about former presidents Johnson and Richard Nixon and the revelations about former Democratic presidential candidate Gary Hart's extramarital love life have shown how important it can be to understand our leaders' intimate human histories. But the boom in personality reporting too often lacks the premise that the only good reason to examine individual lives is as a vehicle for examining ourselves and our culture.

Unless the honest story of one life enlightens, cautions, criticizes, or inspires its readers—resonates in their lives—it has failed. It is entertainment. And most personality reporting today is entertainment, which readers seem increasingly to demand. Fewer newspapers and magazines, I fear, will be willing to pay the high cost of in-depth profile reporting if their editors and owners believe readers will settle for less. For that reason, my newspaper—the *Washington Post*—has earned my deep gratitude. The profiles in this book weren't written simply because I wanted to write them, but because the *Washington Post* was willing to pay for them. That is the bottom line.

In the end, writing the stories in *American Profiles* was for me always an experience in humility and arrogance. Humility, because I inevitably discovered that much of what I believed about people and their worlds was wrong. Arrogance, because after the reporting was done, I still had to decide what I would say about these people—what I would put in, leave out, play up, and play down. That is the real test of a writer's fairness or mean-spiritedness, and I'm not the one to judge that in myself. Every reader should know that these profiles are not the subjects' stories. They are my stories—my renditions of other people's lives. That is an undeniable arrogance hard to justify without reference to the societal benefits of a free and freewheeling press. As for myself, I take refuge in the words of writer Gore Vidal: "What matters finally is not the world's judgment of oneself but one's own judgment of the world. Any writer who lacks this final arrogance will not survive very long in America."

Washington Post photograph by Harry Naltchayan.

KELLY MCGILLIS
Stage Fright, Stage Flight

She wears lipstick and makeup this first day of rehearsal, and, against her black jeans, black cowboy boots, and black tank top, they make her look strange, something neither-nor, as if she couldn't decide this morning whether she was walking out the door for a society dinner or a motorcycle gang picnic. The rest of the cast, naturally, is picnic-bound, sans makeup, in sandals and sneakers, shorts and torn pants, and toting raggedy book bags, scripts, props, and the de rigueur quart of Evian spring water. The woman out of sync is Kelly McGillis, the tall, sleek, beautiful Hollywood star of *Witness*, *Top Gun*, and *The Accused*. She has masked her face today to mask her fear, to make herself think, *I am pretty*, to make herself think, *I can act, I know I can, I know I can*. . . . It's a trick she tried to play on her psyche this morning when she awoke once again with the old terrors, the voice inside telling her, against all evidence, that she is too ugly, too fat, and too untalented to be rich and famous and to command the lead role in the Shakespeare Theatre at the Folger's autumn production of *Twelfth Night*.

The makeup didn't work. It never does. Not on old, deep terrors.

She doesn't *have* to do this, you know, not Kelly McGillis. She can knock down a million a movie. She doesn't *have* to take a job for $563.50 a week to hear that awful damned voice inside her head, for the privilege of playing to a theater of 243 people instead of an audience of millions around the world. No, she doesn't *have* to be onstage in Washington, D.C.—or anywhere! At least that's what Kelly will tell herself again and again during the next month as *Twelfth Night* moves toward its premiere. It's a pose that she, in her fearful, whistling-in-the-dark way, allows herself, although it's fiction. If Kelly McGillis were a bagger at the Safeway, she'd do little theater in the suburbs and skits at the boss's retirement party. It's in the blood.

That's why she's at the Folger doing Shakespeare. Her agent thought it was a lousy, unlucrative idea. Kelly wasn't even sure about it herself, worried that it might hurt her Hollywood bankability. But then, wasn't Hollywood the problem? La-La Land and the arrogance and isolation of fame, the pressures to sell out in big-money flicks. But even worse, movie acting—done in snippets dragged out over weeks and months—often left her feeling empty. The theater was different. Kelly McGillis had felt something that first time onstage in high school—a feeling of leaving her unhappy self, of pristine control, of freedom, a transcendent, unselfconscious, joyous freedom. That feeling had somehow healed her then. She's at the Folger to be somehow healed again.

"It's the greatest high there is," she says. "It's flying."

Trouble is, the agony before flight.

To see her at rehearsal, you'd never guess. Relaxed, making silly faces, she lets out a contagious, guttural laugh, bends down, sticks her butt in the air, peers through her legs upside-down, and suddenly shakes her booty. Yet she doesn't even stand out in this crowd. She's crazy and funny and witty, but so are the other actors in *Twelfth Night,* and so is its director, Michael Kahn, a tall, bald, delicate man who forever stores his glasses atop his tanned head.

Starting with the play's opening scene—in which four characters awaken to find themselves washed ashore after a shipwreck—Michael will analyze every motion, thought, and emotion of every actor for every moment of the play. He'll do this ad infinitum, detail by detail, as in the making of a pointillist painting. In the barren rehearsal hall, without stage, scenery, or costumes, it seems that no final picture will ever connect these thousands of dots. But Michael knows that will come. He has directed more than a hundred plays. And he's the reason Kelly McGillis is at the Folger—the reason she ended up at New York's Juilliard school of drama twelve years ago.

In those days, Michael Kahn taught at Juilliard, and he and two other professors were interviewing prospective students when in walked twenty-year-old Kelly, a Southern California girl. She was poised and drop-dead beautiful, and she already had spent two years at the Pacific Conservatory of the Performing Arts. But she was dressed in what Michael's New York bias saw as well-bred surfer girl attire, which worried him. So he asked her, please, get on the floor and play in the mud. Looking nonchalant, Kelly sat on the floor and, with what Michael saw as delight and abandon, played in the mud.

Kelly was terrified. She'd never played in the mud. But she had played in the snow. So where Michael saw mud, Kelly saw wet, white, plentiful snow. Even then, it was how she acted—paging through her memory and emotions, finding a hit, and then imbuing the pretense of acting with the reality of reality. Naturally, she went home and told her mom she'd blown it. A few weeks later, she was accepted. And for the next four years she was Juilliard's darling—a natural. Even in simple classroom skits, teachers would find themselves forgetting for an instant that this was a girl named Kelly and not, say, Masha in Anton Chekhov's *The Three Sisters*. Word spread that this new girl had the magic. But all the while, the new girl with the magic was terrified she'd be tossed out of school.

She just wasn't good enough!

Twelfth Night is like old home week for Kelly. Besides Michael Kahn, the play's voice coach, Liz Smith, also goes back to her days at Juilliard. She was the teacher who, the first day Kelly spoke up in class, said in her precise British clip, "Miss McGillis, you are a tall, beautiful young woman. Why do you speak like a little girl?" Liz Smith doesn't remember saying that, and she blushes and offers a weak denial when Kelly reminds her.

"Oh, yes, you did!" Kelly says, laughing.

"I probably did. I shouldn't have."

Liz and Kelly are sitting on stiff-backed metal chairs in the gravel alley behind the Folger's Capitol Hill rehearsal hall. A pile of nearby garbage stinks high or low with the breeze, and the bees are dive-bombers. Kelly smokes, and Liz hits the Evian pretty hard. She is a tiny, regal woman with short, thick gray hair and a beautiful, warm smile. She's an expert on the language, poetry, and meaning of Shakespeare. Her job is to see that each actor understands Shakespeare's intent in all 114 pages of *Twelfth Night*, as well as his iambic pentameter rhythm—ten syllables alternating between weak and strong accents within every poetic line. Liz's script is scarred with diagonal accent marks, and Kelly's script is a patchwork of scribbled notes and questions. She has been studying it for a month.

"Now, this next one is really tricky," Liz says, furrowing her brow and shaking her head earnestly. On pages 43 and 44, Kelly has these lines: "No, good swabber; I am to hull here a little longer. Some mollification for your giant, sweet lady." All right, Liz says, let's make a playful joke on the contrasting words "little" and "giant." But to strongly accent both would be unsubtle. So, accent one and find a voice inflection to emphasize the other. "Okay?" she asks. "Let's move on."

In the line "Fortune forbid my outside have not charmed her," strongly accent "out," not "side." In the line "I would not understand it," strongly accent the "would" and the "not" equally. Also, pronounce "usurp" with a Z sound: "uzurp." Says Liz, "U-sssurped is a bit wimpy, don't you think?" Kelly asks a question: "Is it 'taint *their* wit' or 'taint their *wit*'?" Liz heaves a deep sigh: "Oh, boy, yes." She pauses to think. "I believe it's neither," she says finally. "I ·believe it's 'taint their wit.'"

"Oh, of course!" says Kelly.

Seriously arcane stuff. And Kelly McGillis, the movie star, is taking great delight in her decision to return to it. Truth is that despite her fears, it would have been hard for Kelly to say no when Michael offered her the part of Viola. She'd wanted to play the role since Juilliard. One Viola scene, the famous "willow cabin speech," was Kelly's favorite:

> *Make me a willow cabin at your gate*
> *And call upon my soul within the house;*
> *Write loyal cantons of contemned love*
> *And sing them loud even in the dead of night;*
> *Hallo your name to the reverberate hills*
> *And make the babbling gossip of the air*
> *Cry out "Olivia!" O, you should not rest*
> *Between the elements of air and earth*
> *But you should pity me.*

Twelfth Night is probably the best of Shakespeare's great comedies. In his hands, farce becomes sly comment on the masks people wear to hide not only from others, but from themselves. The play spins on a contrived and complicated story line: Viola, a young woman of royal blood, is shipwrecked in the dreamy city of Illyria. Her twin brother, she fears, has been drowned. Disguising herself as a gentleman, Viola takes a job with the duke Orsino, with whom she secretly falls in love. Too bad. Orsino loves Countess Olivia, who, sadly, doesn't love him. Undeterred, Orsino assigns the disguised Viola to woo Olivia for him. Surprise, Olivia falls in love with Viola's male persona. But wait! Viola's twin brother returns. One thing leads to another, and after two hours of hilarious, bawdy twists and beautiful poetry, everyone ends up marrying everyone else.

Viola is the fulcrum. It's a hard role because she must be at once masculine and feminine. She also must be the kind of confident, fun-loving woman who'd undertake such a brash masquerade, while having an emotional depth that rings true with her profound love scenes. Kelly knew she could do drama—tragedy, pain, anguish. She could find these emotions within herself. But how to be Viola? How to be sad and joyful at once? This baffled and intrigued her. An outwardly funny, confident woman, Kelly is always laughing and making people laugh. But that is her own mask. The source of her need to act isn't joy. Never has been.

Kelly was a fat, unhappy, lonely girl who believed she was stupid. She was the firstborn child, and, from the earliest age, she drove her mother nuts. For the first three months, Kelly cried wildly. "She made me a sick and nervous mother," Joan McGillis says. "She made me feel inept." In her youth, Joan had fantasized about being a movie star, and when she decided on Kelly's name, she even imagined how "Kelly McGillis" would look on a marquee. On the surface, she was a tall, beautiful, confident woman—not unlike her daughter today. But inside, Joan had always lacked confidence, and Kelly's arrival intensified her doubts. Sometimes, Joan even felt it was she, not Kelly, who was the child. Kelly's father was a doctor, and Joan's job was to run the household, which she did with a drill sergeant's precision. Everything had a place, napkins were always folded, clothes always pressed just so. Joan could control just about everything, except Kelly.

"My big fear was that I would be judged incompetent because I couldn't raise this child," she says. "That was the damned problem: I couldn't leave her alone. Ours was a struggle for control between mother and daughter, very early on. It escalated into a nightmare."

All Kelly's childhood stages were exaggerated. The Terrible Twos were more terrible. When a newborn sister came home, Kelly hit her with a baby bottle. "I don't like her!" she said. Kelly was always stubborn; if ordered to do something—say, clean up her room—she'd inevitably resist. Occasionally, Joan would awaken in the morning to discover little Kelly wasn't in the house. She'd find her at a neighbor's, chatting and eating breakfast as if she were a grown woman. Kelly's father, Donald, hated to do it, but he occasionally spanked his daughter, who was so high-strung that she sometimes couldn't be calmed down. He just didn't know what else to do. "I'm holding back tears as I talk," he says.

Then came the horrible mistake: When Kelly got to first grade, they tested her and announced that she had an IQ of 85 to 90. "Don't ever expect anything of her," they told her father. He didn't believe it because, despite her stubbornness, Kelly had always been bright and talkative. But the school insisted, and she was lumped with the slowest kids. Her mother blamed herself: It had to be something *she* had done—or not done. "After all, I *was* the mother." In school, little was expected of Kelly, and she came to resent the excellent grades of her younger sisters. She knew the judgment that had been passed upon her: She was dumb.

She also knew this: In her family, dumb was not good. Doctors and lawyers were good. Ambition and achievement were good. Education was the key to it all. And at education, Kelly had failed. Even when the horrible mistake was discovered in junior high, when they announced, oh, gee, sorry about the mix-up, Kelly's really mentally gifted, she's got an IQ of 140-plus, it was too late. She'd never worked in school, never invested her identity in what she was supposedly unable to master, and she wouldn't start then. Her life was filled with tomboy pursuits, with lip-syncing to the Beatles, with holiday skits she'd write, direct, and star in.

Then came age twelve. "She looked eighteen at twelve," her mother says, and this terrified Joan, who remembered the confusing emotions she had felt as a girl whose body had also matured early. "I sensed what she was going through, but I didn't know what to tell her." Joan had buried her fears of her emerging sexuality by immersing herself in teen sports. Kelly took another tack: She got fat, ballooning to 190 pounds. She had few friends. She rarely dated. She was terribly lonely. And at home, the battle for control continued. Kelly broke curfew. "What are you gonna do about it?" she'd ask tauntingly. She skipped school constantly. She once ran away from home for three weeks with only a towel and a bikini.

"You'll never amount to a hill of beans if you don't finish high school," her father would lecture. Yes, yes, Dad, Kelly already knew that.

Then came age fifteen. In search of easy credits, the incorrigible truant Kelly, who had slimmed down by then, walked into a high school acting class, and, snap, her life changed. She suddenly had friends, a focus, a love all her own. After her first play, Jean-Claude Van Itallie's *The Serpent*, she even won her high school's Best Supporting Actress award. But more important than friends or recognition was the *feeling*. "It was such a sense of freedom," Kelly says. "I felt needed, accepted, loved. All those clichés." She had so many emotions that she could only reveal on stage—love, fear, anger. It was blessed release. Her mother saw the change instantly, and felt even more helpless. She'd see Kelly onstage, portraying such anguish, and she knew Kelly wasn't acting, and that she, Joan, had

helped create the well of pain that her daughter drew upon. "It terrified me," Joan says. "I knew I couldn't help her. I immediately
knew she was working out her problems onstage." Kelly, who had
always craved control of her own life, was finally seizing it. Her
mother relented, quit the lectures, threats, and demands. "I couldn't
talk about all this with anybody," Joan says. "I still haven't even
talked with Kelly about it. We let it out a drop at a time."

Kelly may have felt stupid, but she had a passionate ambition to
excel—to prove herself to herself, and to her parents. She quit
school and passed the high-school-equivalency exam, although she
was forever scarred by her academic failures. It's no fluke that this
advice from a high-school acting teacher touched her deeply: "You
don't have to be intelligent to be a creative actor."

"That stayed with me," Kelly says. "It stuck with me for some
reason."

Kelly is changing before her eyes.

Two weeks into *Twelfth Night* rehearsal and she has begun to
exude the manner of a man—swaggering, extending her hand palm
down, standing with feet splayed and fists planted on her hips. She
does this not only in rehearsal but at home, in restaurants, on the
street. She's feeling good, not wearing makeup. Her parents always
joke that they'd like to read Kelly's scripts ahead of time so they will
know who they'll be living with for the next six months. They loved
it when she became so like the serene Rachel in *Witness*. They
endured when she became so like the neurotic woman she played in
a TV movie.

True to form, Kelly hasn't worn a dress in weeks, and she's laughing louder, slapping people on the back. She carries in her mind the
image of a large, strong man, a stranger she once saw eating dinner
on a plane. She noticed that nothing the man did was delicate—his
glass looked heavy when he lifted it, it *clunked* when he set it
down. Even his chewing seemed an exertion. This kind of masculine weight, this heaviness, she hopes to re-create in Viola's male
impersonation. She has stopped reading novels now, stopped watching movies and TV. She so quickly empathizes with their characters
that they compete within her for attention, which must all go to
Viola now. At rehearsal, Kelly looks like an ungainly colt, her limbs
awkward and unsynchronized, and she fears she'll look silly and
foolish onstage, like a woman acting at trying to be a man.

"Just have fun," director Michael Kahn says.

The comedy also is a struggle. Kelly's lack of acting experience at what she calls "comic physicality" is one of the reasons she wanted to do Viola. But right now, her comic gestures and expressions, like her masculine movements, are exaggerated and reminiscent of the Keystone Kops. She looks like someone acting at trying to be funny. But even more pressing is what you might call Kelly's comedic—or noncomedic—attitude toward Viola's predicament. *Twelfth Night* is a thoughtful comedy, but still comedy, and Viola must see humor in the fraudulent love triangle she has created. But Kelly's natural tendency is to see tragedy, everywhere. Viola loves Orsino and, *my God*, she can't tell him! So when Orsino jokes that the disguised Viola reminds him of a woman, Kelly's first reaction is anguish— her face twisting into the grimace of a child who is about to be spanked. Michael gets up and plays Kelly's role himself, with a kind of blushing, feminine charm.

"Find the playful, coy, optimistic side of vulnerability," he says. "Find your natural childishness."

But the magic is bubbling. "Viola is starting to take over," Kelly says. In rehearsing a scene in which Viola woos Olivia, Kelly says the line "My lord and master loves you." Suddenly, Kelly feels a sharp, real pain. She thinks, *Orsino loves you, not me!* And spontaneously, Kelly, or rather Viola, begins to cry. From that instant, each time Kelly acts the scene, she'll seek to rekindle that moment's emotion. In rehearsing another scene, she says to Olivia: "I have one heart, one bosom, and one truth, / And that no woman has; nor never none . . ." And suddenly, without thinking, Kelly, or rather Viola, unexpectedly drops to her knees before Olivia. Everyone falls silent.

"Something has happened here," Michael says softly. "It's lovely."

Yet the terrors nag. When Kelly drops a gun in the play's dueling scene and a fellow actor jokes that she is uncoordinated, she fumes to herself that he's trying to shake her confidence. She angrily tells herself that Michael is turning Viola into a yuk-yuk character, when Kelly doesn't want yuk-yuk. One day, she even wears lipstick. She keeps thinking, *I can't do this.* And after a local press appearance, she suddenly becomes obsessed with the idea that all the city's theater critics will be gunning for her—the Hollywood starlet with the gall to tackle Shakespeare. Judgment—of parents, teachers, critics, of anyone, really—is her great fear.

It's 10:30 P.M., minutes after the play's first stage run-through, and Kelly is standing beneath a streetlight on Capitol Hill. It's cool and damp and moonless, not a star alive. She drags at a cigarette and cocks her head. The lamp reveals a pensive and frightened girlish face. "How was I?" she asks with a studied nonchalance. "Was I bad?" Her voice speeds up now, its intensity rises, and the pretense of nonchalance disappears. "I want you to tell me! All I want to know is will people laugh at me? Will they laugh?

"Will they say I'm no good?"

Kelly is suffering the actor's paradox.

Something deep within makes her act, something strong and intimate and as complicated as life. But that is never enough, because an actor's validation comes not from within, but from without. Acting is reaching out and grabbing the audience with a strong hand that tightens on the neck of its emotions. An actor who can't reach an audience is like an echo without a source: He doesn't exist. Onstage, the great actors forget they're acting and believe, for the moment, that they're living another life. Because if they believe it, the audience may, for at least those heightened instants, also believe they are watching real life. "It's sort of a purist, snobby notion," Kelly says, "but I believe it. You've got to create a world and have the audience lose themselves in it. It's actually a matter of trusting in your life, in your creative ability. Of just being able to breathe and say, 'That's it, that's all my breath, and that's all you get, baby. And you'll love it!' That's the hardest thing in the world."

Trusting in herself. That's the hardest thing. It was hard when she was a teenage loser. And it was hard when she was in drama school in California and not marked as a special talent. She'd stay up all night with her friend Lisa Barnes, drinking coffee and reading Shakespeare, talking about how she'd someday be an actress. "I'm never gonna do ads or be a model, never!" Kelly would say. "I'm just going to do good work." She was desperate for respect. "She never felt recognized or worthy," Lisa says. "She had to prove she was worthy of being alive. She knew people thought she was beautiful, but she didn't want to believe it. Beauty was a vacuous trait. She wanted to be respected. She has a burning, burning need to be respected. But she just knew she'd be an actress."

It was that way at Juilliard too. With Joseph Brutsman and other classmates, Kelly often went to New York's cheap classic-film theaters. Afterward, they'd analyze the movies in that cocky way of students. But Joseph realized one evening that Kelly rarely said a word. "I remember thinking that night that it wasn't that she saw herself as a potential star, but that she intuitively understood what these people were doing in a way we didn't—in a way that analyzing it to death never will. I think she believed even then that she

could someday be at the level of the people we were fawning over—
the Brandos and the Oliviers."

Kelly remembers that she has been frightened of just about everything for just about all her life. "A sad thing to say," she says, laughing nervously. But when it came to acting, she always felt a confidence she couldn't explain. "I'd get these bugs in my ear," she says.
For instance, a director might give advice on a scene, and the bug in
Kelly's ear would say, "No, this is right!" And much of the time, she
came to believe, the bug was right. It's the damnedest thing. She
can't explain it, doesn't want to. It's magic.

Except perhaps it's more than magic. When Kelly was a young
woman with persistent headaches, her father sent her to a neu-
rologist, who gave her a clean bill of health. But in casual talk later,
the specialist told Kelly's parents, "You know, she's the most right-
brained person I've ever met. Her perception, of course, is totally
different from anyone else's." Well, yes, Dr. and Mrs. McGillis did
know Kelly was, ah, different. But this gave that difference a context: In popular parlance, "right-brained" people are more intuitive
and emotional, and rely more heavily on flashes of insight than cold
analysis. That explained a lot, although a bit late.

At Juilliard, Kelly was immersed in what you might call the right-
brained school of acting. Acting isn't acting. Acting is going into
yourself, plumbing yourself to find your character's emotions—
love, hate, greed, fear, pity. It's crossing over, passing through
the impermeable membrane that forever separates observer and ob-
served. Acting is making yourself the character and making the
character yourself. Acting is, well, something like Luke Skywalker's
Force. It's intuition.

So Kelly McGillis was quite a find, a raw nerve of emotion who
could swing wildly from mood to mood. "Like Texas weather," one
friend said. Not so good a prescription for life, but a fountainhead
for acting. Kelly was forever careering about Juilliard, crying, "I
know you're gonna throw me out. It's okay, I know you are." But her
teachers were tolerant. In fact, they marveled. As an actress, the
fragile Kelly was an open vessel into which they could pour challenge after challenge. In show biz, they call this courage. Her desire
to act was enormous, and because of her self-doubts she worked as
hard as any acting grunt who had no magic. So afraid she'd be seen
as dumb, she buried herself in research on her characters. As she
had with her parents, Kelly resented even the most casual advice
from friends about how to run her life. She could, thank you, control her own life. Yet in her acting, Kelly craved, even demanded,

criticism. She was so terrified, yet so willing. "She would take any risk," says Juilliard acting teacher Eve Shapiro. "Some days it was magic."

But some days it was hell, at least for Kelly. She couldn't fake it. In preparing for the role of Masha in *The Three Sisters*, she was baffled that Chekhov introduced Masha reading a book and dreamily reciting two lines from Alexander Pushkin, with no more explanation. What was Masha reading? What was she feeling? How could Kelly know? She couldn't get past this scene. Finally, her teacher gave her a Frederic Chopin tape and told her to play it just before rehearsal. Kelly did, the door to her intuition swung open, and she could play the scene. It's no surprise that Kelly came to admire Rainer Maria Rilke's 1929 book *Letters to a Young Poet*: "You ask whether your verses are good," Rilke wrote to the aspiring poet. "Nobody can counsel and help you, nobody. There is only one single way. Go into yourself. . . . Go into yourself and test the deeps in which your life takes rise."

Kelly did, while playing the stepdaughter in Luigi Pirandello's *Six Characters in Search of an Author*. It's the role of a girl who outside is cynical and tough, needing no one, but inside is pure and vulnerable. "I think maybe," says Eve Shapiro, "that this was Kelly." She had lobbied fiercely for the part, but in rehearsal, Kelly cracked—ran screaming from the room, cursing: "Screw you! I hate this! I hate this school! I'm leaving!" Eve followed her and said, "Let's try it again." To Kelly's bewilderment, she could now act the role. She didn't understand it, didn't want to. *Poof!* Her demons were exorcised.

Like magic, only harder.

If Liz Smith saw the same stage play day in, day out for a hundred years, she'd find something to fix every day. In the theater, reaching for perfection is like reaching for infinity: Every correction moves you forever halfway to your goal. Now, it's only days until the first performance before an audience, and Kelly has goofed up the French. "It's not 'vo,' it's 'vuh,'" says Liz calmly. "It's not 'sir,' it's 'saihr'— 'vuh-truh saihr-vee-teur.'" And in the line "Who does beguile you? Who does do you wrong?," think about strongly accenting one of the "whos" to emphasize the masks that the characters are wearing. And, oh, one thing more . . . "Remember, it's uzzurped, not ussurped."

The woman is a fiend.

Kelly's biting her nails. She keeps telling herself to stop but can't.

Onstage, during lulls, her teeth zip from one finger to another like a runaway lawn mower. But despite the nerves, she's feeling good. For a while, she couldn't figure out why Viola was on that wrecked ship. Shakespeare never says, but—as with Masha in *The Three Sisters*—Kelly had to know. She decided Viola's father, a nobleman, died deeply in debt, leaving his children nearly penniless. They had sailed in search of their fortune. Kelly also couldn't envision Viola's father, so she settled on her own dad—creating in her mind a kind of Elizabethan Dr. McGillis of Messaline, the fictional town where *Twelfth Night*'s Viola had lived. By now, Kelly also has searched the personality of the man playing Orsino, Peter Webster, for qualities that she, Kelly, admires—real qualities on which to focus her real affection. Viola can't love if Kelly can't love. She has settled on Peter's kindness. She also has cut and dyed her hair dark brown to match that of the man who plays her twin brother, and, with the rest of the cast, has time-tripped into costume and into the Folger's Shakespeare Theatre, all brooding wood and beams and pillars. With the stage now a stone castle of pastel hues, Viola appears in silk broadcloth shirt, jaunty cravat, riding boots, jodhpurs, two-button jacket, and a small, round, embroidered cap fashioned by hand from an aged fabric.

With Michael Kahn's gentle persistence, Kelly has tamed her slapstick. She now feels comfortable standing still and has traded her agonizing grimaces for an array of coy, demure expressions and several actual blushes of pleasant embarrassment. In the first shipwreck scene, she even hugs one of the sailors. She has decided that Viola is a strong, optimistic woman who isn't exactly innocent, but who is without guile. Kelly thinks she's a little like that herself. On the mirror in her dressing room, she will scrawl these words with eyeliner: "Light Joy Laughter."

"I'm ready to run," she says, wondering if she has finally conquered the fears that have always made her fall apart emotionally before mastering her characters. "I think Viola might be really good. I think. I can't tell. But I think so."

Go back five years . . .

The pretty young woman who will soon be compared to Lauren Bacall and Grace Kelly sits in a Pennsylvania hotel room and sobs. Shooting starts tomorrow on the movie *Witness*, and she knows she can't do it, can't play the role of the Amish widow Rachel Lapp. In the deep of the night, she calls her old acting teacher, Eve Shapiro, who says, "Trust yourself, Kelly. Live the life of this woman and forget you."

Roll ahead a year . . .

Witness has just opened the Cannes Film Festival, and Kelly McGillis climbs the long stairs to the grand showing as the paparazzi swarm. She's mostly worried about tripping over her gown. At dinner, famed British actor Ben Kingsley taps her on the shoulder and says, "Great performance." She nods, but has no idea who he is. She didn't wear her glasses. On the way back to the hotel, her escort and friend, Paul Millman, says theatrically that she is the toast of the town. Kelly is dejected. She's sure she'll never work again.

The woman just can't savor a good thing. "I feel like I'm not a good person. So why me? Why am I famous? Why am I working?" She is uncomfortable running into old classmates. They seem uncomfortable too. She begins to get calls from acquaintances, "Hi, how ya been? Can ya get me a job?" She tells anyone who will listen that success is dumb luck. Right place, right time. She doesn't deserve it. *She's not good enough!* She becomes suspicious of new friends: What do they want? They can't just like *her.* Says her friend Paul Millman: "Her attitude is, 'Why would anybody want to be my friend? I didn't go to college.' " On the day Kelly learns she has won the part of Charlie in *Top Gun,* she eats lunch in New York with Lisa Barnes.

"It's just luck," Kelly tells her. "It's all luck."

Then she changed. Got into it. The fame thing. She moved to Los Angeles and hung out with the young and the fatuous. She felt twinges of guilt when she remembered the pledge in her all-night marathons with Lisa: "I'm just going to do good work." But she could feel herself changing, thinking that what party she attended and where she ate—and getting her name in the paper for these accomplishments—was important. Then one summer day, she ran into "a very famous young movie actor" on the street, who was reading a Chekhov play.

"You know," he said, "this Chekhov, he's full of crap. He doesn't know what he's doing. He's the worst playwright I've ever read."

"Is that so?" Kelly said.

The next winter, Kelly McGillis was in Washington at the Kennedy Center playing in Chekhov's *The Sea Gull.* Later, she played in the Folger's *The Merchant of Venice.* She set this goal: to be a better actress at age thirty-five, at forty-five, at fifty-five. She went to Israel and made a low-budget film about a band of idealistic Jewish settlers. She moved back to New York. Having been a rape victim while a student in New York, she made a documentary on rape. She began lobbying for victims' rights legislation. She stopped drinking heavily and married a yacht broker named Fred Tillman. When a tabloid said she'd married a "complete nobody," she took it as a compliment. They sold her houses in New York and Los Angeles and bought a farm. Sometimes, through all of this, Kelly would suddenly remember the very famous young movie actor and his disdain for Chekhov. "It was just a chance encounter on the street," she says. "But I realized how shallow and stupid and unfulfilling it was for me. I went, 'Wait a minute, I don't want to be like this.'"

Fame does an awful thing to an actor. It disconnects him from the everyday lives and emotions he must feel and understand to create. Marlon Brando once could sit all day in the Optimo Cigar Store telephone booth on Forty-second Street and watch the strange people come and go. Not anymore, he can't. Kelly decided she never wanted to be that famous. Fame opens doors, and she certainly wasn't going to stop making movies, but her worst acting nightmares had come on big-money films, *Made in Heaven* and *Cat Chaser*. The great Rudolph Valentino once said, "A man should control his life. Mine is controlling me. I don't like it." Kelly shared the sentiment. As ever, she wanted control, over her life and her art. She decided to return to the Folger this year and also began producing a cable movie in which she will star. Based on one of Kelly's favorite novellas, Kate Chopin's *The Awakening*, it's a turn-of-the-century story of a New Orleans woman whose feminist yearnings are, tragically, ahead of their time. Frederic Chopin's music runs throughout the novella and there is this passage:

"To succeed, the artist must possess the courageous soul."

"What do you mean by the courageous soul?"

"The brave soul. The soul that dares and defies."

On her better days, Kelly believes she's a good actress and a good person. "I'm not so bad," she says. She still craves the footlights, needs the affirmation of an audience. But she's learning too that what an audience wants from her isn't always what she wants from herself. Over the last few years, she has grown religious, and she now believes her success wasn't luck, after all, but providence. "I didn't *make* all these things happen in my life, there was some other plan," she says, replacing one explanation that is beyond her with another explanation that is beyond her. She still can't *deserve* her success. Yet, she's taking care of business.

Two autumns ago, while shooting the movie *Winter People*, Kelly did something she'd not done in fifteen years of acting: She called her mother for advice. Joan McGillis, who had once dreamed of being an actress herself, had gone back to college when the girls got older and become a director of local theater. At first, Joan thought Kelly seemed miffed, worried that the mother was trying to steal the daughter's limelight. So Joan was always careful not to comment on Kelly's acting. But then came the call. Kelly said she was shooting a scene tomorrow in which she had to scream horribly, and she just couldn't get it right in her mind. Any ideas? The mother was terrified that she would disappoint the daughter, but she asked Kelly if she'd ever seen Edvard Munch's famous painting *The Scream*, a fearfully contorted, anguished image. Kelly said, yes, she'd seen it. And when Joan McGillis finally saw *Winter People*, Kelly's scream, at least to Joan, was the scream in that painting.

"That was," Joan says, "a wonderful high."

Kelly is in her living room, relaxed and drinking a cup of hot cappuccino, just before this evening's performance, the first before a paying audience. She's dressed all in black—sweat shirt, skirt, cotton tights, and cowboy boots. She smokes. Her husband, Fred, is eating spaghetti when she asks, "Do you think people think I'm a good actress?" This isn't as casual a question as it seems, and Fred gives a long, careful, rambling answer that ends: It isn't what *people* think, but what *you* think that counts.

"I know, I know," Kelly says. "But what do you think *people* think?" On the way to the theater, she says, "I'm not really nervous tonight."

By the end of the first act, she's nearly hysterical. Almost nobody laughs! A few people guffaw a few times, but when no one joins in, they fall silent. At intermission, the applause is, to be polite, polite. Backstage, Kelly is freaking. She wants to disappear. The crowd loosens up in the second act, laughing and clapping, but it's too late for Kelly. She goes home and cries herself to sleep. The next morning, she's still sobbing. Rock music vibrates the room, and she talks in spurts and blasts: "I'm very confused . . . thought it was going well . . . so embarrassed . . . wallowing in my ineptitude . . . scared to death . . . want to go home . . . so overwhelmingly frightened."

"I feel that no matter what I do, no matter how hard I try, I won't be able to live up to expectations," she says. "I would love to go to a psychologist about how I feel about this pain and frustration and insecurity, but I know that there's a big, big part of me that's fundamentally afraid to, because I'm afraid I won't be creative anymore.

And when I'm acting is when I feel the most confident. I know what it is exactly: It's when I have somebody else to focus on other than me. And that's what acting is. I don't feel very comfortable with Kelly, but I feel very comfortable when I can be someone else. You can't completely lose yourself in a character, because that's schizophrenia, right? But you sure as hell can come close. I guess it comes down to why me—why, why, why, why, why? I don't deserve it, I can't possibly be that good. I couldn't possibly be special."

"But why?" she is asked.

"I've done a lot of bad things in my life."

"Like what?"

She has been crying in fits and starts for a long time now, and her answer comes from deep and far away: "I haven't been the ideal child. I haven't been the perfect straight-A student. I haven't. And these things haunt me."

In the afternoon, Kelly takes a nap. When she awakens, she is serene. When she reaches for music, it isn't hard rock but Chopin's Piano Concerto No. 1. She then walks calmly to the Shakespeare Theatre, dresses in a silk broadcloth shirt, a jaunty cravat, and a small, round cap fashioned by hand from an aged fabric—and gives a nearly flawless performance. *Poof!* Her demons have been exorcised. As Rilke wrote in *Letters to a Young Poet,* "Perhaps all the dragons of our lives are princesses who are only waiting to see us once beautiful and brave. Perhaps everything terrible is in its deepest being something helpless that wants help from us."

Tonight, Kelly plays the play. She's not thinking about where her arm is resting or whether a prop is in place. Her frenzy has freed her of self-consciousness of technique and accent, of comic expression, of awkward motion. "Trust yourself, Kelly," Eve Shapiro had said. "Live the life of this woman and forget you." And in the famous "willow cabin speech," when Kelly, or rather Viola, and Olivia are alone onstage, and Viola is wooing her for the duke Orsino, it happens . . .

Make me a willow cabin at your gate / And call upon my soul within the house . . . And Kelly turns away from Olivia and talks to the sky in what she recognizes as the voice of Kelly and the voice of Viola. *Write loyal cantons of contemned love . . .* She has not become Viola, that's too simple. Think of the separate transparencies of a printed color photograph that only become a picture when layered one atop the other. *And sing them loud even in the dead of night . . .* Kelly isn't thinking of the audience watching her, or of herself

watching the audience watching her. She's not thinking of expectations. She's in a stone castle of pastel hues. A child at prayer, Joe
DiMaggio at bat, William Faulkner in conversation with his characters. The place where intuition resides. *Hallo your name to the
reverberate hills / And make the babbling gossip of the air / Cry out
'Olivia!'* . . . And Kelly cries, real tears. It's not so much that she is
in perfect control as it is the absence of all control over her, on the
wing. *O, you should not rest / Between the elements of air and earth*
. . . The theater critics, the audience, they will say what they will.
But you should pity me . . . Kelly's free, believes every word she is
saying, and is thinking as she speaks that Orsino, beloved Orsino, is
the only man in the world with whom she would, at this instant,
like to make love.

This is freedom.

This is the place she lives to be.

This is flying.

OCTOBER 29, 1989

Photograph by Sigrid Estrada.

CARL BERNSTEIN
The Watergate Hero Faces Himself

*T*hat evening, the woman and the man danced the dance of fame.

She was young, twenty-four, dark-eyed and lithe, beautiful and unfamous. He was otherwise. Sweeping into the Washington ball, he wore a black tuxedo and a white silk scarf. He mingled with ease and grace, and, having recently separated from his second wife, soon mingled his way over to the young woman. Oh, she knew his reputation as a shameless seducer, but despite her wariness, she was charmed. Would she like to go out for a drink? the man asked. He was not coy. The invitation exuded sensuality, and the woman thought to herself that if she accepted the man's invitation, she was likely accepting his other, unspoken, request. A drink, she said, yes, a drink would be nice. Outside, in the limousine, the man went straight to his work. The young woman thought: "No matter how this night ends up, I'll have a great story to tell my friends."

A great story. That was for certain.

Carl Bernstein was always a great story.

Legends cling to some men. Carl Bernstein is such a man.

His great achievement, Watergate, became a cottage industry of American truth and myth about how the boys—the wild and crazy Bernstein and his Calvinistic sidekick, Bob Woodward—brought down a corrupt and evil president. Woodward went on to become a virtual Fifth Estate, a one-man branch of government whose books became best-sellers the day they were released. The Wood of Woodstein became a living validation of American values by proving that his Watergate success was no fluke.

But the Stein of Woodstein became validation of another sort— proof for the cynical and the envious that achievement and fame and wealth are dumb luck. As those kinds of people always say, "He was in the right place at the right time." For more than a decade Bernstein foundered. And because legends today are not passed around the campfire, but from gossip columnist to screenwriter,

Bernstein became a comic and tragic figure before millions. His philandering while his wife, Nora Ephron, was pregnant with their second child became the subject of her novel and the movie *Heartburn*. Bernstein virtually disappeared as a writer and blended into the woodwork as a television reporter for ABC. A long-promised book about his family became a pathetic joke, even among his friends. In 1987, the fall from grace came to poetic closure: Bernstein—who had helped bring the *Washington Post* international fame—was not invited to the gala seventieth birthday party of *Post* board chairman Katharine Graham, who had stood behind the decisions to publish the Watergate exposés. Bernstein says he found the snub rude, but amusing. A friend says he was hurt and angry.

That was then. This is now.

Bernstein is back. His new book, *Loyalties*, is a memoir of his childhood as the son of left-wing activist parents caught in the anti-Communist inquisitions of the fifties. It is not a BIG book, *Loyalties*. It is gentle and wrenching, a 260-page memoir of a man facing the revulsion, anger, and resentment he felt as a boy toward both his parents and the government that assaulted them. The book also explains a lot about Bernstein's chaotic life—and about his complicated yearning to be at once an iconoclastic bad boy and a respected member of the Establishment.

The shocker is that Bernstein reveals that his mother, Sylvia, and his father, Al, both of Washington, D.C., were once members of the Communist Party USA—something even J. Edgar Hoover couldn't prove about Bernstein's father. But Bernstein argues that his parents—and others like them—were neither un-American nor subversive, that they fought only for economic, political, and racial equality. Thus, the son who once felt deep shame that his folks were "atheistic Jewish Communists" returns to the scene of their alleged crimes and pronounces them *not guilty*—pronounces them heroes. The irony is that this loyal son of American Communists also grew up to help destroy Richard Nixon, the very symbol of the Communist-baiting hysteria that so altered Bernstein's life and the lives of his parents.

Like Jack, Carl killed the giant. And he, too, entered a fairy-tale land. He became famous. He became rich. He became Dustin Hoffman. He became a dinner guest. Then came the fall. . . . There were women, so many women. There was booze. There were bills unpaid, promises not kept, people treated arrogantly, years and a $3 million fortune lost. As Woodward produced blockbuster books, Bernstein made news by dating Bianca Jagger and Liz Taylor, by getting arrested for drunk driving.

These days, Bernstein rails about the horrors of celebrity in America, about how "celebrity journalism" dominates the news. Not that he's wrong. It's just strange to hear that complaint from a man who has reveled in fame, not to mention profited from it. But, as Bernstein's closest friends say with affection and exasperation, "That's Carl!" He has always had a great ability to delude himself about himself, always seen himself as a victim—Carl against the world, the world against Carl. He has always demanded indulgence from his friends, and the sadness of this is that they have come to expect little of him. He has always craved attention, respect, and recognition, and the sadness of this is that even the fame of Watergate didn't stop his pain. "Fame is that great old illusion, a replacement for love," says Bernstein's friend Eve Ensler. "It's very seductive, but also false." Truth is, Carl Bernstein didn't change after Watergate as much as he stayed the same, which was always the problem. Says a man who has known him for years, "Carl is a nineteen-year-old kid who has gotten older."

Loyalties and rough times may finally have changed that.

But then, Carl Bernstein is forty-five.

Flashback, to the young woman from the Washington ball:

Years later, the woman again ran into Carl at a party. Yes, he offered her a ride home, and, yes, she accepted. But Carl wasn't wearing a tuxedo or a silk scarf that night. He wore a suit. Outside, no limo was waiting. He drove a Toyota. Odd, but its radio was missing. The young woman wondered if Carl was short of cash, short of confidence. He didn't ask her out that night, and she realized this: Without the trappings of fame and wealth, Carl seemed different.

"God," she thought, "he seems so much smaller than life."

The face is like a mask on the body of a younger man. Its skin is pale and translucent, gray like smoke. The body is taut, with skin pulling tightly over good muscles, so taut that Bernstein can still wear purple bikini underwear to the gym. But the face reveals hard time. It sags at the chin, wrinkles deeply across the brow, seems tired in repose. When Carl mentions to his friend Magui Nougue-Sans, who is thirty-one, that he is about the same age as Sylvester Stallone, she looks at the picture of Stallone in the newspaper before her, looks into Carl's face, looks back at the paper, and then back into Carl's face. She does this still a third time before saying, "He looks younger than you." Bernstein laughs and shrugs. What the hell.

This is the new, mellow Carl Bernstein. The change has been a long time coming, and friends who are no longer friends wonder if this is simply a new Bernstein pose. Carl has been apologizing for his flaws, promising reform, asking indulgence for so long that he is like the boy who cried wolf. Yet there are hints of growth. For one, he finished his book, which few people really expected. For another, he isn't *always* late anymore—an irritating and rude trait that goes back to his youth. Bernstein also has cut back on the New York night life that constantly landed him in the gossip columns. He stopped drinking three years ago. His weight is down from 188 to 166.

But most of all, Bernstein is no longer so awfully defensive about his failings. A while back, Woodward, who is Bernstein's closest friend, came into his office to find a dozen phone messages, including an emergency call from Carl. Woodward phoned immediately— only to have Bernstein pull a Bernstein: "Can I call you back in ten minutes?" Woodward, fuming, said he'd returned Carl's call before a lot of other pressing calls and if Carl wanted to talk, then talk! To his delight, Bernstein apologized.

Other hints: Bernstein's apartment on East Sixty-second Street in New York isn't perfect. This may not seem like much, but Bernstein has spent hundreds of thousands of dollars renovating his various digs over the years. The aging two-floor apartment, which rents for $4,500 a month, had plaster falling off the walls when he moved in. He had the faults patched—but left the raw repairs exposed. Bernstein's friend Chip Brawn calls the look "faux decay"—a satiric description he says fits Bernstein well. "It's supposed to look old and flawed and just accepted," says Brawn, laughing. "A lot like Carl."

The old Bernstein, the new Bernstein says, couldn't have lived in this apartment. Besides the cracking walls, he points to a chair that needs to be reupholstered. "I wouldn't have let that chair in my old living room," he says, with the pride of a child who has just mastered his fear of the dark. Bernstein then waves at the many vases of cut flowers around his apartment. An oncidium orchid sits in a cobalt vase inside the front door, purple French lilacs droop on the breakfast table, pink Vivaldi roses rest on the little table with the pictures of Bernstein's two sons. But the flowers are shriveled, their petals rained beneath them; they should have been replaced days ago. The old Bernstein couldn't have tolerated that.

"Perfectionism can drive you crazy," he says calmly. "You're always aware of what's absent in your life and work. I'm not like that anymore."

June 19, 1953, evening . . .

Little Carl, nine-year-old Carl, can't stop sobbing. The tears pour down his freckled face—the face that has won him the unfortunate childhood nickname *Howdy Doody*—and he becomes hysterical. Ethel and Julius Rosenberg were executed at 8:00 this morning, and in the Washington, D.C., office of the save-the-Rosenbergs campaign, which Carl's mother helped organize, little Carl had watched as everyone cried. But this evening, Carl isn't crying for the Rosenbergs. He's crying because he has just realized that if the anonymous Powers That Be can kill Ethel Rosenberg, they can kill Sylvia Bernstein, too. This fear—and the rage Carl feels at his mother and father for doing this to *him*, for threatening *him* so profoundly—has momentarily surfaced.

Nickname or not, this was no Howdy Doody childhood.

For whole summers, on Thursdays and Saturdays, Carl took his mother's hand and marched with blacks up to the whites-only lunch counters of Washington. When twelve people testified before one of the ubiquitous anti-Communist committees of the era, young Carl knew eleven of them. As a boy, he attended the Cooperative Jewish Children's School—which celebrated Passover, the Fourth of July, and the Russian Revolution. Both of his parents were eventually hauled before Red-hunt committees, and his mother, who took the Fifth Amendment, was pictured on the front page of three Washington daily newspapers. When this happened, Carl's sister was kicked out of nursery school, and some of Carl's best friends were no longer allowed to play with him.

Carl's father, who attended Columbia University Law School before moving to Washington during the New Deal, worked at unionizing federal employees. He lost his job when his union folded under government pressure for its alleged communist connections. He defended without charge five hundred people called before closed-door hearings mandated by the 1947 Truman loyalty order, which granted more than two hundred government star-chambers the power to determine whether people were loyal enough to work for Uncle Sam. (One hint of disloyalty: a white person entertaining a black person in his home.) To support his family, Al opened a laundromat on Georgia Avenue.

These were distant drums to little Carl. He doesn't recall seeing the newspaper photos of his mother. He didn't know that his father, in his own Red-hunt appearance, had stood up to a bullying Senator James Eastland. He didn't know this until he got twenty-five hundred pages of FBI documents on his parents—the result of thirty-five years of surveillance. By any standard, the Bernsteins were small fish. But that didn't stop the FBI from attending Carl's bar mitzvah.

Before the Red paranoia became a public spectacle, Carl lived in a beautifully insular world. His family's home on Chesapeake Street in Friendship Heights was woven into an Old World fabric of extended Jewish family life. The boundaries of Carl's world went from his father's laundromat, which the boy found endlessly fascinating, to his grandfather's Columbia Road tailor shop, with its steam pipes overhead. His great-great-uncle's Turkish cigarettes, his grandfather's Saturday glass of schnapps, his Uncle Itzel's Dodge. . . . These threads of everyday existence—not the federal government or senators or the Red hunt—were the fabric of *real* life to Carl. It was a sentiment he would never lose, a sentiment that would become the heart of his journalism, the heart of his adult resentments.

After seven years at the laundromat, Carl's father finally got a good job, and the Bernsteins moved up and out to the prosperous Washington suburbs—and a modern, redwood home on Harvey Road in the woods off Sligo Creek Park in Silver Spring, Maryland. Carl, eleven years old, hated it. It was a culture as foreign to him as his grandfather's cramped tailor shop would have been to his new friends. For the first time, Carl had something to prove.

He knew his parents had been tainted as Communists—and he resented the stain to his own reputation. So he'd become class air-raid warden and gone to Friday afternoon Episcopal prayer services with his gentile friends. He demanded to be bar mitzvahed, though his mother and father, as atheists and secular Jews, didn't encourage it. When they balked, Carl left them a note calling them "atheistic Jewish Communists." Years later, he would be relieved to discover that his Aunt Rose had intercepted that painful note. "You don't want me to be Jewish," Carl angrily told his parents at the time. "And you don't really believe in freedom. It's communism." Carl was bar mitzvahed.

Carl's boyhood dilemma is captured by this line in his book: "In my family Marx and Freud get very confused." With his parents distracted by ominous events, Bernstein's home was a whirl of confusion—his mother unable to run the household, his father withdrawn from parenthood, Carl and his two sisters competing loudly for attention. Sylvia doted on her only son, forever laughing at his wisecracks, worrying and agonizing over him. But Al was an undemonstrative, intellectual man. One of Carl's purest images is of his father standing lost in thought as cigar ashes dribble onto his chest. This gentleness Carl mistook for weakness.

Obviously a smart kid, he did poorly in school. By the time he was a teen, Carl's anger and demand for attention had turned outward: He and a gang of boys broke all the windows in the house of an old anti-Semitic woman. For this and other offenses, he narrowly avoided reform school. As part of his rebellion, young Carl also eschewed politics, particularly left-wing politics, although he did adopt his parents' disdain for Richard Nixon. "It was a surefire way to get a rise out of Carl or his parents to say something nice about Nixon," says his boyhood friend Ben Stein. "They just hated him. It was rich, rich psychic meat for Carl to get Nixon."

Carl came to believe that his parents' politics had cost him that to which he felt entitled. He remembers vividly the day Stein lugged out a huge red book. It was *Who's Who in America*, and Ben's father, Herbert, who eventually became chairman of Nixon's Council of Economic Advisers, was listed. "I'll never forget that," says Carl. "Here was my father, who could have been God-knows-what in the government, clearly among the brightest of his generation, and he ended up in a damn laundry, and has been in the paper for nothing short of treason." Carl felt cheated. He wanted to fit in, wanted his folks to join the country club; they refused.

His childhood friends understood none of this. To them, Carl was one *cool* kid. While most guys cruised the Hot Shoppes, he hung out at the pool hall. With a gang of teen friends, he once visited a whorehouse in Hagerstown. Even then, Carl was Carl. He'd phone a kid at 3:00 in the morning and act as if it were 3:00 in the afternoon. He greeted his friend Stan Sitnick's older sister with, "Hi, babe!" Playing his guitar, he introduced his sheltered suburban friends to the class-conscious lyrics of Woody Guthrie and the protest songs of Bob Dylan. He was the best jitterbugger in Silver Spring.

Not much penetrated Carl's facade of confidence. The only time Stein recalls seeing Carl shaken was at report-card time, when he'd say he wished he could get straight A's like Stein because it would make his mother so happy. But he never did. Instead, he asked Stein to correct the spelling on his homework. "Which I did," says Stein. "He was my friend."

On Harvey Road, Bernstein also developed his weird habit of borrowing money and not paying it back, as if it, too, were his entitlement. With a charming I-gotta-have-it, Carl coaxed loans out of his friends. Kids often had to go to his parents to get repaid. "It was such small sums," says Stein. "The most was $20." But as Carl got older, the amounts got larger—$200 from Sitnick, who says with a laugh that he can't recall if Carl paid him back, but probably not. Later, when Carl was out of high school, he borrowed $500 from an old high-school sweetheart. He didn't repay her. When the woman complained to Carl's father, Carl became indignant, acting as if she had wronged him. Even when Carl had a full-time job, he'd parcel out his payments to the woman, say, $10 at a time. Twenty-five years later, she says, Carl still owes her $325.

Is she angry at him for this?

"Not at all," she says with a laugh. That's Carl.

Ben Stein recalls this telling story: When Carl discovered Stein had a ping-pong table, they played and Stein beat him badly. Day after day, Carl insisted they play. Finally, he won. From that day on, Carl lost interest in ping-pong. "It wasn't really a game for him," Stein says, "but a competition."

Carl had something to prove—and his way of going about it set a pattern for his life. Here was Carl—yearning *not* to be the son of Communists, yearning to join the country club, to be an Episcopalian or at least be bar mitzvahed. At the same time, he was visiting a whorehouse, getting arrested, hanging out at the pool hall—a suburban, Jewish James Dean.

Carl wanted it both ways: to be accepted, to be a rebel.

January 17, 1989 . . .

"Mr. Bernstein, Mr. Bernstein," the waiter hollers.

In the Cypriot Corridor, just outside the restaurant in the Metropolitan Museum of Art in New York, Bernstein turns and waits for the young man in the white waiter's jacket to catch up. A check pad in one hand, a pen in the other, the young man, in one breathless sentence, says, "Mr. Bernstein, I'm not really a waiter, I'm an actor and in acting class I'm getting ready to do a scene from your book *All the President's Men* when you were a copy boy and they asked you to wash the carbon paper and you got it all over your new suit, and I wonder if I could just ask you a few questions about it?"

"Sure."

"Did it really happen?"

"True story."

The goofy-looking sixteen-year-old kid standing with dripping hands outstretched in the bathroom of the *Evening Star*, ink and water all over his new cream suit and the sink and the mirror, hardly seemed destined to be a set-piece character in anybody's acting repertoire. Yet that day, Bernstein's first day in a newsroom, did change his life. The place was *real!*

The sounds, the smells, the action, the perpetual action—garrulous shirtsleeved men yelling "Copy!," typewriters clacking, cigarette smoke rising, martinis after deadline at Harrigan's. Old-time newspapering was both glamorous and tawdry—a perfect fit for Bernstein. It also was aggressively unideological—and you didn't have to be a shrink to see the appeal of this to a young man reacting to his parents' politics and persecution. "One of the things that attracted me to journalism," he says, "was its utter absence of absolute belief."

At the *Star*, Bernstein continued to hone his tough-guy demeanor, modeling himself after crusty city editor Sidney Epstein. "There's always been a pose there of being tough," says Bernstein. "The fact is I'm not very tough." Again, nobody noticed. Soon, Bernstein was lord of the copy boys, and he seemed destined to become a reporter—until Sid Epstein insisted he get a college degree. Cocky and arrogant, the *real* world before him, Bernstein refused. He quit and headed for a little paper in New Jersey, where he quickly won three statewide journalism awards. A year later, 1966, he was back in Washington, a reporter for the *Washington Post*.

Bernstein describes his *Post* career this way: "The editors at the *Post* have always had a view of me as someone of great ability, but they had to put up with an awful lot of crap for the work they got." That about covers it. Brilliant but erratic. A moocher of money and cigarettes, a moocher of everything. From a neighbor he borrowed silverware, liquor, firewood, a can of spaghetti. He was a slob, with a desk that resembled an archaeological dig. When *Post* executive editor Ben Bradlee once made Bernstein clean his desk, staffers sat enthralled as Carl unearthed old lunches in reverse chronological order. But if a person's father died, it was Carl who showed up at the funeral. If a person was sick at home, it was Carl who stopped by.

As always, there was a disarming charm about Bernstein, who was popular with his fellow reporters. To the bewilderment of other men, the gawky Bernstein (behind his back women still called him Howdy Doody) also was a tireless and successful Casanova. He certainly enjoyed life. He could take endless pleasure in a walk with a friend through the park, but at the same time he was manic and nocturnal, calling friends at 4:00 A.M., asking them out for a snack.

Bernstein didn't like to be alone and he was always the life of the party.

At the *Post*, in a newsroom of dark suits and preppy suspenders, Bernstein copped the uniform of the sixties—jeans or casual pants, long hair. "I used to think this kid must drive Ben Bradlee mad!" says Douglass Lea, a friend from those days. "Here was the *Post* trying to acquire a suffocating respectability, and this guy was running around right out of 'The Front Page.'" Ironically, it was Bradlee—confident, swaggering, tough—to whom Carl had begun to look as the new model for his own studied, tough-guy persona.

Surly and arrogant, Bernstein griped about even small changes to his stories. But no doubt, he was a fine writer, composing long, graphic stories on the city of his childhood, its neighborhoods and people. The evocative feature story became Bernstein's signature. Government and bureaucracy weren't *real*, Bernstein argued, people and their moods, the looks on their faces, the smells in their kitchens—these things were *real*, and evoking them was the true mission of the journalist.

His attitude, his knowledge of Washington, and his unusual childhood and life gave his reporting an edge over that of the many Ivy League graduates who populated the *Post* newsroom. Bob Kaiser, now the *Post*'s managing editor, remembers going out with Carl to Washington's infamous Clifton Terrace housing project as a young reporter and watching him put people at ease, get them to talk naturally. Kaiser, a Yale graduate, realized that in Clifton Terrace, anyway, the oddball Bernstein was the better reporter.

But Bernstein never felt appreciated at the *Post*. Reflecting the era and his bent, he aspired to three reporting jobs: covering the counterculture, Vietnam, or rock music. Twenty years later, it still pains him that Bradlee gave him none of these jobs. Yet this was no surprise. Bernstein was like a foreign object transplanted in the organism of the *Washington Post*, a transplant that seemed slowly on its way to being rejected. Once again, he wanted it both ways. He wanted to be appreciated—even as his loud, arrogant, and unconventional manner repudiated the values of the people whose respect he craved. "He was the kind of guy," says former *Post* national editor Peter Osnos, "who does something amazing or he sinks without a trace."

Enter Watergate, a Pulitzer Prize, and Dustin Hoffman.

September 1973, Naples, Florida . . .

Bernstein is chained to his typewriter on the patio of Woodward's mother's house. Sunny and hot. Carl wears green shorts, no shirt, no shoes. He's skinny and white-skinned, his hair long and stringy, parted in the middle. A cigarette, a Kool, hangs from his mouth. Woodward has confiscated the car keys. After fifteen months of working with Carl on the Watergate exposés, he's tired of Carl's erratic work habits, the crazy excuses, the endless trips to the store for cigarettes. But this day, Bernstein sits down and writes a section of the book that will become *All the President's Men*, a section about how Woodward and Bernstein felt during the deepest days of Watergate. They are beautifully written pages, capturing Woodward's own emotions perfectly.

Sixteen years later, Woodward still marvels at them.

When the split came, the men barely spoke for more than a year. Woodward believed Bernstein hadn't carried his weight, not anywhere near his weight, on *The Final Days*, the now-classic 1976 book on the last horrendous months of the Nixon presidency. The men were already celebrities, and by the time Nixon resigned in August 1974, Bernstein's stringy hair had been styled. He was spending time in New York, hanging with the glitterati, courting New York writer Nora Ephron. *The Final Days* was originally Bernstein's idea, but when Woodward and two research assistants, Scott Armstrong and Al Kamen, buried themselves in Woodward's house to begin interviewing 394 people for the book, Bernstein was nowhere in sight.

"At the beginning I was not pulling my weight," he says today. "And then I made up for it in a major way, I think, both in terms of interviews and in the writing. I essentially became the book's editor." Bernstein says he ran the entire book "through my typewriter." His is a charitable interpretation.

"I'm sure Carl did twenty interviews, maybe twenty-five," says Armstrong, who with Woodward later coauthored *The Brethren*, a best-selling book about the Supreme Court. "But if you said he did thirty-nine, I'd have to call you a liar." Woodward was furious at Bernstein. He would rant that Carl was a "cheater," swear he'd never work with him again. But then, as a sympathetic explanation for Bernstein's irresponsibility, Woodward would tell Armstrong he had to realize that Carl was "unexplainably driven" to seduce women, which took up a lot of his time. But in the end, even Woodward's sympathy failed. Armstrong remembers that Bernstein once dropped off about twenty pages of manuscript. Woodward chortled: "Here's what Carl's done for the last couple months—twenty pages." When

Woodward angrily complained to Bernstein about his performance, Bernstein—as he had once done to the woman he owed $500—tried to turn the tables: "The difficulty is your anger," he told Woodward.

"Goddam right I'm angry!" Woodward snapped.

He was so angry that he told Armstrong and Kamen he wanted them to be coauthors. But when Woodward talked with his editors at Simon and Schuster about adding their names, he came up against the lucrative new business of celebrity journalism—the business Bernstein would deplore years later. He was told that Woodward and Bernstein were an entity, Armstrong says, and that Simon and Schuster had contracted with that entity. No way was anybody else's name going on *The Final Days*. In the end, Armstrong says, Bernstein wrote a small portion of the book and lightly edited about half. Bernstein's share of the book brought him more than $1 million.

Of *The Final Days*, Woodward now says only, "It was not the most productive time for Carl." Bernstein edited the whole book and improved it immensely, he says, but he doesn't deny Armstrong's overall critical version of events. Over the years, Woodward also has told intimates privately that he doesn't recall Bernstein running *The Final Days* through his typewriter, as Carl contends. "Look, I owe him a lot," Woodward says. Indeed, during Watergate, Bernstein used his charm and brains to get in the doors of people who knew they shouldn't talk. It was Bernstein who found the laundered check that linked the Nixon reelection campaign to the Watergate burglars. And it was Bernstein who first suspected Nixon's involvement in the scandal: his painful childhood had given him an intuitive sense of the darker side of power.

"*The Final Days* was his idea," says Woodward, pleading. "I never would have thought of it. I never, ever would have thought of it. It was his idea to do *All The President's Men*, too. I have enormous gaps, and he filled them in. I was at times able to capitalize on his gifts, probably more than he was. I've had my own personal and professional rocks in the road, and I can't help but be sympathetic."

But back in 1976, after *The Final Days*, Woodward kept his vow. He would not work with Carl again. Bernstein tried to talk Woodward into doing another project with him. He even went to Armstrong and asked him to intervene with Woodward to sell a Bernstein idea: The duo would write an investigative political column. It would become a Washington institution, Bernstein told Armstrong, and it would be worth a fortune. Armstrong was speechless at Bernstein's chutzpah: "I remember the irony of Carl wanting me to argue in his favor with Bob." But that's Carl. Armstrong took the idea to Woodward, who gave it a flat no.

And Woodstein was no more.

September 24, 1977 . . .

Bernstein sits in his magnificently renovated apartment in Washington's trendy Adams-Morgan neighborhood. He has spent a fortune turning it into a page out of *House and Garden*, and it is perfect. But Carl still is not perfect. He has recently written an article in *Rolling Stone* magazine exposing secret cooperation between the CIA and the American press, and the story has been harshly attacked as exaggerated. Even Ben Bradlee—whom Bernstein still reveres— had pulled Carl aside at a dinner party just the night before and told him that he, too, believed the *Rolling Stone* article was flawed. Bernstein, the son of banished left-wingers, is now a prince of the Establishment—but the Establishment has turned on him. He is shaken.

"I've gotten too comfortable being everybody's favorite little hero up there on the silver screen with Robert Redford," Bernstein writes to himself this day. "I worry too much about how I'm perceived, particularly by people in the profession." It is time, he decides, to get back to being himself—and stop worrying about preserving his legendary Watergate fame and his place in the Establishment. It is good advice, not taken.

Without Woodward, Bernstein was adrift.

It wasn't that he lacked confidence, says an intimate from that time; it was simply that he didn't know what to do. But he had told his wife, Nora Ephron, about his family's history on their first date. She immediately saw that Carl's life *was* the story: the son of parents persecuted by the likes of Richard Nixon reaching out across the generations as God's hand of justice and retribution. Carl quit the *Post* and began a magazine article on his family for the *New Yorker*. But by now, he was deep into doing things for the wrong reason: "I somehow needed to know that I was working on something that was going to be something, that was going to be a book," he says, laughing at himself. "I got maybe self-conscious, too accustomed to being the object of attention."

Bernstein doesn't acknowledge it, but he was feeling great pressure to live up to the Watergate mystique. "He talked about how much was expected, but he didn't know if he had it," says Carl's friend Barbara Howar. "Bob was going on to great things and he wasn't." For his book, Bernstein got a $400,000 advance from Simon and Schuster, drawing $100,000 immediately. This was a great deal of money for a book about Bernstein's family. But the name *Carl Bernstein*—the famous name that had been required on *The Final Days*—would be on this book. Except that there was no book. After a year of interviewing his parents and their old friends, Bernstein finally was overwhelmed by the revulsion and anger, pain and fear he felt from his childhood. Also, his folks opposed the book. They'd been devastated by their experiences, and reminding people that they'd been shunned seemed insane. Bernstein wrote fifty pages and could write no more. Soon, he was repaying the $100,000 to Simon and Schuster.

It was the beginning of rough times—what Bernstein calls his years of "turbulence." He and Nora had moved to a country house in the Hamptons on Long Island, and there Carl sat, unable to write, missing the action of daily journalism, missing Washington, missing Woodward. After Woodward separated from his second wife in 1978, he and Bernstein reconciled. Carl told him, "I know it hurts," and invited Woodward to visit. They took long walks on the beach, and Bernstein poured out his frustration. Woodward had never believed this street-savvy reporter should write what Woodward saw as a self-indulgent, navel-gazing book. He'd already told Carl he disagreed with Nora's idea, but Carl took that with a grain. After all, Woodward had never liked Nora. He told people he believed she was too worried about whether people wore tasteful shoes or served the properly crisp lettuce. He told people he believed that Carl, too, had come to worry too much about material things, good taste, people with good taste. "He's very concerned," Woodward once said of Bernstein, "about not just being a little guy from Silver Spring who didn't go to college."

On the beach, Woodward told Bernstein he was planning to jump into the race to succeed Ben Bradlee as editor of the *Post*. The men then hatched this bizarre scheme: They would go to Bradlee and propose that they become coeditors of the paper's Metro section. From there, each would compete for Bradlee's job with the platoon of other *Post* editors in the running. They went to Bradlee, who listened intently, though he knew the idea was wacko. First, only one person could be Metro editor. And besides that, Bradlee was dead certain that Bernstein wasn't management material. As usual, Carl was unable to see himself as others saw him. After seeming to think over the proposal, Bradlee said no, but suggested that Bernstein still return to the *Post*. Bernstein agreed to come back, but then had second thoughts. After all, people at the *Post* hadn't appreciated him. He also saw himself returning to enter a race with Woodward. They'd just renewed their friendship, and Carl didn't want that screwed up again. But in his own way, he also knew this race with Woodward was one he couldn't win. Woodward always got along better with *Post* publisher Katharine Graham, Bernstein says, still not acknowledging that he wasn't equipped for Bradlee's job. "I've got a lot more rough edges," he says.

With all this brewing, ABC-TV executive Roone Arledge made Bernstein an offer he couldn't refuse: the job of ABC Washington bureau chief for $150,000 a year, plus a $50,000-a-year expense account. Though he had no experience in TV news, Bernstein took the job—once again for the wrong reason: "There was something appropriately grand being the Washington bureau chief," he says with self-mockery. "It seemed to me that this was a step up the institutional ladder, which might have been expected of someone who had done what I had done. This was a great mistake."

In no time, he was a disaster. Being bureau chief wasn't a reporting or editing job but a managerial job—drafting budgets, sending out film crews. As Bradlee had known, Carl was no manager. Power seemed to go to his head. "It was as if the bureau existed for him," says one network correspondent who knew Carl well. "I gotta tell you, at ABC, he was just a terrible screwup. It's awful to say it. It was awful to watch it." About this time, people noticed that Bernstein was drinking more heavily.

His life had gone beyond chaotic. While Nora was pregnant with their second child, Bernstein had what became a notorious affair with Margaret Jay, wife of the British ambassador to the United States. "He just fell head over heels in love with another woman," says a Bernstein friend, as if that explained it. Ephron lashed back. She published *Heartburn*, a novel that portrays a Bernstein-like character as an emotionally empty, self-absorbed, narcissistic man capable of having sex with venetian blinds. Says Bernstein, "The book has nothing to do with the truth, the truth of our marriage or its dissolution." Bernstein eventually received joint custody of the couple's two sons and court-mandated assurance that the impending movie version of *Heartburn* would portray him as a conscientious and loving father.

Carl maintained his facade of bravado. But the word *vulnerable* began to creep into descriptions of him. Margaret Jay says Carl's failure at ABC rocked him. "He was trying to not just live on the old myth and the old fame, and it didn't work out," she says. "I think it damaged him. I do think he felt under pressure. He would talk about it. He was very aware of what the critics were saying." Some times, she says, Carl—cocky, brash, confident Carl—even wondered if the critics weren't right.

After little more than a year, Bernstein left the job as bureau chief and became an ABC reporter. Other reporters recall this as a face-saving move for Bernstein and Arledge, but Bernstein did do good stories for ABC. Yet he was working only about quarter- to half-time by then, says Georgeanne Thanos, his assistant at ABC, and he often arrived late or missed appointments entirely. "That was probably the worst time of Carl's life," she says. "He was getting divorced; Nora had the book out and was getting ready to do the movie."

And his money woes mounted. Even on his ABC income, Bernstein couldn't always pay his credit-card bill on time, and he bounced checks, says Jane Brooks, who, as Bernstein's secretary at ABC, paid his bills. At one point, Woodward loaned Carl $16,000, which he later repaid. The Jerusalem Post wasn't so lucky. Once, when Bernstein was scheduled to be a guest at the paper, he asked its editor, Ari Rath, to bump up his plane ticket from coach to first class, promising to pay the difference. Bernstein never paid; he says he simply forgot and that he'll now repay the money. But Rath isn't miffed: While Carl was in Israel, Rath's nephew died. "When I saw Carl at the funeral," Rath says, "I was touched to tears."

The chaos peaked in July 1983 when Bernstein was arrested for drunk driving in Washington. The next day, he had a car accident that resulted in a civil suit later settled out of court. That's when Woodward thought he heard an echo. He'd been in California interviewing friends of the dead comic John Belushi for his book Wired. Again and again, people told him they'd known Belushi's life was running out of control, but they hadn't known what to do. Woodward took the hint and went to Bradlee and the Post's then managing editor, Howard Simons, warning them that Carl was in trouble. That afternoon Bradlee and Simons went to Bernstein's apartment unannounced and convinced him to see a psychiatrist and check into a hospital. There had been a time, closer to Watergate, when Bradlee knew that any tarnish on Bernstein's name also meant a tarnish on the Woodstein legend—and thus a tarnish on the legend of the Washington Post. But by now, his concern for Bernstein was personal. Woodward drove Bernstein to Sibley Hospital. He emerged determined to get his life together. Typical of Carl, it didn't happen overnight. But he cut way back on his drinking and eventually quit with a day-to-day regimen that he has followed for several years now.

When the time came to renew his ABC contract in 1984, Bernstein announced that he wanted to be stationed in New York, where his sons live, plus he wanted a signature news segment of his own—Carl Bernstein Reports. It was no go. Again, Carl's opinion of himself didn't match the opinions of those around him. He was offered a year's extension on his contract, no signature segment. "The last thing that you want to be at the network is just another reporter," Bernstein says. "You get lost and your work gets lost." Your work and you get lost. *Attention. Respect. Recognition.* Bernstein—all grown up and famous beyond imagination—still craved these things. As he had at the *Post,* Bernstein felt unappreciated at ABC, and he quit. He says, "I did not sense that they really wanted me."

Carl went back to his book. And when he read the pages he'd written years before, they were no longer painful. He decided that was because of the pain he himself had since been through—and because he was now a father who realized that his own father had certainly loved him, though he hadn't always seemed to show it. Bernstein eventually cut a $1 million, two-book deal with Simon and Schuster. Big money for a man who had written next to nothing in a decade. But he was still Carl Bernstein, though a chastened Carl Bernstein with a secret emotion.

"I was frightened," he says, "genuinely frightened."

January 23, 1989 . . .

Hulk Hogan is at New York's Madison Square Garden in a one-fall grudge match with Big Boss Man, and Bernstein is here to see it with his nine-year-old son, Max, a pro-wrestling fan. "You know anything about pro wrestling?" Bernstein asks. "I don't either. I'd like to." So while Max hoots, howls, boos, and cheers, Carl works the crowd.

"He does this all the time," says his friend Magui Nougue-Sans with a sigh.

With this audience, the famous Carl Bernstein is in no danger of being recognized, and before the evening is out, his instincts take over. He learns that the wrestlers are told who will win or lose their scripted matches just before they enter the ring. He discovers each wrestler's income and that the big money is in TV, not live shows like this. He discovers how much Titan Sports, the corporate promoter, grosses in a year, how much profit it makes. Bernstein beams with a cub reporter's pride.

"That ain't bad—9:46 and I got it all figured out."

Failure can be redemptive.

Bernstein has learned that much. But is it enough?

"I feel good," he says, "because there were two periods of serious pain in my life—and the result of them both is this book. I was trying to do the best work I could, deal with my children, my ex-wife. Was my production as high? Absolutely not. I was trying to hold the roof up. Instead of it being seen as a period of me dealing with painful realities, they were scorecarding it by whether it's up or down. That's craziness! At some point I had to say, 'I have to be the person I am, and I have to get rid of some of this stuff, this anger, I've been carrying around all these years.'

"The point when I was able to do that was when I got the hell out of Washington. It's the ethic of the place—things aren't measured in terms of real life down there. It's about deals and minutiae. It's about fading stars and shooting stars. That's crazy. The real thing is what kind of person you are underneath. Other people's feelings perhaps were not one of my priorities when I was young. Being late has got nothing to do with being famous, and it's truly selfish and something that I've had for much too long. Clearly, I had a problem with money. I was selfish. I hope I'm a different person these days.

"But I'm not going to put myself on the psychoanalytic couch for the public. I like being Bernstein, I really do. One of the things I've learned to do that I didn't do, except with Woodward, is say, 'Hey, I need some help. I need my friends.' I think in those days I did try to give the impression of being invulnerable. I've changed in that regard. I think I've learned something about humility. What you make out of difficult periods is who you are. That's how I measure people and that's how I want to be measured. And that's not about winning and losing."

Carl Bernstein is never short of eloquence—or self-justification. Once again, he asks indulgence: Don't judge him by who he was; judge him by the person he has become. But Carl is still Carl. He's miffed that people are calling *Loyalties* his comeback. Anyone who knows him well, he says, wouldn't say that. But it is Woodward who has said it. Carl will still visit a person's home for a week and never offer to wash the dishes, until he's asked. Then he'll cheerfully do them as if the idea had simply slipped his mind before. He will still get star-struck when a friend successfully impersonates

Debra Winger on the phone and invites him to a party. Do you think she wants to go to bed with me? he'll ask. Yet when the joke is revealed, he will laugh at himself harder than anyone. And if a person's father dies, it is still Carl who shows up at the funeral. If a person is sick at home, it is still Carl who stops by.

As they've always said, "That's Carl."

Even as he changes, he stays the same. "Carl has extreme self-awareness and extreme self-delusion," says a friend. "He will say, 'I've screwed up and hurt people and spent too much money.' And then, after all this regurgitation of self-awareness, he'll do it all again."

After everything—after all the pain, the struggle, the revelations—still nothing comes easy to Carl. When he gets somewhere on time, it's still a pleasant surprise. Even writing *Loyalties* was a typical Bernstein ordeal. Woodward nearly locked him in his Georgetown house to get him writing. He told Bernstein: "Carl, you've done fifty pages in seven years and you're going to do the last several hundred in the next three months. Tell me how that's going to work?" But it did. And that is the test.

Passing the test of fame is another matter. "I don't think that I handled it great," Bernstein says, acknowledging that his arrogance was only worsened by his early fame. Until *Loyalties*, Bernstein had become the very caricature of a man who was famous for being famous. New York's satirical magazine *Spy* named him to its list of journalistic "coasters"—people living off their past glories. After tailing him one night as he wandered from party to bar to bar, *Spy* also chose him as runner-up in its Ironman Nightlife Decathlon.

Bernstein flashes the old bravado: The *Spy* article didn't bother him. But with friends, he isn't so cocky anymore. He asked Chip Brawn, "Does it make me look like a gadabout, jumping from car to car?" Says Brawn, "He's hurt by it. He's obviously a little image-conscious, and it bothers him." Yet the mocking press may have one advantage for a man who has always craved not only respect, but also attention and recognition. "It preserves his fame," says his friend Magui. "The fact that he is losing his fame bothers him. He would not like to let it bother him, but it does." Says his friend Eve Ensler, "Carl is a man who is struggling. How Carl perceived fame then and now is very different. He's really at odds with it and asking why it has meant so much to him. Carl is trying to redeem himself."

These are Carl's new friends. Among his old friends, the skeptics abound. "To tell you there is really a true-blue, sterling, plug-ahead person there," says a woman who has known Bernstein for twenty years, "I don't believe it anymore. Carl is almost fifty years old. I mean, it's grown-up time." Even Ben Bradlee, the godfather of the Watergate legend, has told friends he has given up on Carl. He feels guilty about this because of Bernstein's stupendous contribution to the Washington Post, but Bradlee doesn't respect Bernstein's life-style or the thoughtless way he has treated people. Today, says a friend of both men, Bradlee holds Bernstein in "near contempt."

"Why do we go on loving him and liking him?" one Bernstein friend asks. "He's like a great black hole that gobbles up the friend-ship. I have come to carefully monitor and edit my friendship with Carl. I like him and enjoy him, but I don't take him too seriously. He just takes more than he gives."

But at least Loyalties is finally done.

And it's a niche Bernstein was never able to find before. Its writ-erly grace harks back to the early, evocative pieces he fought to do at the Post. With Loyalties, Bernstein is once again the outsider on the attack—assaulting the Establishment that ran the witch-hunts, glo-rifying his own left-wing roots, clearing his parents, purging him-self of the guilt and rage he has felt for a lifetime—and blaming it on Washington, the city in which his parents were assaulted, in which he was made mythical. Yet Loyalties also is an Establishment book. Ted Koppel has praised it. It has kept Bernstein living in luxury. It has received an extraordinary amount of publicity—in Vanity Fair, Fame, New York and Rolling Stone magazines—not only because of its content but also because it is the long-awaited return of the Watergate legend. It has made Bernstein once again a talk-show guest on everything from "Good Morning America" to "Late Night with David Letterman." In today's America, Loyalties could be as comfortably excerpted in Reader's Digest as in the Socialist Review.

Bernstein has finally done it.

He finally has got it both ways.

February 2, 1989, evening . . .

Bernstein is lecturing tonight in New York's Andy Warhol Ball-room, where the old wooden floor is splattered with lavender, blue, white, red, pink, and green paint, creating the illusion that it was in this very room that Warhol memorialized America's modern celeb-rity culture. Celebrity Carl Bernstein sees no irony in speaking in this room with two washed-white busts of Warhol posted like smirk-ing sentries behind him. About a hundred sophisticated people talk in gentle voices, wearing a lot of black and gray, holding a lot of cigarettes. Tama Janowitz, John Gregory Dunne, Victor Navasky—

they all have come to hear Bernstein talk about the city of Washington and to read aloud from *Loyalties*.

"What must my father have thought when he looked at Eastland's fat face?" Bernstein asks. Washington, he says, was a small, segregated town in the fifties, and his parents and other idealists tried to change it, improve it, as they did the nation. For this, they were attacked and shunned. That is the larger truth. Then Bernstein says, almost casually, "The people I knew best suffered as a result of these actions."

It is impossible to avoid the thought: Bernstein could be speaking of himself, of the suffering child who is now the man who for a lifetime has carried the debilitating shame and confusion that shaped and distorted—will forever shape and distort—his life. That is the smaller truth, Bernstein's truth, the *real* truth.

MARCH 19, 1989

RUTH AND BUCKY JENKINS
In the Wake of a Son's Suicide

*R*uth and Bucky Jenkins are suspended somewhere between despair and redemption. It has been that way for several years now, ever since their son, twenty-two-year-old Ricky, killed himself. Ricky was always trouble. Or at least always *in* trouble. He'd break the rules and charm his way out. He was so charming. And caring, not at all mean-spirited. It's just that for as long as anybody can recall, no one could tell Ricky Jenkins what to do, not his folks, his friends, his teachers. As a boy he broke windows, vandalized the local pool, rigged a water fountain to drench Sister Claire. His father was a fireman. Ricky set a field on fire.

It's so easy to look back now and say Ricky was crying out for attention, for respect. Nobody saw that then. He was just a bad boy, and his troubles only grew with age. He discovered drugs at thirteen and went on to get a girl pregnant, skip school, bounce from job to job, become addicted to, of all things, model airplane glue. Life became a labor. Even as a boy Ricky talked about escaping, finding what he called freedom, a mysterious thing that seemed vague and fantastic to those who loved him but seemed very real to Ricky. Finally, at a time when life appeared better for him, Ricky waited until everyone was gone from his parents' house, went to the little shed in the yard, closed the door, started his motorcycle, and died from carbon monoxide poisoning.

Ricky wanted to be free of his emotional pain, free of his imagined worthlessness, free of a closing circle of high expectations and repeated failures, free of his addiction. And he wanted his parents to be free of him. But they are not. Because Ricky wasn't only the cause of his family's troubles, but also their reflection. And nearly three years after Ricky's death, that is what Ruth and Bucky, ages fifty and fifty-two, are still confronting. Every day they ask themselves why Ricky did this—to himself and to them. Because the suicide of a child leads parents into a dark tunnel of soul-searching that descends into their histories and psyches, reawakening fears long buried. Those who emerge are stronger. Yet some don't emerge.

49

For them, life after the suicide is never better than before. How do you take responsibility but not blame? That is what Ricky's parents, particularly his father, are struggling to learn. They haven't yet found redemption. But God knows, they're trying.

Bucky and Ruth Jenkins pulled into their driveway that Saturday night in 1984, and right away Bucky noticed that the lock on the red storage shed to the right of the house was hanging open. Bucky, who rose from rookie to assistant fire chief of Arlington, Virginia, noticed that kind of thing without effort. He was a detail man, a man who believed that a life's achievements were constructed one brick at a time. He'd done well that way. It also was like Bucky to feel a rush of irritation that one of the kids, Ricky or his then-twenty-eight-year-old brother, Lee, would have gone off and left the shed open while their folks were in the mountains. Most likely, Ricky was the culprit. Even a loving father couldn't argue with history. Ruth went to the house and Bucky to the shed. Before latching the lock, though, he glanced inside. That moment is forever captured in stop-motion in his mind: There on the floor, lying atop a bed of storage blankets, was Ricky, motionless, his eyes closed. Anger flashed in Bucky at the thought that his boy would play so sick a joke.

"Get up!" he said curtly.

His words and his horrible recognition came simultaneously. He bent down and touched Ricky's skin, cold and firm. As a fireman, Bucky had touched a score of corpses, and he knew instinctively that his boy was dead. But he ran to the house, ordered his wife to call for help, and ran back to the shed, where he tried to revive Ricky. No chance. Bucky stroked his boy's hair and sobbed, which no one had ever seen him do. Through his tears, he kept asking, "Why would he do this? Why would he do this?"

Bucky was close to hysteria that night, and he was not a man prone to hysteria. He ranked no manly virtue higher than being in control—in control of himself and, by virtue of his role as provider, in control of his wife and children. They were his responsibility, and he was proud of that. When Ruth went back to work after twenty years of child-rearing, Bucky insisted she spend her income only on herself. Bucky would provide for the family. Bucky was the strong one. The posture was something of a loving joke in the family, because Ruth and the kids knew Bucky was cotton candy beneath the gruffness—"a soft touch," they called him. He'd rant and rave, bark orders, but they knew he wasn't so strong as he pretended, as they allowed him to pretend. The funny thing is that Bucky also knew this about himself. And he knew his family knew. It was just a game they agreed to play. That night, though, Bucky lost it. "Why not me!" he screamed, again and again, revealing almost immediately his terrible guilt about Ricky's life and death. "Why him?" he asked plaintively. "Why not me?"

Ruth, obedient wife Ruth, was not herself that night either. "Shut up!" she roared. "He's gone, he's dead! There's nothing you can do about it, so shut up!" Shocked, Bucky shut up and regained his control. In the next few days he handled all the arrangements with military precision. But he also became obsessed with finding a suicide note. They nearly tore the house apart. Ricky's younger sister, nineteen-year-old Janet, even looked in Ricky's secret drug-stash compartment in his bedroom, but no note. Bucky kept saying Ricky wouldn't do this, not without a note, but everyone else concluded he had. Then Ricky's older sister, twenty-five-year-old Linda, mentioned that the passage her mother had marked in the daily book of readings in the upstairs bathroom was oddly relevant to the suicide.

A look that Linda will never forget flashed on her mother's face, and she tore up the steps. "I didn't mark this passage," she said calmly when she returned. They had found Ricky's note: "*I surrender my will to the wisdom of a loving God.*" The words comforted the Jenkins family because it meant to them that Ricky hadn't killed himself to punish them. He didn't *blame* them. Says Janet, "Ricky just wanted out."

It was a sentiment easier to voice than to truly accept.

Ruth McNey was sixteen and Bucky Jenkins was eighteen when they married, and both were running away from their childhoods. They met when Bucky's best friend, also Ruth's boyfriend, asked Bucky to entertain her while he was in California for a few weeks. Bucky did, and the old story played out. In time, Ruth and Bucky had a son, Lee. Suddenly, they felt helpless. Raise a child? How do you do that? Of only one thing were they confident: their childhoods were no guide.

She'd grown up in the Maryland suburbs of Washington, D.C., and her father was a clerk at the patent office. It was a good job, but he was an alcoholic. She wasn't beaten or abused, but the house, a nice little house, was always in turmoil, with her mother riding her father about his drinking. He was a weak man, warm and loving with Ruth, an only child, but forever sad. Her mother, a strikingly beautiful woman, worked as a secretary before most mothers worked,

and Ruth was at home alone a lot. But despite the sometimes desperate atmosphere, she always felt loved, if lost. Life got worse in
her teens when her mother, too, became an alcoholic. By the time
Ruth had kids, her folks were riding a hopeless seesaw of drunken
regrets and recriminations. She never asked their advice, and they
never offered.

Young Ruth was a quiet, lonely, and frightened girl. She was
pretty, but she believed she was ugly, especially next to her mother.
Short, five feet two inches, petite and well-formed, Ruth had an
infectious smile. But like her father, she also harbored an abiding
sadness and fear. She hated arguments; she'd heard enough, and
she'd do nearly anything to keep from arguing, especially with
Bucky.

In those days, Bucky had a touch of the know-it-all about him.
But then, he'd come up the hard way, perhaps the hardest way, and
if his confidence was part show, it worked. He knew even then that
determination was his life's advantage. Bucky had grown up in Ber-
ryville, Virginia, on a 263-acre farm owned by an old bachelor.
Bucky's grandmother, the old man's housekeeper, had taken Bucky
from his alcoholic mother at age one, after she had beaten him. His
father was already dead. After that, Bucky's mother disappeared,
except for rare visits when mother and son would end up at a local
bar. Bucky laughs and says, "She thought nothing of reaching across
the bar stool and smacking me."

Grandmother—Granny, as he called her—was Bucky's family.
She was a tough one, Granny, and Bucky was rarely hugged or
kissed. But she loved him dearly, even if he was too young to understand it. She wore ragged clothes and had holes in her shoes, but
not little Bucky. No way did Granny have enough money to spoil
him, but Bucky never stood out at school as a Raggedy Andy, like
some of the other dirt-poor farm kids.

With no other children near the farm, Bucky was without playmates but not without responsibilities. A tiny boy with short legs
and a wide chest and shoulders, Bucky could heft two fifty-pound
buckets of feed by the time he was twelve. He was proud of that
then, and he is proud of it still. He was a gentle, vulnerable boy who
always adopted the runts from the farm animal litters. Usually,
they'd die or be killed by their parents or siblings or the old man.
But if Bucky got them first, he'd nurse them and protect them. And
when he walked across the farmyard it was with a menagerie of
yelping, quacking, squealing runts behind him.

One animal stands out in his mind: a crippled Black Angus steer that couldn't bend his front knees. Bucky, nine years old then, was walking in a far corner of the farm in the first cold of early winter when he came upon the newborn calf with its mother. She was cleaning him with her tongue, her breath rising in the chill, and nudging him to stand, but he couldn't. Bucky knew the calf would die if left overnight, so he bent down on one knee and lifted the calf, probably fifty pounds, and draped its legs over his shoulders. Then, with the mother mooing ominously and bumping him as he walked, Bucky trudged back to the barn. The old man took one look and started out for his gun.

Bucky begged him not to kill the calf. "I'll raise him, I'll take care of him," he pleaded, giving the kind of promise suburban kids make about hamsters and goldfish. Reluctantly, the old man relented, and the Black Angus, which came to be named Benchleg, lived, learning to use his front legs like a spry, elderly man uses a walker, hopping along on them in synchronized motion. For years, wherever Bucky went on the farm, Benchleg, 900-pound Benchleg, hopped along behind, more like a dog than a steer. "Lord, I loved that animal," Bucky says.

Bucky was thirteen when his grandmother died. She'd been sick, but, deep in his child's world, Bucky hadn't understood the gravity of her illness. When she died, he was struck with a deep guilt. At the funeral, he recalled a gift she had given him as a young boy—a Navy uniform with a white cap and a whistle and a red string that hung over the shoulder. He'd seen it in the Sears catalog and coveted it immediately. One day it just showed up. He'd taken it with glee, of course, probably even said thank you. But it wasn't until the funeral, when it was too late, that Bucky realized that Granny had likely paid a month's wages for that Navy uniform. And all the other gifts: shoes, pants, shirts, toys that he'd taken without a thought. Why, only days before she died, he'd asked for spending money, and she'd given him two dollars. It was her last two dollars, Bucky knew that, but he took it anyway. Suddenly, Bucky realized that the things she'd given him, things he'd taken thoughtlessly, had been wrapped in Granny's love, silently, without display. Her love was not in the items themselves, but in the sacrifices she had made to give them. It was a keen, empathetic insight for a boy entering his self-absorbed teens. But to Bucky the lesson wasn't that he was only a child, as Granny most certainly knew, but that he was ungrateful and, in his own word, worthless. "Besides Ruth, my grandmother was the only person who ever loved me," he says, "and that's how I repaid her."

Bucky left the farm after that and moved to Maryland's Washington suburbs, where he lived with an aunt and uncle he knew only vaguely. "They were good to me," he says, "but they really didn't have time for me. They had a family of their own. I was just a pain, another mouth to feed. Nobody is going to help you."

Bucky grew to be a muscular young man, short, five feet eight inches, but strong, especially in his upper body. He was outgoing and popular, a leader of the hot-rod gang he hung out with, seemingly confident, even cocky. He dressed sharply, liked nice cars, and had plenty of girlfriends. And he followed a hard philosophy: "The only person I can trust 100 percent is me. I trust me. The only time I've been hurt is when I trusted someone 100 percent."

After Ruth and Bucky married, she stayed home with the kids and he worked as a carpet layer. Bucky earned $8,000 in 1955, had a company car and an expense account. But Bucky always wanted to be a fireman, and the next year he took a $3,720-a-year job as a rookie with the Arlington, Virginia, fire department, just outside Washington. By then, though, he and Ruth were used to the big money, and to make up the shortfall Bucky worked side jobs, as many as four in twenty-four hours. He laid carpets, worked in a factory, drove a limousine. Then he'd go off and drive a taxi, not only for money but also to learn the streets so he'd be a better fireman. He started a housepainting business. On the side, he got his high-school degree. Nobody ever accused Bucky Jenkins of being lazy.

But Bucky's ambition also meant he wasn't home much, and when he was home he was exhausted and short-tempered. Bucky was not naturally at ease with kids bouncing on his lap. He hugged them, told them he loved them, played with them, but somewhere deep inside he felt uneasy showing his emotions. They hinted at dependency; taking love implied that a man needed love, needed others, needed even to trust others, perhaps 100 percent. Bucky was the kind of man who enjoyed giving gifts, but who squirmed nervously when it was his turn to receive them. It was never easy for him to accept love. It still isn't.

He was a calm, steady man, but Bucky also was a man with a boiling intensity. And if his gentle words weren't heeded quickly, they were likely to become loud, blunt commands, with his firemen or his children. But kids have a way of not listening, of being beyond precise control. And Bucky remembers that most of his time at home was spent disciplining the kids or asking them to leave him alone because he was so tired. He'd lose his temper a lot in those days, snap, go into a rage, break a dish, threaten, spank the kids, order them to their rooms. "I was wrong in most cases," he says. Then Bucky would feel bad. The next day, he'd go out and buy them a gift or an ice-cream cone—offerings always wrapped in his love, silently, without display. It became a pattern that Bucky now regrets.

"I didn't understand," he says. "I just knew my children, my wife, my family had to have a home, a place to hang their hat, which I never did as a boy. If I came home with ten dollars in my pocket, I did good. No matter what it cost me. The children don't understand. They just know you're not there. I tried to buy their love. It was always monetary, trying to buy my way through life. Ricky was smart enough to see through it."

Bucky was hard on himself as a boy, and he is hard on himself today.

Ricky was different from the other kids from the start. At eight months he climbed out of his crib. His folks installed crib extenders on the sides, so he climbed over the ends. At two, he wouldn't go to sleep. He'd run around the house until midnight and then just drop over on the floor. The doctor gave him sedatives, but they seemed to make him worse. By the time Ricky was three, Ruth had four kids, but Ricky took more out of her than all the others.

"Sometimes I thought I'd lose my mind," she says.

Nobody thought Ricky had a problem then. He was just Ricky, as everyone in the family came to say. "That's just Ricky." He was always in trouble. "I know he got a lot of spankings," says Ruth, "but they didn't seem to have any effect on him." Ricky turned out to be the smartest of the kids, talking very early and acquiring a twinkling curiosity that only meant more trouble. And he was stubborn, no surprise. Ruth was stubborn, demanding that the kids keep their rooms meticulously tidy, nagging them about small failings. "I thought all you had to do was work at it and you could be perfect," she says. "Just work at it—and make everyone else work at it." And Bucky, well, Bucky was stubborn by everyone's account. But Ricky was the worst.

"If he didn't want to do something," says Ruth, "he didn't."

They called him Dennis the Menace. He was so cute, small, and sensitive, like his father had been, and outgoing, precocious, and popular. He was an intuitive boy, and it sometimes seemed he could read people's minds, or at least their emotions. He was always quick to notice if someone was angry or sad, quick to cheer them up. He brought home wounded birds galore. But his sensitivity also gave him a way to put things over on people, and he was relentless at using his charm and brains to get his way.

Ruth and Bucky tended to see their children's behavior as a reflection of themselves, and they often tweaked the kids' guilt when they misbehaved: "How can you do this to me?" they'd ask. In no time, quick-witted Ricky was tweaking his parents' guilt. Once he brought home a stray dog and Ruth made him take it back. For years after that, whenever they argued, Ricky would suddenly say, "You made me take my dog back!" Ruth wasn't able to see this as artful manipulation. "I felt very bad, an inch high," she says. "Ricky always knew how to push the right buttons."

So eloquent was little Ricky that they often joked that he could talk you out of your last dollar. Among his friends he was known for getting reluctant pranksters to ignore their better judgment. His reputation for being in trouble got him accused of pranks he hadn't even committed. He was always rounded up with the usual suspects. Like so many kids of the type, Ricky was an underachiever and his grade-school report cards inevitably included a teacher's remark: "Richard does not work to his full potential." Ricky soon came to see himself as others saw him. On his mom's birthday card he once wrote: "I know I've made it hard over the years, but I love you for putting up with me." And in a childhood will and testament in which he left his eyes to science, he wrote: "Maybe someone can use them to see things the right way."

The first two Jenkins kids, Lee and Linda, made it through childhood with the usual bumps and scrapes. Linda was a "goody-goody" and not very rebellious, though she did go off and get married early. Lee and Bucky had some rough times during Lee's teens, with a lot of yelling and a little shoving. But Lee also had his father's ambition. Always, he had a paper route or a job. Like his dad, Lee tended toward the know-it-all, and they clashed plenty. But Lee had a quality that made life easier: He'd back down, not push every minor dispute to the wall. Ricky never backed down. As a boy, he often refused to say "I'm sorry." Says little sister Janet, "Ricky was never afraid of my father, and that used to drive my father crazy."

It wasn't until seventh grade that Ruth and Bucky began to take Ricky's troubles seriously. The Catholic school he attended insisted that Ricky go for counseling, and the counselors reported that Ricky was like a "clenched fist." That shocked Ruth and Bucky, because Ricky seemed so lackadaisical. He didn't take anything seriously, rarely finishing projects. To Bucky, he seemed like a quitter. It was recommended that Ricky be given more responsibility, at home and at school: He was on too tight a rein and chafing at the bit. Ruth talked to the principal about that advice and was told that Ricky was a troublemaker who would conform or be out. Ruth now believes that a strict Catholic school wasn't the best place for a boy looking for any petty rule to resist.

At home, they tried to give Ricky more responsibility. They hadn't entrusted him with much because he handled it so badly. They had let Ricky's older brother and sister baby-sit at his age, for instance, but not Ricky. After the counseling, they tried: The experiment ended with Ricky's little sister calling her folks in tears—Ricky had held her down and sat on her.

The Ricky stories just went on and on. At ten, he and a friend stole beer from the refrigerator. He once got caught climbing on the roof of his school. Before he was old enough to drive, he took a car out for a joyride. When he was old enough to drive, he had a series of accidents and tickets and lost his license. He once called his father to say he'd gotten the family car stuck but didn't remember where. Bucky found it axle-deep in a field of mud; it had to be lifted out by a crane. In high school he would run away for days at a time and return for the inevitable guilt-inducing lecture from his parents: "We love you. Why did you put us through this?" In fourth grade Ricky had scored as high as the ninety-second percentile on his achievement tests, but by high school his scores had fallen drastically. He dropped out of school with two months to go.

"I just can't hack it," he said.

And the glue he had begun to sniff years before was now a daily ritual. Modeling glues then were a cheap, mildly hallucinogenic high. But the toxic chemicals in the glue—now removed from most glues—also could contribute to depression and aggressiveness. Because Ricky built models, his parents for a long time didn't suspect. When they learned, a battle that lasted a decade ensued. There were raids on his room, ultimatums, counselors, psychiatrists, drug rehab programs. Ruth stopped buying brown paper lunch bags, because Ricky used them to sniff glue. Nothing stopped him.

"I just like it," he'd say.

Even his friends, who were as rebellious as Ricky, couldn't understand his habit. "A slummy drug," said one friend. "Disgusting," said another. Glue containers were all over the house, his breath reeked of it, his clothes were spotted with it. His friends rode him fiercely to stop, knowing it was dangerous. Besides, it changed Ricky. Normally, he was outgoing and upbeat, ready for action, even if it was troublesome. He'd do any favor for a friend. He never forgot a birthday, and he bought Christmas presents even for mere acquaintances. But after sniffing glue, he was lethargic. *Life sucked. It was a waste, no use.* And sometimes he was mean, occasionally hitting his high-school girlfriend Denise during an argument. Then he'd immediately become "the other Ricky"—the sweet, vulnerable, repentant Ricky. He'd apologize, swear he'd never do it again, that he'd quit glue, that he'd kill himself if she ever left him. She'd forgive him, but he never changed.

Ricky and Bucky were at each other constantly by the time Ricky reached high school, with Bucky now seeing Ricky's rebelliousness as a taunt. Once, when he discovered Ricky was growing marijuana in the yard, Bucky asked angrily, "Are you trying to make a fool out of me?" It got so Bucky hated to come home. "You love a kid, but you know that you can't come home without getting on that kid," he says. "Every day, you have to come home and say his name in a nonloving way. Every day." It even got physical. Ricky's friends recall that it was always Ricky who tried to slug his father after, say, Bucky had smashed Ricky's glue-sniffing bottle. But Bucky could be threatening too. "I can still kick your ass out the door!" he once bellowed at Ricky. After a dispute, though, Ricky's friends were always amazed that father and son made up so quickly, as if nothing had happened.

Yet for all the anger, Ricky idolized his father. As a boy, he had collected firemen's memorabilia, and every time Bucky won a promotion, Ricky would hang banners in the house congratulating him. To his friends, Ricky often talked about how brave his dad was, about the lives he'd saved, about how he'd made it in the world on his own, without help from anyone. Says Ruth, "He had an unrealistic view of his father." Ricky's close friends couldn't recall a time Ricky spoke badly of his dad. On the contrary, he often talked about how much he loved him, how much his father had done for him—or tried to do for him. He talked about it so much that some of his teenage friends thought it was weird.

But Ricky couldn't break out of the descending spiral. His parents were admittedly hard on him, demanding he do better, try harder, straighten up. After all, he had so much potential. But Ricky seemed determined to prove he didn't, that he wasn't worthy of the hope people placed in him. He was hard on himself, unable to behave yet racked with guilt for his failings. To girlfriends—the people Ricky seemed to confide in most—he talked about how he was "nothing," how he was "worthless," how he had let himself and his folks down by not living up to his potential. Despite the bravado, Ricky felt powerless. He even dabbled in Satanism, a renegade philosophy that attracts society's losers, people desperately trying to bolster sagging egos.

"You'd better watch out," Ricky once told Denise ominously. "I have powers you don't know." Yet for all his swagger, Denise and Ricky's friends knew he was deeply insecure. Ricky once quit a job when he discovered that a girlfriend made more money in her job. He wouldn't date girls who were taller. He threatened suicide so often in high school that Ricky's friend Charlie Hale finally ignored the threats. Ricky also was horribly jealous, and Denise recalls that after a man once talked to her briefly at a nightclub, Ricky grilled her all night long: "What's that guy got that I don't have?"

Ricky fancied himself a loner, a man who needed no one. It was a philosophy much like his father's, but Ricky didn't have the determination or strength to live it. He was naturally artistic and often drew pictures of a lone wolf howling in the night. He was a musician with a natural ear, and he played a decent electric guitar and wrote good lyrics. His songs are full of the lone wolf's cry, of the desire to be free, to get on his motorcycle and go somewhere faster than the cops could go after him. Ricky loved speed, loved to dirt-bike and drive fast. He would sometimes drive seventy miles an hour on suburban streets, scaring his passengers witless.

In time, his girlfriend Denise learned an important clue to Ricky's character: The more she complained or screamed or demanded that he slow down, the wilder he drove. If she said nothing, acted calm, Ricky would soon slow down. It isn't so shocking, really. Ricky gained control by making others, particularly his father, lose control. Chaos was his upper hand.

Ricky's great dream was to be a rock star. He could almost see himself onstage. He wrote: "Now I'm all grown up, playin' in a rock 'n' roll band / All those schools didn't even give me a hand." But Ricky didn't have the fire. A musician who played with him said he was good, but lazy. He played rhythm to a dozen or so simple rock songs but refused to take on the hard job of learning lead guitar. Ricky was tossed out of one band after only two practices because he insisted on playing songs the band didn't play.

Yet mixed in with Ricky's rebel tunes were sad ballads that cried out for love and conformity. He wasn't always Ricky the rebel. He envied his older brother's success, for instance, and craved a house, a good job, a wife. When he and one of his girlfriends once moved in together, Ricky insisted they get plants, a cat, and a dining room table. Then the shocker: He insisted on place mats. During the last year of his life, Ricky dated a woman named Connie, and she recalls that he often talked about the nice things they'd own someday. This, at the same time he couldn't keep a job. Toward the end, the fantasies may have become too fantastic even for Ricky.

To Ruth and Bucky, though, Ricky's life at twenty-two seemed better. The horrible arguments had stopped a few months earlier. Connie had laid down the law about the glue, and Ricky had taken a stash of tubes outside and tossed them away. He seemed calm and relaxed. He was talking about going to computer school. "Everyone just seemed so happy," Ruth says.

But if Ricky's life looked brighter on the outside, it was more of the same on the inside. A week before Ricky's death, his old friend Charlie Hale had fired him from Charlie's housepainting business. Charlie and Ricky had learned the painting business in high school from Ricky's father, and Charlie had started his own company after graduation. Bucky had tried to give his housepainting operation to Ricky—including clients, trucks, equipment—but Ricky had refused, saying he wasn't going to be painting houses all his life. Now he was painting houses for Charlie. But Charlie had gotten lots of complaints about Ricky's work. He would talk to Ricky, who'd apologize and cheerfully say, "I guess I missed it." Ricky was even bucking for a raise. Then Charlie found him doing glue on the job, and that was it.

Ricky also was having trouble with Connie, though nobody knew it. He had promised her he would stop the glue, but he hadn't. When they were vacationing in the mountains, she found Ricky's hidden glue stash. She didn't say anything. But she too had had enough. She could no longer bring herself to say "I love you," and Ricky was very upset by that. When he called, she often found herself too busy to see him. She denied to him that she was pulling away, but looking back she knows that she was. And if Ricky was good at anything, it was reading emotions. He most certainly knew.

There were other pressures too. One of his oldest friends had told Ricky he didn't want to see him again until he stopped doing glue. Ruth and Bucky, adjusting to the kids' having grown up, were having marital troubles, and Lee and his wife, whom Ricky adored, were separated. Ricky also was having trouble finding modeling glue that contained the chemicals that made him high, because stores had taken it off the shelves. Bucky had even found Ricky sniffing automobile lacquer in the basement one day.

Yet perhaps the greatest hint of Ricky's desperation was that just before his suicide he made a pass at his younger sister, who rebuffed him. For several nights before his death, Ricky asked her to come to his room to talk. She refused, afraid he'd try again. She felt that he wanted only to get closer to her emotionally. But she says, "That's not something I should have to put up with."

Nobody knows what went on in Ricky's mind, because he apparently told no one of his plans. He had gone to his girlfriend Connie's house at 5:00 A.M. a few months earlier, shaking and crying, saying that he had gone to the shed to commit suicide, but that he couldn't. He told her that all he could think about was how much his family loved him. And he couldn't do it. That morning, for the first time, Ricky told Connie that maybe he needed help to overcome his glue addiction. Certain that Ricky had scared himself out of suicide, Connie told no one.

Who knows why, but on that last night, Ricky showered, put on clean clothes and a gold necklace, and, without doing glue, drugs, or booze, killed himself.

Ruth worried that Bucky wouldn't live through it.

Ricky's suicide hit everyone like a Mack truck at sixty miles an hour. It was like an actual physical pain that wouldn't subside, like aching joints or migraine headaches, but a pain of the spirit. So drained were they of joy and optimism that sadness seemed to curl their bodies like bentwood. Bucky was wiped out. He didn't go back to work for two months, and Ruth wondered if he ever would, or if he'd take early retirement. He sat in his stuffed chair in the basement rec room with a box of tissues on the table next to him, and he cried. He was defeated. Not only was Ricky dead, that was anguish enough, but it was also as if everything Bucky had ever believed was suddenly, in a single flash of horrible light, revealed to the world and to himself as wrong and shallow and flawed. For the first time in his life, Bucky was face-to-face with himself.

For a year, husband and wife were no use to each other. Bucky withdrew into himself, taking no consolation and giving none. Ruth found him crying in the shed one day. "Leave me alone!" he snapped. She ran to her bedroom and cried by herself. Then Bucky threw himself into his work. He seemed to blame only himself. On the other hand, Ruth was angry at everyone—Bucky, the kids, the psychiatrists, counselors, and teachers. But thankfully, she wasn't angry at herself. She believed that she'd done about all she could to save Ricky, that he hadn't been able to save himself.

Ruth had begun this transformation even before Ricky's death. She'd gone to work against Bucky's wishes and found she felt better about herself if she voiced opinions rather than always trying to keep the peace. Ricky's little sister Janet had developed her own set of serious problems as a young teen, partly as a way to steal the spotlight from Ricky. When Ruth, who drinks no alcohol herself, took Janet to alcohol counseling, Janet's life turned around almost overnight. Ruth then attended meetings of Al-Anon, a network of support groups for the families and friends of alcoholics, and she was struck by the Al-Anon philosophy that each person is responsible for only his own life.

On the surface, it rang of Bucky's philosophy of self-reliance. But with a subtle difference: If each person is responsible for only his own life, no person is responsible for the life of another. We are in control of no one but ourselves, and to change another's behavior we must first change our own behavior. So that is what Ruth tried to do. She came to realize that she'd been deeply scarred growing up as a child of alcoholics. Like Ricky, she scapegoated, blamed others when things didn't go her way. Her notion of acceptable behavior was narrow and rigid. Ricky had never fit the mold, so she tried to make him fit. She did this not only because she believed it was right for Ricky, but because she needed Ricky's life to serve as an affirmation of her own. This, she came to believe, was selfish.

"I spent fifteen years of my life worrying about Ricky," she says. "But I was always quick to judge. Things were black and white. I got my feelings hurt a lot. I expected people to do things my way, and if they didn't, I'd sulk and get mad. Just like Ricky's manipulation of me—I never thought of it, but it's true. Whenever Ricky got in trouble, all I could say to him was, 'How could you do this to me?' I didn't think of others. I thought of myself."

The last years of Ricky's life, Ruth struggled to break her cycle of nagging and then fighting with Ricky, of trying to guilt-trip him into changing his behavior for her. She told him she didn't want drugs and drinking in the house. If he broke that rule, he couldn't live there and his pickup bands couldn't play there. Then she tried to drop the subject. She'd praise him every chance she got, having gleaned another simple insight from Al-Anon: Praise works better than criticism. Yes, she regretted that she hadn't done this earlier, that she hadn't seen her own manipulative behavior for what it was. Yes, maybe that would have saved Ricky. But Ruth knew intuitively that she wasn't to blame for her painful childhood or her ignorance as a parent. She had made choices and some were wrong, but they weren't mean-spirited. She had tried her best.

In the end, perhaps Ruth Jenkins loved herself too much to take the blame. Ricky's death beat her badly for a time. "It was like an elephant sitting on my chest," she says. But after more than a year, she began to heal. She went to suicide counseling sessions and couldn't hear enough about how people had responded to suicides in their families. She joined a suicide survivor group and eventually became its head. Looking back at Ricky's tumultuous life, Ruth finally concluded that his suicide was inevitable. "They tell people that the person gives you a gift with his suicide," Ruth says. "It's hard to believe at first. Bucky still doesn't want to hear it. But I like myself now. I'm a better person. I'm more attuned and sensitive to others' pain. I take the damn time to listen to people and their piddling problems. I look back and don't like the person I used to be. I believe my new compassion is what Ricky has given me."

It has been harder for Bucky. He wasn't able to accept that Ricky's suicide was inevitable. He struggled to control Ricky and he failed. "I can rationalize with myself that I would never have control over his actions," Bucky says. "But when I say 'responsibility,' I mean your thoughts when you say your prayers in a quiet room. That is what I mean by 'responsibility.' I can accept that I am not to blame. I can say that. But when I get in that quiet room and ask 'Why?' I can't come up with an answer. I can't for the life of me let go and say I couldn't have made a difference, because dead is dead. I am the breadwinner. I am the provider. If I don't provide for my family, I can't blame the family. I blame myself. With Ricky, somewhere along the line, I missed something. And I don't know what that is. To be so oblivious to the fact that the kid was going to take his life!"

Ricky's death forced Bucky to face what he and his family always knew—Bucky wasn't so strong as he claimed. Bucky was deeply embarrassed by his emotional breakdown. A few times when Ruth was having a rare good day, Bucky became so severely depressed that he pulled her back into her depression. Then, with Ruth out of control, Bucky could again regain his control. He would put his arm around her and say that everything would be fine. "This happened a couple of times," says Ruth, "and I decided I didn't like it." It was as if she had to be weak so Bucky could be strong, but she would no longer play.

"I never thought you'd be the strong one," Bucky told her.

Ruth and the kids tried to be understanding of Bucky's remorse, but as it dragged on they began to send the same harsh, stiff-upper-lip message he had always preached to them. It was not helpful. The older daughter, Linda, called him "pathetic." Ruth flew into a rage. "I want my husband back! I want my husband back!" she screamed, forgetting that her old husband had died with Ricky. They had all lived through the same death, but Ruth and the kids didn't understand that Bucky's grief was more intense than their own. It is a truth: Those with the most ambivalent feelings about the suicide victim—those with conflicting emotions of love and hate, anger and sorrow—will suffer the most. As father to a profoundly rebellious boy, Bucky had more to resolve.

He went to group counseling with Ruth, but he couldn't stand it, all those people pouring out their anguish so publicly. "It was not my way of handling it," he says. Ruth and the kids believed Bucky wasn't handling it. But unknown to them, Bucky was doing what he could. He'd sit for hours going through Ricky's belongings, looking for answers. "I listen to his tapes until I embarrass myself," he says. "I feel like a damned fool sitting in the house crying, listening, trying to make sense, searching for a clue. And in some of his songs you can detect his insecurities and his feelings. In one song, he almost tells you how deeply frustrated he must be, how much he hurt. In the words of his songs—songs I didn't know existed."

Soon after Ricky's death, the family wanted to tear down the shed where Ricky died. Bucky went wild, said that if they tore it down, he'd leave, they'd never see him again. Linda came to see the shed as a monument to her dad's guilt, a reminder that he should never forgive himself. Actually, it was more like a chapel. For two years after Ricky's death, Bucky would sneak off to the shed, close the door, and sit. Sometimes he cried, sometimes he talked out loud to Ricky. He always asked why. His family had forgotten, but when Ricky was a boy, he and Bucky had built that shed together. They may have fought constantly, but Ricky and Bucky always worked well together, unlike so many fathers and sons. In the shed, Bucky kept Ricky's favorite tools. He kept a cache of old Washington Redskins posters they'd collected together. He kept a clipboard on which Ricky had estimated a painting job.

But these weren't the biggest of Bucky's secrets. He had a secret that he kept not only from his family, but for a long time even from himself. Because while he and everyone else believed Bucky was angry only at Bucky for Ricky's death, he also was furious at Ricky—poor, helpless, confused Ricky. Anger at Ricky was an emotion Bucky repressed, one that even Ruth and the kids were unaware of in Bucky. It isn't easy for a parent to acknowledge anger at a child who has taken his life, because the parents are supposed to be to blame. But Bucky finally came to do it.

"I am angry at Ricky," he says, his anger and his voice quickening as he speaks. "I can say it to myself. I'm not sure I even told Ruth I have this anger. My feeling with him now is extreme anger. Oh, yeah! And it probably always will be. I was a loving father and gave him a good home. I tried daily to make him take responsibility for his life. For failing to complete these things and failing to be the man I wanted him to be, I feel shortchanged. I never got to see any of it.

"With Ricky it never worked. You had to do things the hard way. He could have had a dozen good jobs, but they weren't his bag. Ricky wanted to be the boss, but not do any of the boss's work. He wanted to walk on the job and say, 'I'm the boss.' But not do the billing or the estimates. He didn't want to work at it. I've done all the nice things for my child. Is this my reward? Ricky never gave me the opportunity to be nice to him in the later years. It was always constant correction. Go down to his room and ask for the glue. He'd deny it. I'd find it. It went on like that every day of his life. I think that in his own way, his suicide said to me, 'Kiss my ass!'"

Ricky's suicide touched Bucky's deepest insecurities, those his tough exterior and his self-reliance had long hidden. Bucky was just a young man when he decided upon his hard philosophy of life: "The only person I can trust 100 percent is me." Yet Bucky's pain at Ricky's suicide announced to everyone that he was not an island, that he couldn't always be in control, and that, like it or not, he needed the love of others. His very life depended on it. "Bucky really didn't think he needed anybody," says Ruth. "Nothing could happen that he couldn't take care of. Then it did."

Bucky knows now that this is the real message of his anguish. But it is so hard for him to be weak so that he might be strong. He has a nine-year-old grandson, Billy, who reminds him so much of Ricky. But at times Bucky must pull away. To play catch with Billy is to remind Bucky of all the times he didn't play catch with Ricky. To Ruth, Billy is a second chance. To Bucky, he is a reminder that he has been hurt before, that he could be hurt again. In his darker moments, Bucky still wonders if he is that sad, worthless little boy abandoned by a dead father and an alcoholic mother, that selfish boy who was ungrateful for his grandmother's sacrifices. Sometimes he wonders why his wife stays with him. Sometimes he wonders if he did something, some sin he can't recall, that has caused him to be punished. The power of intimacy still is a mystery to him, and sometimes he thinks about his boyhood friend, Johnny. "He was poor as dirt but with a father and mother," Bucky says. "The father was rarely home, and when he was, he was drunk. And they'd steal money off him. But all their kids lived, prospered, and married. And here I am, worked my ass off, sent them to good schools, worked myself to the bone. I could have done better with nothing."

Yet Bucky is not the person he was three years ago, and he knows it. He is less demanding, more accepting, more free with his emotions, less certain of himself. These changes sometimes seem like weakness to him, though he knows they are the first steps toward healing. Sometimes he even feels optimistic, and just recently, he went in for the complete medical exam he had been putting off for years. After three years, Bucky knows now that he must let Ricky go, accept that Ricky was his own master in life and certainly in death. He knows that if Ricky's suicide was not inevitable—and Bucky believes it was not—then his own failings as a father didn't inevitably lead to his son's death. And he knows now that he is no island, that he needs his family and friends as much as they need him. These are hard lessons, cutting to the heart of Bucky's character, lessons learned at the cost of a renegade son. But most important, Bucky knows after years of struggle that Ricky wasn't seeking revenge, that he couldn't have known how profoundly his suicide would scar his father and his mother. How could anyone have known? Bucky knows all these things now. And on his good days, he is even able to believe them.

So why did Ricky do it?

"Ricky just wanted out," his sister Janet said, and she is probably right. *"I surrender my will to the wisdom of a loving God."* Ricky Jenkins sought redemption. So does Ruth and so does Bucky. They haven't yet found it, but they are trying. God knows, they're trying.

JUNE 7, 1987

Washington Post photograph.

LYNDA BIRD JOHNSON ROBB
Daddy's Little Girl Grows Up

$\mathcal{S}$he is her daddy's daughter.

The older she gets, the more she looks like him, with the gangly frame, the long, awkward arms always seeming to search for a place to hide, the pinched, chaotic face, the nervous energy, the natural and ingratiating intimacy, the shoulders that must forever hunch toward a world of shorter people, the air of entitlement, the craving to be respected, the gnawing ambition. Her mother, Lady Bird, sees Lyndon Johnson in Lynda Bird all the time. The way she remembers faces, names, birthdays, little stories about people met in passing years ago, the beautiful, seamless, relentless way she works a room, handshake to handshake. But most like Daddy is the way Lynda suffers criticism—not well or easily or gracefully. She, too, hungers to be liked. But like her daddy, after a lifetime in the fishbowl, she has come to despair of ever being understood by others as she understands herself. So they are a lot alike, Lyndon and Lynda, daddy and daughter. Except for one mammoth, insurmountable, unchangeable difference.

Daddy was a man.

She is her husband's wife.

Lynda and Chuck stand beside each other, posing with a small crowd for one more meet-and-greet photo, this one being shot at the Strawberry Hill horse races in Richmond. *Ready, here goes . . .* And at just that instant, the Democratic senator from Virginia rises up on his tiptoes, giving him and posterity an imaginary extra inch or two on the crowd and on his very tall wife. *Ready, one more time . . .* And Chuck Robb does it again—rises up, up in his very own organic elevator shoes.

In one man's shadow, Lynda lived as a girl. In another man's shadow, she lives as a woman. She has never quite gotten used to this, still bridles at being an appendage to the men in her life. But she knows this: It's not nearly as bad as it was when her mother was young. It's not nearly as bad as it was when she herself was young.

And certainly it will not be anywhere as bad for her daughters, who will soon be going out into a very different world. These girls will have the chance, will even be expected, to stand on their own tiptoes. Lynda has seen to that, made certain they will have what she didn't, made certain her own life has been the fulcrum for profound change across three generations of Johnson women.

But still, there's always . . .

The hair.

If only she could do something with the hair.

It's raining, and before the day of politicking through Tidewater Virginia with her husband is done, Lynda will fuss about her heavy raven hair so many times it will seem like an extra guest on the trip. "Mah hair!" she moans. "Ohhh, mah hair!" She excuses herself to go to the ladies' room—that last soda, you know. But when the outer door swings open a moment later, there's Lynda, at the mirror, fussing with her hair.

But wait, stop, this is exactly the kind of intimate, invasive, seemingly insignificant little story that drives Lynda Bird Johnson Robb nuts. It drove her nuts when she was a teenager living in the White House during her father's presidency—people gossiping that she was fat, frumpy, and aloof, unmannered and clumsy, hickish—and it still drives her nuts today, at age forty-five, even after her husband has served as Virginia's lieutenant governor, governor, and now U.S. senator, even after Lynda herself has become thin, poised, and confident. It's the kind of story that once soured her on politics altogether. The kind of story that made her resist her husband's ambition to get elected. I mean, whose business is it if Lynda is in the bathroom fluffing her hair? What's it got to do with war or peace, the deficit? It just makes her look, what, silly, self-conscious, frivolous? After all these years, Lynda still doesn't like that kind of story, can't get used to it, refuses to accept it as the price of being a princess of American politics.

But still . . . That no-account hair runs like a mysterious reprise through Lynda's life. As a little girl, her hair would be curled by the Johnson family nanny, Helen Williams, and it would just hang limp. Little Lynda Bird would accuse Helen of not *really* trying to curl her hair, because if she were *really* trying, it would come out as soft and full and pretty as the hair of her younger sister, Luci Baines. Eventually, Helen gave up on Lynda's hair, and she wore it in a bob. Thirty years later, on the night of her husband's inaugural ball, that hair was still giving Lynda fits. The new first lady of Virginia was in the dressing room forever, gowned and made-up, sitting at the mirror going at that hair, which was wound in a coronet with a single, beautiful braid. Her Washington hairdresser, Evind, was in town for the occasion, but still Lynda couldn't get it just right. "She was so worried about her appearance," recalls a friend in the room that night. "It manifested itself in her worrying about her hair. We all said she looked like a fairy princess."

As ever, the princess was fearful of her public—all those people looking and whispering, judging her by her unruly hair or her too-big-for-her-face smile or her skinny legs, judging her by what is least important in life, just as they had done since she was a girl, the cameras always clicking, always seeming to freeze-frame her goosey neck or her pointed nose. The camera isn't always kind to Lynda, nor was it kind to her daddy, who would maneuver to get his left profile, which he inexplicably believed to be his best, before the lens. The logjam in the dressing room that night finally ended when Governor Chuck Robb, stiff and erect in black tie and dinner jacket, came in and said sternly, "Lynda, don't spend one more minute with your hair." Says Lynda's friend wryly, "It would have been more helpful if he'd told her how beautiful she was."

It's odd how often Lynda's friends, mother, sister, husband, daughters mention that she is beautiful. Lynda does look awfully good today, especially compared with her old photos. She's striking, even charismatic. She's so tall, with pure soft white skin against black hair, with a voice and a laugh that carry. Heads turn when she enters a room. But beautiful, well, that seems a bit of a stretch, though perhaps those closest to Lynda know what she needs to hear, or still believe they must refute an image shaped long ago.

Lynda Bird wasn't a pretty child, and she knew it. Her mother and father constantly told her she was beautiful, but it didn't take. "I hate to say Lynda was an ugly duckling," says an old friend of the Johnsons, "but it was sort of that way." It was Luci, almost four years younger, who was the swan in the Johnson home. And Lynda Bird knew that too, was hurt by the talk that Luci was Daddy's favorite. Luci was charming and flirtatious, easy with people. Lynda Bird was her reverse image—serious and studious, the brain, shy and lacking in social confidence. She read constantly, disdained small talk and girlish frivolity. While her girlfriends played, Lynda Bird might sit off to the side, half watching, reading a book. Sometimes she wished she were a boy. She thought Daddy wanted a boy.

The studious Lynda Bird took a great interest in her father's job in the Senate. Of course, if she wanted to see her father, she had little choice—he worked night and day, every day. She'd follow him on his weekend rounds, sit on the lap of legendary House Speaker Sam Rayburn, who adored her, while the men talked politics. Lynda Bird never thought of herself as a kid. She devoured history books and loved to spout facts and correct tour guides. She once told White House curator James Ketchum that a display had to be changed because it said Abraham Lincoln's Emancipation Proclamation had freed the slaves, when, in fact, it had freed only those slaves in states still at war with the Union. It was vintage Lynda Bird: blunt to a point just this side of rudeness, eager to impress, quick to flaunt her knowledge. If she'd been a boy, they would surely have said, "That kid's gonna be president someday." But she was not a boy, and they did not say that. Indeed, her mother can't recall ever thinking that Lynda Bird might grow up to have a career.

Lynda's was a strange childhood. Lyndon Johnson was a man consumed by ambition and power and achievement. Even Rayburn, his mentor, once said he'd never known a man "as vain or more selfish than Lyndon Johnson." Lady Bird—who had been a painfully shy, serious, and studious young woman who thought she was unattractive—believed it was her duty to put Lyndon's needs before those of her daughters. Johnson biographer Robert A. Caro, in his book *The Path to Power*, portrays Johnson as a man who dominated, even psychologically brutalized, the defenseless young Lady Bird. In public, he ordered her about. At home, she brought him coffee and newspapers in bed, laid out his clothes, filled his pockets with money, pen, and cigarette lighter. Johnson's extramarital flirtations eventually became gossip for Washington insiders, and Caro writes that only a few years after his marriage, Johnson was leaving Lady Bird behind while he went for weekends to the Virginia estate of his lover, Alice Glass.

Yet Johnson also could be loving, generous, and supportive of his fragile wife. "He was awful and wonderful to Lady Bird at once," says a woman who knew her well. Johnson told Lady Bird she could do anything she put her mind to, and he made her believe it. In the game of politics, he also relied heavily on her unassuming warmth and charm. And, at least in her later years, says a friend of Lady Bird's, she "rapped Lyndon's knuckles" plenty in private as she became increasingly self-reliant. It pained Lady Bird to leave her daughters behind while she campaigned or attended congressional sessions with Lyndon, but she did, and Luci and Lynda were often left with surrogate parents such as Helen Williams. Luci was angry at her father for this, accused Lady Bird of not being a "real mother," played on her guilt. Not Lynda Bird. She was the good soldier.

Talking with Lynda about this today is a little like talking to a diplomat reciting the official position of her country: Daddy was just so committed to public service, and Mother believed her first duty was to her husband. They did what they thought best. That is that. No hard feelings. Besides, when the family was together, she says, her parents were so attentive and affectionate. Lynda then repeats a Johnson family story told again and again: Whenever Mother and Daddy went away or whenever they called home while they were gone, they always told the girls, "Know that you are loved."

"I never questioned that I was loved," Lynda says. "I'm selfish enough to have wanted more time with him, but I don't think Daddy ever thought, 'Oh, my gosh, if I do this, I won't get to be with my family.' That was not a conscious decision on his part. But I don't think he loved us any less. I don't ever remember having any anger about it then, and I don't now."

Johnson family intimates paint a darker picture. "It was just so sad," B. A. Bentsen, the wife of Texas senator Lloyd Bentsen, says of the little Lynda. "She wouldn't cry, but you could just tell she wished things were different." Says another family friend, "Lady Bird was so subservient and under the spell of Lyndon Johnson that it made it difficult for the kids."

Eventually, Lynda Bird came to think of her mother as her best friend. But her father wasn't so much a friend as an adored object. Johnson biographer Doris Kearns Goodwin argues that Johnson needed to be adored, that he could tolerate nothing less. He was fiercely loyal and generous, but in return he demanded adoration. "I believe Lynda was more hurt by her father," Goodwin says. "He was very affectionate, but he could also turn on the people he loved." Says B. A. Bentsen, "Lynda wanted his approval of everything she did, but they all seemed to work so hard—the mother and the daughters—to please him."

Soon after Lady Bird married Lyndon Johnson, he began insisting she abandon the dowdy clothes she wore in favor of tight, body-hugging dresses in bold reds and yellows. He put her in spike heels. He put her on a diet. "I don't like muley-lookin' things," he said. And, "You're sellin' yourself short." Even after they'd been married thirty years, even after Johnson was president and Lady Bird was first lady, he wouldn't hesitate to tell her in front of others in the Oval Office that her dress was too long.

He did the same with his daughters, who were named so that their initials—like those of Lady Bird Johnson—read LBJ. Every night for dinner, if Daddy was coming home, Helen Williams dressed the girls in pretty, feminine clothes. It pleased him. As they got older, the girls learned that Daddy liked clothes that made them look slim, not dresses made of heavy "saddle blankets," as he put it. This was always a problem for Lynda Bird, who as a teen wore a size fourteen. Even in college, she kept Daddy's taste in mind, once declining to buy a deep red velvet dress because Daddy didn't like any color verging on purple. When Johnson once visited Lynda Bird at the University of Texas, he surprised her with a batch of new dresses. Then, while Vice President Lyndon Baines Johnson, Daddy, sat in willing judgment, Lynda modeled every dress.

"I loved my father," Lynda says today. "I feel very loyal to him. Certainly, he wasn't perfect. No person is perfect. But I learned a long time ago not to speak for him. He doesn't need me to. My experiences with my father were very positive. I have no 'Daddy Dearest' stories."

Lynda Bird didn't want to leave Texas for Washington, but after President Kennedy's assassination, her folks feared for her life, and her mother wanted Lynda and Luci to have the once-in-a-lifetime experience of living in the White House. Besides, Lady Bird needed Lynda, needed someone to talk to honestly without fear that something she said in anger or humor would end up blown back in the newspapers. It was a Johnson family axiom: "Never say anything you don't want to read on the front page of the *New York Times*."

Except, that is, to family.

So Lynda Bird, nineteen years old, moved to Washington, where she went to George Washington University and followed the front-page-of-the-*New-York-Times* rule, trusting almost no one. As she'd done when she was the little girl left at home, she didn't complain. But her resentment showed in peevishness. She believed she'd sacrificed a lot because Daddy was in politics. The problem wasn't Daddy, who was the kind of man who believed it was more important to invite Richard Russell, the Senate's lonely bachelor eminence, over for Sunday breakfast than it was to spend the time alone with his family. No, it wasn't Daddy's fault. It was politics. Lynda Bird was wise, though, and this became her favorite saying, one she still uses today with humor and irony, one her daughters also use: "It's not fair!"

When Johnson became president, Lynda Bird and Luci became

presto! prototypes of the mythical American teenager—Gidget goes to Washington—and they knew they would be judged against that standard. "I'm not worried about you," Lady Bird would tell them. "But it's just what people might say." So Lynda Bird didn't stay out too late, she adored Johnny Mathis, she used hair spray. In the rebellious sixties, she was a girl of the fifties. Luci relished the attention; Lynda Bird hated it. Forever shy, she still felt awkward and unattractive. Lady Bird had always told the girls that politics was a life of trade-offs—Lynda lost her privacy, but she got to meet poet Carl Sandburg. She was not convinced. After all, what teen wants her "weight problem" broadcast to the nation? Yet, the story Lynda and Luci both tell to show the pain of life in the limelight came not from press sniping but from Daddy. "I will never have to worry about either girl," Johnson once said. "Lynda Bird is so smart she'll always be able to make a living for herself. And Luci Baines is so appealing and feminine there will always be some man around wanting to make a living for her." Lynda Bird's translation: "He makes it sound like no man will have me."

It wasn't until she dated actor George Hamilton that Lynda discovered brains weren't enough, that if she wanted to feel good about herself, wanted men and Daddy to feel good about her, she had to compete in the feminine world of grace and beauty. With Hamilton's encouragement, Lynda Bird reinvented herself. A Hollywood makeup man did her face, sculpted her brows. She swept her hair up to reveal a face made thin by a one-meal-a-day regimen. She jet-setted with Hamilton in Acapulco, London, Hollywood, New Orleans, on John Wayne's yacht. When her old friend Carolyn Curtis asked the secret of her new image, Lynda answered with blunt clear-sightedness: "There's no trick to it. You have to spend a lot of money on clothes and have a place to go. It's no big deal." Yet it was a big deal, and Lynda Bird's confidence soared. "He made me feel beautiful," she says of Hamilton. "I enjoyed it."

But the other Lynda Bird, who had returned to graduate from the University of Texas—and who might have made Phi Beta Kappa if she'd been able to spend four years there—also was all dressed up with smarts, seriousness, and ambition, but with no place to go.

It was 1966. She was a Johnson woman.

Two decades later . . .

She doesn't call herself Lynda Bird anymore. She calls herself Lynda, a name Luci has never gotten used to. "Lynda Bird . . . I mean, Lynda," she says. Their mother, whose real name is Claudia,

tried for years to dump the nickname hung on her by a family nurse-
maid. "Why, she's as purty as a ladybird!" the woman had ex-
claimed. No use. They'll put Lady Bird on her grave. Lynda Bird,
whose husband and friends now call her Lynda, has had better luck.
Somehow, it's nearly impossible to say Lynda Bird in the East without giving it a phony Texas twang, without implying just the hint of
pickup trucks and prairie towns. The name Lynda is more dignified, and, fortunately, it has stuck.

Says Lynda, "There is no more LBJ."

As a girl, Lynda thought about becoming a history teacher, imagined that she might become an archaeologist. Daddy encouraged
her to go to law school. But when she looks back today, Lynda
knows she saw those careers only as interludes, a year or two or
three before her marriage, when she would quit, take care of a husband, and raise a family. Naturally, she'd do volunteer work, as the
affluent wives of successful men had always done. After college,
Lynda did go to work for *McCall's* magazine. "We were before the
revolution," says her old friend Phyllis Bonanno. "Girls after college went to New York to work at magazines. That was something
acceptable." The editors of those magazines were men. No one
thought that odd.

Lynda had only one strict rule about her future then: She would
never, ever marry a politician. She'd lost too much of her life to that
game. She married Chuck Robb—a young, strapping Marine. "I
thought I was marrying a general," she says, laughing. If she needed
more proof that she didn't want a life in politics, it came during
Johnson's last year as president, 1968, while Robb was in Vietnam.
Lynda, pregnant with the first of three daughters, lay awake in her
White House bedroom listening to the protesters in Lafayette Park
chanting, "Hey, hey, LBJ, how many kids did you kill today?"
Lynda, who took criticism and rejection as badly as her father,
didn't see the war as a political or military exercise. No, she was
tormented by the vision of her father being broken and nearly destroyed by Vietnam. Lynda, the good daughter, saw it this way:
After all Daddy has done for America—civil rights, Medicare, the
poverty program—this is how they repay him. After all the sacrifices, the days, weeks, years he and Lady Bird spent away—*away
from their little girls!*—this is how they repay them. And Luci. And
her.

Since then, a lot has come down.

The biggest surprise: The strapping young Marine who was supposed to become a general became a politician. Lynda wasn't coy in

her objections. "She said, 'Hey, I've been there and you haven't,' " recalls Chuck's old friend Douglas Davidson. "But I don't think he wavered in what he wanted to do."

That is one way to look at it. Another way is through the prism of Lynda's image of herself as a woman who simply would never have vetoed—with threats of divorce or a refusal to campaign—her husband's ambition. She is asked, Would that have stopped him? "Well, you want to believe in your heart that he cares that much about you," she says. But it never came to that. "Because down deep he would resent the fact that I kept him from it, and I didn't want that."

The Robbs' marriage was traditional, and Chuck proved more willing to risk resentment on Lynda's part. "It was a fairly gradual thing," Robb says of his emerging interest in politics, and by the time he actually decided to run for lieutenant governor in 1976 Lynda no longer objected. Otherwise, he says, he'd never have run. Still, the cynics have always whispered that Robb married Lynda less for love and more to use her name as his political launching pad. Says Lynda, "I have never felt that Chuck used me. I've fussed at him about a lot of things, but that's not one of them. I never knew he was going into politics. But I don't think he had that plan, either."

Robb thought of the marriage as a kind of business contract. He was to go out and make his way in the world, and Lynda was to stay home and handle family life. They'd be a team. A certain kind of team. In the early seventies, Lynda and a group of other wives of law school students in Chuck's University of Virginia class asked their husbands if they would quit their jobs, as many of the women had done, and move to a little southern city so their wives could go to law school. Only one man said he would. Lynda remembers that Chuck was not that man. Chuck remembers that he missed that meeting.

Naturally, Lynda's choice of husband pleased Daddy. "I'm sure one of the things that attracted her to Chuck," says B. A. Bentsen, "was that he reminded her of her father." Robb was a lot like Johnson: confident, competent, ambitious—so ambitious, it turned out, that he too had time for little else. So ambitious that he too was willing to put his family after his ambition or, depending on the perspective, after his desire to serve the public. Both men also had pulled themselves up by the bootstraps—up with the help of their wives. Johnson first ran for Congress with $10,000 Lady Bird had borrowed from her father against her inheritance. Robb's marriage to Lynda made him a Democratic money magnet, but more important, it linked him to that magical name. Face it: If not for his marriage, Charles Spittal Robb could never have launched his political career running for Virginia lieutenant governor.

Lynda may have surrendered to Chuck's ambition, but, for a time, her resentment again showed through in peevishness. On the campaign trail, after a disagreement over political tactics, she told Chuck in front of onlookers, "It's my money, after all." She seemed spoiled and petulant. But be assured, Lady Bird never stood up to Lyndon like that in public. And after Robb's victory in 1977, Lynda did something else Lady Bird had never done: When Chuck went to Richmond, she stayed in suburban Washington—leaving him to commute on weekends, not moving the family to the Virginia state capital until he became governor in 1982. Lynda saw the family's new life in politics not only through her own eyes or those of her husband—as Lady Bird had done—but also through the eyes of her daughters. Lynda had been there.

"It's not a slap at my parents," she is careful to say. "I have nothing but good things to say about my parents."

"Oh, absolutely," Lynda says. "You look back and say, 'How would my life have been different if . . . ?' "

Lynda's no worrier about choices past and dead. She's a Johnson, a doer. But so much has changed since she was a girl happily dressing up for Daddy. "Sometimes I think," says Lynda, "that parents live out their ambitions through their children." Lynda's twenty-year-old daughter, Lucinda, will be a senior at Princeton this fall. She plans to go to law school. For years, she said she'd never marry. Now she has mellowed: Maybe she'll marry at thirty-one, maybe she'll have one child, just one. For an ambitious firstborn daughter, the world is born anew, and the family says this about Lucinda: "She'll be president someday." Cathy, a nineteen-year-old sophomore at the University of Virginia, is less clear about her future, less ambitious. But of course she wants a career. And, no, she'll never, ever marry a politician. Eleven-year-old Jennifer, well, she's a basketball star whose father recently realized that she scores more baskets than he did at her age.

The third generation is a new breed.

"There's definitely a feminine culture in our family," says Lucinda, who knows that her mother is simultaneously at the heart of that culture's stability and its change. Lady Bird was an only daughter, Lynda had no brothers, the Robbs have three girls. "We call them all turkeys," says a smiling Lucinda of the family's men. "I mean, the women do have to take care of these guys."

At family dinners, Chuck Robb sits quietly at the head of the table while the girls, including Lynda, compete to describe their days, to debate the news. With tongue in cheek, Chuck may make some provocative, old mossback remark about women—and the debate will fly. It's a family adage, "Lose your breath, lose your turn." After Daddy's done eating, he then gets up and performs what has become a family ritual: Starting with Lynda, he goes around the table and massages the shoulders of each of his girls. "Chuck's harem," they call themselves. Occasionally, they all go and plop on the bed to watch rented movies, everyone wrestling for a spot next to Dad. In Johnson tradition, Daddy is royalty.

But in the family's new feminine culture, there is an edge. Lynda, exasperated by Chuck's failure to give her directions on some political task while he was in the statehouse, once quipped to a friend: "If he only told me what he wanted to be coronated for when he left here, I'd know what to do." With feigned seriousness, Cathy calls him "My father, the senator." The girls tease him about how he must have been born in a three-piece suit, about being in the Senate's Old Boys Club. They eat the chocolate and vanilla, leaving only the strawberry, in the Neapolitan ice cream, knowing that it irritates their obsessive dad—a guy who every night after dinner, without fail, eats only two Hydrox (never Oreo) cookies. Once, they jokingly dubbed him "the Supreme Being" and suggested he run for pope. Even Jennifer, says a family friend, once broke into an imitation of her father by becoming stiff and somber and saying in her deepest little girl voice, "Do I sound like Chuck much?" The friend looked at Lynda, who looked at the friend—and they both broke out in laughter.

Lynda has buried her own ambitions in those of her husband, but the tension remains. When Chuck ran for lieutenant governor, for instance, Lynda wrote a magazine article about being back in politics. It was mostly chatter, but it ended this way: "I'm doing all this for someone else—why not for myself?" Regrets? Maybe not. Ambivalence? Absolutely. Because even growing up in so powerful a patriarchy, if Lynda were ten years younger—had been a serious, studious, ambitious, well-connected young woman who graduated from college in 1976 instead of 1966—she probably would never have asked that question of herself.

"She really should have been a lawyer," confides Lady Bird. "I think that may be one of her buried dreams." Even today, Lucinda and Cathy urge Lynda to go to law school—again, seeming to know what it is their mother needs to hear. "Mom's bright," says Lucinda. "She could be in Congress. She'd be great."

Lucinda is asked, Is Mom a better politician than Dad?

With a devilish smile, Lucinda says, "She'd love it if I'd say she was better."

Yet there is this paradox: If the girls coax too hard, get too insistent that Mom do it, really go to law school, they hear the voice of an unfamiliar, less certain, more docile generation: "Oh, I couldn't do that," Lynda tells her daughters. "Who'd take care of your father?"

To see Lynda and Chuck together is to see the power of image versus flesh and blood. In Chuck's photos, he looks strong as iron, jut-jawed, straight-backed. In person, he isn't so tall, really, a little over six feet, his chin isn't so rugged, and his shoulders aren't so broad. In fact, they slope a bit, and his eyes carry deep circles. In person, Chuck Robb isn't imposing. The camera just works some magic. For Lynda, it's the reverse. Photos often diminish her, as they did her daddy. But in person, her physical awkwardness, her pensive hesitancy, her self-deprecating humor, her twang put people at ease. As with her father, Lynda's lack of sophistication isn't the absence of style, but the essence of her style.

Finally, she is confident of that. Her friends even believe she has secretly come to enjoy politics, because she discovered what other women before her discovered: There's more price than payoff in being a political wife—until husband dearest hits the big time. Lady Bird discovered this, so did Betty Ford, when their husbands became president. Suddenly, they didn't only have to put up with invaded privacy and absent husbands. Suddenly, they had staffs, projects, and the public's attention. It happened to Lynda. When she became Virginia's first lady, recalls Eva Teig, now the state's secretary for health and human resources, Lynda was slow to lead the charge for her own pet project—a massive study of the mostly ignored role women have played in Virginia history. But before long, Lynda was aggressively drumming up money, support, and interest. Again, her confidence soared. "Being a politician's wife is a conservative, anachronistic, full-time profession," says Lucinda. "You get everything but paid and everything but credit. If you're always being described as somebody's else's other, you wonder who you are yourself. That's why mother enjoyed being first lady—she had a job, a staff, and she got credit."

Lynda went on to set up the Good Old Girl Network, an ironically titled but deadly serious group of influential women in state government who met to talk about their problems and how to win more clout. She has been on the board of Reading Is Fundamental for twenty years. Her schedule is always packed. But it's her role as a member of the National Commission to Prevent Infant Mortality that consumes her. She gives speeches and lobbies members of Congress and newspeople—loudly arguing that it's an outrage that babies in the United States die at a higher rate than babies in eighteen other developed nations of the world.

The timid Lynda is gone. "I don't know if I'm ready for people to know that," she says. "It's very safe to be seen as boring and bookish." She then tries an old tack: "I'm still just as nervous and shy and, really . . ."

"You're still the ugly duckling?" she is asked.

"I'm still the ugly duckling."

Then she smiles broadly. It is true no more.

What is still true is that Lynda resents life in the fishbowl. The published accounts of her father's philandering and his selfish, manipulative ways have hurt her deeply, and she refuses to read them. But the curious, intellectual Lucinda did read excerpts of Robert Caro's critical Johnson biography—and, suddenly, the human cost of political life was passed on to the next generation. "If he was a bad person," Lucinda agonized to herself after reading the articles, "am I a bad person?" Last year, the human cost of politics again came home when published reports claimed that Robb—unknowingly, he said—had attended private parties where cocaine was used. Lucinda says her mother—with hard-earned and unerring political intuition—had warned Chuck early on: "I'm not sure I approve of that crowd." Robb listened too late.

And there are still the trivial irritations. A while back, a woman told Lynda about a friend who'd had her birthday party at a male strip joint. Lynda would love to go to a bash like that, but no way could the wife of the honorable Chuck Robb be spotted sticking a dollar in some guy's G-string. No more than the daughter of the honorable Lyndon Johnson could have been spotted wearing hippie beads in 1966. Lynda ran into George Hamilton recently at a party in California. He asked her to lunch. She wanted to go but feared the publicity. She could've asked George to bring along, say, his son as a chaperon, but it was too weird a thing to ask of so old and dear a friend. So she said no. This pettiness gets tiring.

But here's the irony: Lynda is no longer just a child of politics. She's also mother to her own children of politics, and she finds herself giving her daughters much the same advice her mother gave her. Think of what people might say. Be careful about going to parties where kids might be doing drugs. Remember, something you say to a friend in confidence might land on the front page of the *New*

York Times. When the girls gripe that this is unfair, Lynda says, "Oh, yeah, you think that's bad, well, listen to this . . ." Things change but they stay the same. That worries Lynda. She looks at her daughters—and all their ambition and opportunity—and she wonders how they will do it all: compete with men, raise families, be good wives. When she meets a younger man, she grills him: Does your wife work? Do you have kids? Who does the housework? Who nurses sick kids? What percentage of men your age share the domestic load equally? The questions aren't academic. Says Lynda of her daughters, "I worry how they will do it."

Chuck worries too, but in his own way. "Rightly or wrongly," he says, "society looks to the mother for the most important nurturing. I'm not saying that's as it ought to be. I'm just acknowledging that's the way it is."

He is told, Perhaps it won't be society but young women themselves who will solve this problem by their choice of husbands. Perhaps your daughters will choose not to marry a man like you, or a man like Lyndon Johnson, a man so absorbed in his work and who expects his wife to be part of a team of which he is captain. Robb nods.

Lucinda agrees. So does Cathy.

They are asked, Could you marry a man like your father?

Lucinda: "My marriage will be more of a two-way street."

Cathy: "I don't think so. It'd be a bit much."

Lynda loves Chuck dearly. After twenty-one years, she'd marry him again tomorrow. Yet men of his generation were sexists, she says. They couldn't help it, they just were. But what they didn't realize was that it isn't only the wives and kids who suffer when Daddy lives to work. When her father had grandkids, Lynda says, even he discovered how wondrous is a child. "I think he realized what he had missed," she says.

Indeed, before Johnson died, he'd been reading Carl Sandburg's biography of Abraham Lincoln. Yet, he told biographer Doris Goodwin, he couldn't conjure up a vision of Lincoln in his own mind. If Sandburg couldn't bring so great a president to life, he asked, who could ever bring him, Lyndon Johnson, to life? Johnson had finally realized, Goodwin says, how hard it is to be seen as great in the unforgiving eyes of history. In a rare moment of introspection, Johnson then told Goodwin, "Maybe I should have put my bets on immortality in my children and my grandchildren."

Lynda fears this kind of regret will grip Chuck someday. The first two girls grew up spending only rare moments with him. And even those, say the girls, came because Lynda made heroic efforts to fit them into Dad's wind-tunnel schedule. But there's hope, Lynda believes, because Chuck, who just turned fifty, has begun to cool out, something Daddy never did.

Lynda refuses to reflect critically on her father, but she has realized this: It wasn't only his being in politics that determined the way he treated his family, but also the person he was, the choices he made. Once, when Chuck told her he knows many high-powered men in professions other than politics who rarely see their kids, Lynda shot back: "So what? You should all be spending more time with your children! That's a cop-out." Chuck has finally done that. He sees a lot of eleven-year-old Jennifer. And last Christmas, the girls were amazed and elated when he took a whole week off, rather than his usual two or three days. "He used to work all the time," says Cathy. "But Dad has really mellowed out." Says Lucinda, "My father was very sober and distant, but I'm not going to psychoanalyze him. I don't think parenthood comes naturally to anyone, but he grew into it. He's more a part of the family now."

For that, credit goes to Lynda. For all her fragility and fear, the woman has fiber. She built a family that works, and from her weird childhood she took lessons, not bitterness. Knowingly or unknowingly, she didn't marry Daddy, as people have said. Chuck is not Lyndon. Chuck has listened and changed, if not as easily as a younger man, more easily than an older man. And for the Johnson women, Lynda has been a bridge linking her mother and daughters in a journey from the dark ages of Lady Bird's early marriage to the space age of her daughters' lives.

The price for Lynda?

In sipping both worlds, her thirst is quenched by neither.

Chuck Robb is asked, If Lynda could change you, what would she change?

"If she could start all over with a clean slate and chisel me," he says, haltingly, uncomfortably, "she would make me certainly more attentive, more visibly caring, more emotional."

He is asked, What would you change about her? His answer— given Lynda's concerns, given the era—is remarkable.

"I wouldn't say Lynda is a natural in terms of housework."

"Oh, he says that?" Lynda asks later, her voice rising. "Well, I think it is true. But I'll just tell you, I've run the vacuum many more times than he has." Then she smiles, and chuckles, ha, ha, ha—but with that edge, that edge emergent in the Johnson family's new feminine culture, that edge of Lynda Bird Johnson Robb's own making, her own awakening, that edge born of her own regrets, ambitions, and resentments, and of her own hopes for the future.

JULY 9, 1989

Since this article appeared, Virginia senator Chuck Robb has become embroiled in more controversy about his private life. He has admitted that he received a massage from a former Virginia beauty queen in a New York hotel room, but denied that he had a sexual affair with the young woman. His political future is considered to have been severely damaged by the revelations. Lynda Robb has stood firmly behind her husband during the controversy.

ROB THATE
Who Kidnapped His Baby Boy?

$\mathcal{F}$or a long time, Rob kept the woman's picture tacked to the wall by the stairs leading down from his apartment. On his way out, he'd stop and stare at her, or at least at the face that had come to belong to her. It was a dull, expressionless face, with a square, hard-set jaw and eerie, demonic, dead-zone eyes, eyes without color or emotion. In his mourning and rage and confusion, Rob decided he had met this woman before, for an instant perhaps, in the K Mart or the Giant. He was certain of it. But then he'd stiffen, and wonder if that thought was only a dream. By this time, he seemed to dream when he was awake, and he wasn't always sure whether his dreams and reality weren't washing over one another. When the face would begin to resemble Meredith Baxter Birney, Rob would close his eyes and shake his head free of the image, and start again.

He would stare so long and so hard at this picture, an FBI composite drawing, that Rob even believed, or maybe he dreamed, that he understood the woman in the picture, the woman Rob was convinced had stolen his baby from his hospital bed two months ago. Certainly, the woman feels guilty for what she has done to him and his wife and their children, Rob reasoned. No matter how insane, she must have a conscience, didn't God give everyone a conscience, even lunatics? And certainly she's afraid she'll be caught. She covers her face, changes her hair when she goes out, even to the 7-Eleven. She lives furtively, unable even to tell friends that she has a new baby, afraid her son—Rob's son, really—will be taken from her any time.

Then Rob would wonder: What name has she given him? Not Jeremiah, his real name, the name Rob gave him, the name he took from the Bible. But she knows the name. Of course. It was on TV for weeks, it's on posters all around Washington, D.C. She knows the name, all right, and someone, somewhere, knows this woman has Jeremiah Thate, son of Rob and Terry, brother to Jessica and Patrick. She can't hide a baby! Not from a husband or friends or neighbors.

Photograph by Steven Pumphrey.

Somebody, somewhere knows she has Rob Thate's boy, and someone, someday is going to turn her in, out of love or anger or, more
likely, greed. The reward is more than $16,000, and Rob is aiming
for $50,000. His attitude has a cold and ominous and desperate cer-
tainty about it: It may be today or it may be twenty-three years from
now, when Jeremiah will look just like his daddy does now—tall
and spare and delicate, with blue, deep-set eyes and dark blond
hair—but someone, someday, will turn her in, for a simple reason:
   This woman stole the wrong baby!
   She stole Jeremiah Thate! Rob's boy!
   Blood of blood, bone of bone, heart and soul.
   This woman is gonna pay!
   Jeremiah may be cradled in a stranger's arms tonight, feeling
what he imagines is her love for him. But what Jeremiah is feeling is
really this woman's love, or maybe her hatred, for herself, and he
will learn this someday. That is what Rob believes. Because somehow, Rob doesn't know how, Jeremiah is a vessel. Good things come
from bad, the Bible says so, and this is a plan, God's plan. Does it
sound pathetic? A father grasping at purpose in the purposeless.

Think whatever, but this demented woman with dead-zone eyes has, of her own free will, become a player in a performance beyond her control. That is what Rob believes. If he saw it any other way, he'd go crazy.

Let the police pussyfoot around and call her only a "possible suspect," let the police remind people that composite portraits don't always resemble their subjects, that this woman could be totally innocent, that Jeremiah could by now have been sold to an unwitting couple in Oklahoma, Ohio, Kansas. No! Rob has studied this woman, and evil has a face: She did it, she has his baby, she lives here. And when she is caught, Rob will calmly tell her, face-to-face, what she has done to him and to his family. Then she must tell him why she did it. Rob has to know. It had something to do with her father, Rob imagines. That is, if she ever had a father.

Rob Thate works as a cartographer, meticulously etching onto emulsified film, hour after hour, the details of roads and bridges, streams and abutments, county lines. It is appropriate work, because Rob has always seen the world about him in tiny pieces, close-ups, tight shots. He's an artist and a sculptor by avocation, though he has only rarely sold his artwork. He gives it to friends or keeps it around the house. He does small ink sketches of small things—four sapling birch trees growing in a cluster. Even his sculptures are small table pieces, parabolic shapes that lead the eye around corners without breaking vision at the edges. When he sculpts Rob imagines a person at a museum—one arm crossed at his chest, the other thoughtfully stroking his chin—as he is compelled to circle a sculpture to see its meaning from all directions, the artist shaping the form that leads the eyes that lead the feet that lead the mind, all unconsciously, always in a closing circle. It's what Rob believes life should be about, coming round with meaning.

When he was a boy, Rob almost died. If his grandmother hadn't been there to pound on his back, the sourball would have strangled him, and Jeremiah would never have been conceived or born or stolen. Maybe the devil keeps an eye out for the dangerously good, Rob wonders, intervenes when he can, strikes at the righteous early. But it all seems so haphazard sometimes.

If Rob hadn't overslept that Thursday, if he hadn't stayed home from work, if his old Plymouth hadn't been on the fritz, Rob would never have gone to the hospital earlier than usual to see Jeremiah. He wouldn't have gotten to the sixth floor about four that afternoon and found his son sleeping on his stomach, head turned to the left.

He wouldn't have held the duffel bag filled with incidentals in his right hand, reached out with his left, and softly touched his son's back. He wouldn't have suggested to his wife, Terry, who had slept in Jeremiah's room for the several days he was hospitalized with pneumonia, that they leave Jeremiah and go down to the canteen for dinner. If Rob hadn't overslept, Jeremiah, three weeks old and without sin, wouldn't have been alone for the twenty minutes it took for someone to strike at the righteous. But Rob wonders: If there is a plan, would any of it have mattered? Would Jeremiah have gotten well only to be stolen later from the supermarket or the park? Who knows. Rob wishes he had not overslept.

Rob and Terry met in a science-fiction class at Prince George's Community College in the Maryland suburbs of Washington when he was eighteen, she nineteen. She was so pretty, with a way of flicking back her long blond hair as she laughed, always with energy and confidence. She was the kind of woman Rob figured he needed, a strong, self-reliant woman who would keep him on the straight and narrow. He was confused then, without direction, a hothead, rebellious and angry at the world, it seemed, though he was mostly angry at his father for being a father. Fathers are so important in the lives of their children, Rob believes, much more important than mothers. It was that way for Rob, and that way for Terry and most of Rob's friends. He knows this for sure because he has asked.

Terry was a born-again Christian. She gave Rob a Bible, and he was born again too. They laughed a lot in those days, Rob sent roses, they held sweaty hands and imagined raising a family. Terry told Rob he was the kindest, most sensitive man she'd ever met. They married the next year. His folks protested: Life isn't *Romeo and Juliet*, you know.

The couple soon had a daughter, Jessica, and four months later, Terry got pregnant again, unexpectedly. Rob didn't take naturally to fatherhood, and he began to wonder if his parents hadn't been right: Maybe there was more to life than a wife and kids, empty pockets, and a dinky, run-down, one-bedroom apartment. Marriage or not, Rob was still confused, still unable to make decisions, still, as Terry lovingly called him, "a wimp" who would break down and cry during, say, a sentimental TV segment of "Webster."

Yet Rob also came to discover that Terry was not exactly the woman he believed he had married. Her confidence and self-reliance weren't deep. Her older brother had been hit and killed by a car when she was five, and after that her mother withdrew from the family for a long time. Terry's most searing childhood memory is of her mother sitting motionless in the living room, cradling a picture of her dead son as the song "The Green Berets" played on the stereo. There were other problems too, and by the time Terry was a young teen, she felt lonely and unloved. Her sophomore year in high school she found Christ. It was only then, Terry believed, that she became the woman Rob fell in love with.

When Jessica was born, Rob hadn't been able to stay in the delivery room, with the screaming and the bleeding and the tension. He apologized to Terry for weeks after Jessica's birth, and when Patrick came he did better. But then, at the moment of Patrick's delivery, the boy got stuck. A nurse jumped on Terry's bed and pounded on her stomach. Patrick nearly died and Terry bled horribly. For a few moments she lost her vision and Rob became a pale ghost. He looked into the doctor's face for reassurance, but instead saw fear. Rob left the room again, this time to pray in the bathroom: I don't want you to take 'em, Lord, but they're in your hands. Everyone came out fine.

With Patrick, their lives finally fell together. Terry stayed home with the kids, leaving them broke constantly, but for the first time the Thates were really happy. It was a wonderful year. For fun, they'd go for walks, window-shop at malls, or, on an extravagant night, go bowling. It was the happiest year of Terry's life—the only happy year so far, she'd say, laughing.

The doctors had told Terry it could be dangerous for her to have another child, but the next year she told Rob she wanted another baby. He was reluctant. They were poor enough. But then he got a raise. They called Terry "fertile Myrtle" for good reason, and the next month she was pregnant again. Terry hoped for a girl. Rob said he didn't care, but when Terry mentioned that she was having a birthday sleep-over for Jessica after the baby came, Rob said, "Great, I can take the boys camping that night." Terry said, "Rob, the boy will only be a week old." Rob said, "Well, maybe next year."

Jeremiah was born without trouble, and Rob finally made it through a delivery. They were ready for this one, even videotaped it. Rob had an uncontrollable, geeky smile on his face, and Terry cried joyously. For the first time, she got to hold her new baby on her chest rather than see it rushed off to intensive care. Then the doctor handed Rob the scissors to cut Jeremiah's umbilical cord. Rob expected the cord to be soft, fleshy, but it was tough, more like rope. He tensed his hand to finish the cut, and at that instant—with the click of the scissors—Rob had the odd, fleeting, magical sensation that he had just brought Jeremiah to life.

That last night, Rob and Terry were shuffling around Jeremiah's hospital room, wanting to go for dinner but anxious about leaving him to sleep alone. A nurse's aide came by pushing a little girl in a stroller. Terry knew the girl because she'd heard her crying a few nights earlier and had walked into her room, stroked her hair, talked to her softly, melodiously. The girl had stopped crying and slept, and Terry told Rob cheerfully that she was still a good mother, she could still put a child to sleep that fast.

A nurse assured Terry and Rob that Jeremiah would be fine, and so they headed for the canteen. At the elevator, though, Rob had a vague, dark intuition when he noticed a burly man wearing a red lumberjack shirt and a trucker's cap walk into pediatrics. The man had a wide gap between his front teeth, and he stopped to crush out his cigarette in an ashtray near the door. Rob watched the man walk down the hallway and thought that he looked out of place, somehow frightening. But Rob was no worrywart. He was used to shrugging off the usual moments of blind fear, the kind that would come, say, when Terry was a little late getting home and Rob was suddenly certain she had crashed the car, the times when a sense of doom touched him with a brief but cold and certain shiver. Then he'd feel foolish for, like an Alfred Hitchcock film, imbuing the trivial with the horrific.

But this happened when Rob and Terry returned to Jeremiah's room: Rob walked through the door first and saw that the crib was empty. He said, "Hey, where's Jeremiah?" Terry was behind him and to his left, her vision blocked, and she said, "What?" Rob saw the clear-plastic IV tube that had been attached to Jeremiah's arm dangling at the floor, a small, oval pool of translucent liquid beneath it. He bent down, picked up the tube, and held it to his face, where he saw that it had been cleanly cut. He said absently and without panic, "This isn't right." Oh, don't worry, Terry said, an air bubble probably got in the line, that's all. As they returned to the hallway, Rob heard a baby cry—Jeremiah, he was certain—in an examining room across the hall. Rob confidently pushed open the door, and several strangers looked his way.

Rob and Terry didn't run down the hall to the nursing station, but they did walk quickly. Terry asked lightly, "Where's my son?" The nurse looked at her blankly. And then her look changed. Nurses were soon running everywhere and Terry began to cry. Like a chant, she repeated, "This is not happening. It's not real. It's a dream. I'm gonna wake up."

In the chaos Rob felt a sudden composure. He told himself to stay calm, to remember what he saw, to move quickly. He ran to the elevator, where a candy striper was standing inside the open doors. He pushed for the main floor and waited, nothing. He glanced over and saw the young woman, looking very proud and professional, with her left hand on the "hold" button. Rob cursed and she looked at him fearfully, as if calculating the chances that a crazy man had randomly fallen upon her. She removed her hand slowly, never losing her studied poise, but never taking her eyes off Rob.

On the main floor, Rob sprinted, yet the doorways and the people he passed moved in slow motion. With a robotic efficiency, he looked in everyone's arms. A woman carried a shopping bag; he looked inside. Out the doors, across the drive, and over a grassy knoll, past three people standing at a bus stop. Rob ran to the hospital parking lot, up the off-ramp, and stood before a woman leaving in her car. They stared into each other's eyes, and she looked momentarily confused. Rob looked for a baby, saw none, and ran on, through the lot and back into another hospital door. The stairwell had just been painted, and as he ran past he heard a fat woman with short hair complain bitterly about the odor. Up and down stairways, past gawking nurses, secretaries, administrators streaming home for the day. When Rob reached pathology on the first floor, the smell of formaldehyde was overpowering. He remembered: the burly man with the lumberjack shirt and the gap between his teeth. But back in pediatrics, the man was still there, with his wife, visiting a child. He looked so benign. The man had not been evil itself, only one of its shadows.

The other night, Terry thought she heard noises on the back steps, outside the kitchen door. Then Rob thought he heard noises. He got up, checked the lock, peered out the windows. He jammed the straight back of a kitchen chair beneath the knob. He couldn't sleep. He heard more noises. He walked the dark apartment, his heart pounding, working himself into a frenzy. He sat nervously in his favorite stuffed chair. Terry tried to calm him. Rob said, "I'm sick of being afraid. I'm getting a gun." He raised his left hand to his chest, cradling the barrel of an imaginary shotgun. He tightened his right hand around its stock and suddenly snapped his left hand up and down, *click-click*, the sound of a shotgun pump setting its shell. He did it again, *click-click*. The next day, they laughed about how groaning floorboards aren't scary without the enveloping darkness. But even then, Rob stood in the living room and assumed the pose, *click-click*. Maybe a Beretta, a fifteen-shot Beretta, he told Terry. Maybe that was what he needed.

The FBI and the police have no hot leads on Jeremiah. Except for the woman in the composite. In the days before Jeremiah disappeared, several people noticed a woman—whose presence the FBI has been unable to account for—wandering from room to room in pediatrics. The FBI sketch that is burned in Rob's mind is based on these eyewitness descriptions. The woman is not an official suspect in the case, but police would like to question her. The odds, based on other baby-snatching cases, are good that Jeremiah was taken by a sick person craving a baby, that he is still in the area, that he is unharmed. These are the good odds. Rob doesn't dwell on the bad odds—that Jeremiah is dead or sold or living halfway across the country. With the help of people at their church, the Thates found a lawyer who set up the Jeremiah Recovery Team Foundation to keep Jeremiah's name and the woman's face before the public. Rob wants the foundation to someday give advice to other parents caught in similar tragedies.

So much of the advice the Thates got was ludicrous. People said, "Good luck." *Imagine it!* They said, "Good luck." Only a week after Jeremiah's abduction, one intimate told Terry, "You've got to put Jeremiah out of your mind and get on with your life." And just about everybody said, "I can't *imagine* how horrible it must feel." Rob would think, *You're right, you can't imagine.*

The FBI went hard at Rob as a suspect for several weeks, as is customary in these cases. He passed a county police lie-detector test, but the FBI polygraphs were inconclusive. Then one night, an FBI agent looked Rob in the eye and said he believed Rob had arranged his son's abduction. He asked if Rob believed in psychic phenomena and could he communicate with Jeremiah to learn his location? Or could Rob, because of his faith in Christ, ask God to divinely inform him of his son's whereabouts? Rob answered the questions, but later sobbed angrily to Terry, "They think I stole my own son!" Finally, along with the police, the FBI concluded that Rob was not a suspect.

Rob doesn't exactly know why, but he found himself wearing a cold public mask after Jeremiah was stolen. At home, Terry was inconsolable. Little Patrick would walk into the bedroom, smile, and vomit. Jessica, always so cheerful, was whiny and cranky, though she only dimly understood why. She said, "A bad person took Jer-e-MI-ah." Gentle Rob yelled at the kids. He and Terry argued about socks and underwear on the floor, unwashed dishes, a catsup bottle left on the table. Rob tried to limit his sobbing to the shower. But in TV interviews, he didn't seem broken enough for the living-room jury. The etiquette of public mourning demands emotion, tears, crack-ups. Rob could give none of it. He had to be strong, he told himself, for Terry and the kids. And for a deeper reason: Rob imagined that the kidnapper—locked in a weird sumloss psychological game with him—might draw strength from seeing his weakness.

The interviews, the investigation, the letters of consolation gave the first few weeks afterward an air of unreality, as does the rush of family support after, say, a husband or wife dies. Rob expected the tension to ease, but it worsened. After Jeremiah's abduction, there were frantic warnings that he might die if not returned to a hospital for medical treatment. But because Jeremiah had been on antibiotics for several days before his disappearance, doctors now believe it's likely—though not certain—that he would have recovered from his pneumonia if cared for properly, even by a kidnapper.

So in Rob's mind, Jeremiah lives. He and Terry consent to every interview, every talk-show request, and they repeat the story, over and over, because any of these could generate the phone call, the tip that will free Jeremiah. Each time, they are drained and empty for the day. At home, they have had horrible fights, over nothing, really. Once they were in the bedroom, bellowing at each other, and Rob said, "I just feel like killing someone." Terry said she couldn't take any more, she was leaving with the children. Rob could only think, *This is it, divorce!* Then Terry slugged him. Slugged him in the face. She said, "Go ahead, hit me!" For some reason, Rob had a baseball in his hand. He shifted it from hand to hand, hand to hand. *No,* he told himself, *I won't, I won't lose control.* Then, like an explosion, he fired the ball at the bedroom wall. It shattered the plaster and bounced back. He threw it again and again, before Terry grabbed his arm. She spoke softly now, "Stop, stop, we can't go on like this." Then they sobbed.

Every night, Terry was in and out of bed, checking the kids four, five times. She imagined kidnappers in their room. Sometimes, Patrick and Jessica would wake up screaming. Rob dreamed of walking down the street pushing Jeremiah in a stroller with Terry and the kids around him. The most trivial things became frightful: One day Rob noticed a ladder leaning against the house next door, opposite the kids' room. He thought, *A madman could tilt that lad-*

der this way, climb in, and take the children. At night, Terry would stay up past midnight by herself, until she fell asleep on the couch from exhaustion.

She remembered how her mother had withdrawn from the family after Terry's brother was killed. She didn't want to abandon her children to grief, so she stopped listening to the moody, inspirational Christian music she loved. She watched only game shows on TV. All the others seemed sad and tragic. There were kook threats against the kids. One day Terry came home to find the yellow ribbons she'd strung around two trees in front of their apartment ripped down. Another day, she saw two men sitting in a red car, talking, and glancing at Patrick and Jessica playing in the yard. Terry hurried the kids into the house and called the police. When they arrived, the red car was gone.

This became Terry's ritual: Almost every day, she would change her hairstyle, put on sunglasses, and wander around shopping malls. There was a report that a woman resembling the composite had been seen at a shopping center that Terry had frequented, and she came to believe the woman had seen her there, realized she was pregnant, and planned the abduction. So Terry went to this mall often, looking into the face of every baby. Her fantasy: She would find Jeremiah, grab him, and order the crowd to tackle the woman as she fled: "Stop that woman! She stole my baby!" Then Terry would walk up to the woman and slap her and slap her and slap her and slap her . . .

Late one Saturday night, as Terry sat once again rocking, rocking and crying in the darkened living room, it came to her: the good carving knives. Tomorrow morning she would feign illness and stay home from church. She'd then run to the store and buy a six-pack of beer. She'd have to be drunk. Then she'd cover the floor with plastic garbage bags and put a note on the door telling Rob to leave the kids outside. Rob had once told her that people not serious about suicide cut their wrists the long way. She would slit them across.

Suddenly terrified, Terry shook herself out of it. When she told Rob, he didn't know what to say. He asked, "Do you think if a person commits suicide, he goes to Hell?" But Terry was beyond caring. She had already raged at God out loud, "I hate You! How could You do this to me? I had one good year!"

Rob said, "This woman has got to know what she did."

If life hadn't gone berserk, Rob might not recall the things about Jeremiah that are now all he has left to recall. That when Terry was pregnant and asleep on her side, Rob would reach around under the covers and gently poke her bulging stomach—and Jeremiah would poke back. That when they brought Jeremiah home after his birth, Rob didn't like the way he slouched in the infant seat, so he stopped and spent thirty-nine dollars on a new seat, and said, "There, little guy, isn't that better?" And in the last days, when Rob took Jeremiah down for his chest X-ray at the hospital, he laid him on the table and noticed how cold the table was against the back of his hand, compared with the warmth of Jeremiah's naked body against his palm.

Rob believes the person who took Jeremiah figured it this way: The Thates already have two kids, so they won't miss this one. There was a time when Rob might have seen some crazy logic in that, but now he knows it's like saying because people have two legs, they won't miss the one that gets cut off. He laughs at rediscovering the wheel: You don't know what you've got till it's gone. Rob never thought he'd be famous. Then he lost his son and ended up on TV, on the front page. He met the TV news stars he'd always figured had the life, boy. And they were just people, people who didn't seem any happier than he. Suddenly, Rob wanted from life exactly what he once had—simplicity and anonymity.

This woman, *this woman!*, had stolen these things too.

But she will be caught. Rob is certain. He has refused to go on TV and beg Jeremiah's abductor for his return, though reporters have asked him to do this again and again. This woman is a criminal, Rob has explained each time. If we beg criminals, they win. They are in control. And this woman is not in control. God is in control. And with His help, Rob is in control. It is as if Rob is locked in a personal war of wills with the woman in the composite. When he talks, it sometimes seems he is talking directly to her, as if he can see her out there in a room somewhere, Jeremiah on her knee, as she drinks her morning coffee and reads Rob's words: "I just want this woman to know she's not gonna get away with it. There's not gonna be a day she doesn't have to look over her shoulder, because one day, I'm gonna be behind that shoulder. She's gonna go into a store to buy a gallon of milk and, bam, someone's gonna recognize her and she's gonna be history. I'm gonna find her. Even if she goes to a deserted island and eats bananas, I'm gonna find her. This lady took the wrong baby. Because Jeremiah was my baby."

Every morning, Rob offers the same prayer: God, bring back Jeremiah and help me and Terry and the kids come through this. Then Rob asks for one more thing, that God help him come to love the woman in the composite. The only good thing—and it is not a small thing to Rob—that has come out of Jeremiah's disappearance is that Rob's faith is stronger. He cannot understand why Jeremiah was stolen, but he trusts that God knows what He's doing. Rob told Terry with astonishment, "All the things I said I believed about my faith—it turned out I really did believe them." Then he smiled.

It hasn't been easy. Rob has imagined slipping under a table where the woman is sitting and slicing her Achilles tendon so that forever when she walks she'll remember what she did. He has imagined throwing her to the pavement and driving his knee into her back. Rob tells himself: The Bible says get angry, but don't sin. Yet he has imagined worse for this woman, this woman with the dead-zone eyes, the cold, vacant, reflectionless eyes. *This woman . . .* she has shattered Terry's life and faith, sapped Rob of trust and joy and naiveté, forever imbued the trivial in their lives with the horrific. *This woman . . .* Rob the rageful wants to kill her! *This woman . . .* Rob the faithful wants to heal her! *This woman . . .* Rob the seeker of meaning wants to ask her a single question: "What was your father like?" Oh, *God!*, the man must have been a monster.

OCTOBER 11, 1987

Washington Post photograph.

ANTON SZANDOR LAVEY
In Search of Satan's Power

"*Oh, we've spared no pains and we've spared no dough;*
And we've dug at the secrets of long ago;
And we've risen to Heaven and plunged Below,
For we wanted to make it one hell of a show."
From *The Circus of Dr. Lao*, one of
Anton LaVey's favorite "satanic" novels

*I*magine Satan as a sentimental, middle-aged guy running a seedy bar in San Francisco. The lighting in his tiny place is dim and dreamlike, as if you were walking through a thin, refractory mist where depth and focus are out of sync. Reach out to touch Gwen's knee and you miss, and must reach again, a few inches more this time. She sags against the bar, nearly passed out, her legs splayed, her garters exposed, a puddle of urine on the floor beneath her. She's tired and wrinkled, sad to see. But Steve, the smiling sailor with her, is on a short leave from the war, World War II, and he's not tired at all. Across the room, Bonita, hard and cynical and confident in her fox wrap, tight sweater, and peg skirt, glowers at his intentions. She's with Fritz, the cabbie.

Welcome to the Den of Iniquity, where proprietor and American high priest of Satanism Anton Szandor LaVey is playing "Lover Man" on his old Hammond organ, its iridescent blue, red, and green keys illuminating his bald head, goatee, quirky smile, and missing teeth. As always, he wears black.

"I've known people who come in here and actually get nauseated," LaVey chortles.

The Den of Iniquity is not *real*—at least not real enough that you can walk in off a foggy street and buy a shot of Ten High. No, Gwen and Steve, Bonita and Fritz are LaVey's creations—polyurethane manikins molded with his own hands on his own kitchen floor. Down to the clothing, the jewelry, the posters, and the Rock-ola jukebox, the Den of Iniquity is LaVey's magical warp in time, circa 1944. His basement tavern, he says, is more satanic than a black mass. This night, the Den of Iniquity also includes two real-life

99

LaVey creations—Terry, twenty-six, and Blanche, twenty-four. Their hair is blond and styled in the way of the forties. They wear tight dresses, seamed stockings, garters, spiked heels. They are Satanists, and the fifty-five-year-old LaVey is their fashion adviser. He plays to them for hours: "Down on the Farm," "My Man," "It Had to Be You."

"I love old songs," says Terry, a shy woman who has never made friends easily. "They make me dream and escape. They don't play this kind of music anymore."

"Oh, they will!" assures LaVey. "They will!"

LaVey, a magus, or master of magic, is seeing to that—tonight and most every night he sits at his organ or his music synthesizers and imbues the atmosphere with magical vibratory frequencies. He believes they are changing the psyche of the world and creating a new romantic, yet satanic, revolution. You thought Linda Ronstadt's Nelson Riddle album made you don a tuxedo and go ballroom dancing, that Madonna made your daughter turn to black lace, that Pia Zadora made you rediscover Gershwin? No, the spirit of the devil did it—with a little help from LaVey, who deftly segues into "Ragtime Cowboy Joe."

"I can see the girl on the stage, twirling the lasso," sighs Terry. "Doctor, it makes me dream!"

And then the magic happens: In the infinite reflection of the mirrored walls it is, for an instant, impossible to tell which LaVey creations are human and which are humanoid—the hair, the stockings, the scent of musk, the air of sordid romance, the clink of ice in a whiskey glass.

"I wish I *was* one of those dolls," Terry says, lost. "It's like walking into the past. I wish I *was* one."

"It was a strong satanic ritual," LaVey says of the bizarre evening, as he heads to Jack-in-the-Box for breakfast hours later. "We had the right people and right moment. We were immersed, swept into another time, another place, another era. Time stood still. At the eye of the madness and mystery."

It's been twenty years since Anton LaVey shaved his head and declared himself high priest of the Church of Satan. His was a pop diabolism, a Machiavellian atheism with cloven hoof. "Satan is a symbol, nothing more," LaVey says. "Satan signifies our love of the worldly and our rejection of the pallid, ineffectual image of Christ on the cross." LaVey believes in neither God nor Satan, and his satanic "religion" is a parody of Christianity—with a heavy dose of magic, as in "Sorcerer's Apprentice" magic. LaVey doesn't worship

Satan. The devil is a symbol of man's carnal nature—his lust, greed, vengeance, but most of all, his ego, all drives LaVey says Christianity has unfairly labeled "evil."

But LaVey's Satanism also lashes out at the rubes who take the Ten Commandments seriously. Satanism, he says, is already the ad hoc reality: The strong, not the meek, inherit the world! LaVey, like anyone, loves his friends, wife, and children. But there is a venom in his Satanism that goes beyond parody. Among his teachings: "Death to the weakling, wealth to the strong."

Two decades of Satanism have been good to LaVey. He collects classic cars and has several luxurious homes and a 185-foot yacht at his disposal. A follower pays his medical insurance. He's parlayed Satanism into a business consulting Hollywood horror-film makers on authentic satanic ritual. He charges $100 a session for satanic counseling, and there are the royalties from his several books. LaVey's religion of the darker side, however, does have a darker side. "What I have done is open a Pandora's box," he says. Since he founded his church, Satanism has come a long way: The devil has become rock music's nihilistic symbol and there have been the Satan-tinged murders—from Charles Manson to the Night Stalker.

"These people are not Satanists," says LaVey, eyes closed, voice a whisper. "They are deranged. But no matter how many they do, they'll never catch up with the Christians. We have centuries of psychopathic killing in the name of God."

LaVey, it turns out, is a law-and-order man. He hates rock music—with or without satanic lyrics. He insists he's misunderstood. "The Catholics were once thought of as devils by Protestants. The Protestants were devils to the Catholics. The Jews were considered devils by both. The white man was considered a devil by the Chinese. The American Indian was considered a devil by the white man. Now who really is evil? Who is to say who is evil?"

Anton LaVey is not a cartoon Satan. He's far less frightening than you might imagine, because he is admittedly a carnival hustler. Yet he is still terrifying, because he touches, if not the mystical darkness, then the psychological darkness—the hate and fear—in us all. And because he, sadly, knows a haunting truth: Everybody wants to feel better than somebody. LaVey is a junkyard intellectual, a philosopher of the sordid, a savant, an ingratiating and funny man. He's a man who could find no faith, until he discovered magic. But Anton LaVey worships only Anton LaVey. His religion is egotism—and his church, his Den of Iniquity, his dolls, his women are shadows of that ego. And that, as LaVey would say, is truly satanic.

It's a hard winter in San Francisco, and LaVey's house, with shades always drawn, is dark and cold—cold as, well, cold as a tomb. But sit down in Rasputin's sled chair and relax, thumb through LaVey's collection of girlie calendars: "A uniquely American art form," he says. Look closely at the Jivaros shrunken head from Ecuador, examine the Aztec knife that once cut hearts from human victims, or study the torture hook from the Inquisition. "All done in the name of religion," LaVey says, laughing. Tonight he wears a black ascot with his black shirt and slacks and relaxes in the eerie glow of his purple sitting room, where he explains the magical power of being different for difference's sake.

"The word *occult* simply means hidden or secret," he says. "Go to the record store, to the corner where no one else is, where everything is dusty and nobody ever goes. Mussorgsky's 'Night On Bald Mountain' is mystical music, dramatic, Gothic, satanically programmed music. But it's not occult music. 'Yes, We Have No Bananas' would be an occult tune. It's occult because when you put that record on that turntable, it's a lead-pipe cinch that there is not another person in the entire world who is listening to that record at that time. If there's anything, any frequency, any power that exists anywhere in this cosmos, in this universe, you're gonna stand out like a beacon! It truly makes you elite."

LaVey's house must beam like a zillion watts. It's a museum of the weird. On the Victrola is "The Love Nest Medley Fox Trot." His collection of such odd melodies runs into the thousands. He loves Irving Berlin's "Stay Down Here Where You Belong," in which the devil proclaims: "You'll find more hell up there than there is down below." And don't forget the classics: Liszt's "Mephisto-Waltz" and Saint-Saëns's "Danse Macabre." Are freaks your interest? LaVey has hundreds of production stills from the 1932 film *Freaks*. It did poorly, but he likes it because the freaks eventually overpower their "normal" prison keepers.

All of this is a long way from the seventeen-year-old Anton LaVey who ran away from home to work as a cage boy for circus lion tamer Clyde Beatty. LaVey later became a carnival mentalist and hypnotist, then a bump-and-grind organ player for a stripper named Marilyn Monroe. His friends in those days were hustlers, con men, and carny freaks. He recalls once going to the store with three-eyed Bill Durks, who wore a cap to hide the eye in the middle of his forehead. Said the man at the checkout: "What's a matter, buddy, ya embarrassed to take off your hat?" So Durks did—the man got sick and had to be helped away. "He had it coming!" laughs LaVey. It was a world turned upside down: Saturday nights the young LaVey played the organ to a male crowd at the carnival sex shows; Sunday morning he played the same organ for the same men—now with their wives and kids—at the evangelist's tent.

In the fifties, LaVey left one seedy world for another, becoming a San Francisco police department crime scene photographer. Yet his growing obsession with magic also led to the "Magic Circle" gatherings at his home, and the flamboyant showman LaVey became a gossip column staple.

The Church of Satan seemed like more of his old carny act: Nude women sprawled atop a satanic altar, black masses, scarlet robes, horned caps, the blasphemous cries of "Hail, Satan!"—much of it available for film at 11:00. It was a freak show. But then, in 1967, LaVey performed a public satanic wedding: Fifty reporters attended and the *Los Angeles Times* ran a front-page photo. Presto, Satan had his first mass-media minister—a minister who didn't even believe in Satan! But the Christian view of the devil as pure evil was, ironically, a media magnet: *Life, Look, Time, McCall's,* and hundreds more told the story. Jayne Mansfield joined the church. LaVey played the devil in Roman Polanski's movie *Rosemary's Baby*—and, abracadabra, became a satanic consultant to Hollywood. He published *The Satanic Bible,* now with more than 500,000 copies in print. He did Johnny Carson. As a favor to Mansfield, he put a curse on her lawyer—who soon was dead in a car accident. Unfortunately, Mansfield died with him. The tragedy only spread LaVey's legend.

But the weirdness also began. The church was popular with Hell's Angels, Nazis, and sex-starved men. There were death threats against LaVey, and his daughter was harassed at school. Suddenly, the satanic circus was no fun anymore. So, in the seventies, LaVey went underground, stopped all public ceremonies, recast his church as a secret society—and pushed deeper into his private world of "madness and mystery."

Today, the man is truly occult. He collects not only old records, but Horatio Alger books, satanic artifacts, and "satanic" movies that portray man's darker side as tragically heroic. "The most satanic film character ever?" asks LaVey. Perhaps Edward G. Robinson in *The Sea Wolf,* which opens at a page from John Milton's *Paradise Lost:* "Better to reign in hell, than serve in heav'n." Or Walter Huston as the cynical prospector who keeps his decency in *The Treasure of Sierra Madre* while that of the naive Humphrey Bogart disintegrates in greed. Or the benignly deluded Peter O'Toole in *The Ruling Class,* in which he believes he is Christ until his aristocratic family convinces him it's more respectable to be Jack the Ripper.

"My all-time favorite quote is novelist Somerset Maugham: 'If only the good were a little less heavy-footed,'" says LaVey, who is forever reaching for this or that quote, turning to just the right page and reading it aloud. He reaches for a Maugham biography and quotes him again: "I had Rev. Davidson rut in bed with Sadie Thompson in *Rain* . . . Some said I had set back missionary endeavors around the world a hundred years . . . Actually, Rev. Davidson was closer to spirituality in bed wildly fornicating with Sadie Thompson than at any time in his life."

That, in a nutshell, is the philosophy of Anton LaVey.

The purple room is so cold tonight that everyone wears overcoats. It's 3:00 or 4:00 in the morning, but a few Satanists have dropped by—Terry, Blanche, and Gene, a close LaVey friend and the owner of an auto repair garage. Like the Den of Iniquity, the tiny, freezing room is oddly disconnected from any mooring outside itself. The evening's topic is the abundance of fools in the world, and LaVey goes to the shelf for his collection of photo-essay books on Middle Americans—books that seem to tell more about the people in the purple room than they do about the people in the pictures. LaVey sits in his recliner, in black shirt and lavender tie, gold loop earring in his left lobe. He leans over the coffee table, his books and his guests spread before him.

"It's really depressing," he says in his raspy whisper. In the dim light LaVey resembles Christopher Lloyd as the whacked-out genius in *Back to the Future*. "The paper tablecloth. The Tide box. The metal folding chairs. Wonderful! The good life!" His friends pick up the theme and begin to poke fun at the pictures of people in their Military Order of the Louse fraternal uniforms, the people sitting in their tacky living rooms, the people smiling gawkishly from every imaginable vacation boardwalk. LaVey thumbs the pages of Michael Lesy's *Time Frames*, a heartfelt social biography of average American families, although LaVey doesn't see it that way. "Who would read a whole book about these people's lives?" he asks. "Yes, it's very satanic. You know why? Because the average person thinks that his life *means* something, that people will give a crap about it. This guy has taken real nonentities, people who nobody would give a crap if they ever lived or died. It's satanic because it comes full circle. It's not just dignifying them. It's like putting the microphone in front of the drunk. It's really being sadistic."

"It's like *The Circus of Dr. Lao*," Blanche says.

"It really is," says LaVey, and he goes to the shelf for a passage from the obscure 1935 novel by Charles G. Finney, a scene in which the widow Mrs. Howard T. Casan visits Dr. Lao's mystical circus and insists on hearing her future from Apollonius, a fortune-teller who must forever speak the truth: "And for all the good or evil, creation or destruction, that your living might have accomplished," Apollonius tells her, "you might just as well never have lived at all."

"The pretentiousness of these people!" LaVey says angrily. "Thinking that their little, petty, insignificant lives really have some effect in the scheme of human existence. I mean they're lumps. They're ciphers." The other day LaVey talked about a man he saw at Jack-in-the-Box, a man who walked in, pounded on the counter, and then looked around with a weird smile on his face. What would the world miss if he were dead? LaVey asked. If someone put a gun to his head and blew him away, who would care?

"They're not even zombies!" Blanche says. "Because they never had a life in the first place. They're just zeros! It's frightening."

At 4:00 A.M., in a freezing purple room with a bald Satanist in a lavender tie and two Adele Jergens look-alikes, this bolstering of egos at the expense of everyone else seems suddenly far more sad and frightening than fat people in their Military Order of the Louse uniforms. It even seems evil. "Satan is important as the accuser, the prideful angel," Gene says. "He was kicked out for thinking he could run things as well as the big guy. He is a symbol of the ego. And that's why these books are satanic. They point the finger, act as the mirror to humanity and say, 'Look, look at what you are! You are no better than this. And this is nothing.'"

LaVey whispers: "Behold your glorious handiwork, Brahma, Buddha, Christ. These are the people you have exalted."

The file cabinets are overflowing with church applications ($100 for a lifetime membership), and Blanche works full-time keeping up with them—plus the mail, the updating of LaVey's books, the selling of Church of Satan medallions ($50), the typing and mailing of his 2,000-circulation newsletter, *The Cloven Hoof.* The Macintosh computer helps. Blanche pulls out stacks of church membership applications, which include questions on everything from sexual preference to favorite jokes to political philosophy. Among the applicants is a forty-nine-year-old former Catholic nun. She is a lesbian who enjoys Rod McKuen and Maurice Ravel, Abbott and Costello, Bruno Bettelheim and Sherlock Holmes. She is a substitute schoolteacher. Of LaVey's satanic Bible, she says: "It speaks to me and touches me like few written pieces. I want my anger expressed. I want to finally be real with myself."

The applicants seem so normal, so mundane—like the neighbors in *Rosemary's Baby*: the office manager from Beverly Hills, the musician from Chicago, the plumber from Indiana, the retired Army sergeant from the South, the farmer from Nebraska whose photo shows him sitting on the couch with his wife and two children. These and the half-dozen Satanists who come and go through LaVey's home all say there is no anthropomorphic Satan with red suit, pitchfork, and horns. He is a Christian myth to scare people into the pews. But there are those who confuse myth and reality: the nice middle-aged woman who sat a few feet away on the couch the other night and said the devil—with horns and cloven hoofs—makes love to her in her dreams, sometimes gently and sometimes violently. She said she'd do anything for Satan, even kill.

Sociologists who have studied LaVey's church say its members often had serious childhood problems, like alcoholic parents or broken homes, or that they often were traumatized by guilt-ridden fundamentalist upbringings, turning to LaVey's Satanism as a dramatic way to purge their debilitating guilt. But another trait also seems to repeat: Satanists profess to believe that, except for themselves, the world is full of idiots, fools, and chumps.

"They *want* to be different," says LaVey of his followers. "They *feel* different. They *are* different."

It's another desperately cold night, but the whiskey helps. LaVey's vitriolic anger of the other evening has receded, and he's in a good mood, cracking jokes as he flicks switches on his bank of seven music synthesizers. They are set against a wall mural of the devil enveloping a city as its inhabitants sleep. Magic, LaVey explains, is always best performed while people sleep, because they are then the most susceptible. So from his kitchen-cum-magical laboratory, LaVey has for five years, night after night, tried to change the world. "My goal was to use music as a magical weapon to change the face of society—to provide new options through the New Romanticism."

The rock revolution, he says, has meant the dominance of hostile, pounding music—the beat, beat, beat. "It's been the end of romance," he says. So LaVey decided music must return to an earlier, melodic time, to tunes that made people introspective, imaginative, and nostalgic—the tunes, it just so happens, that were popular when Anton LaVey was young. Magic, he says, simply taps the unrecognized energy of human emotion: love or hate, fear or joy—emotion is emotion. People able to unconsciously feel the emotional power in LaVey's nostalgic tunes are magical people. They are his new elite. Let the hard-rock fans with their satanic lyrics live like the losers in the movie *Escape From New York!* he says. With LaVey pouring magic into the ether nightly, he expects a younger generation of his superior romantic beings—people far less infected with Christian guilt than their parents—to flock to his Satanism.

"I don't believe in 'supernatural' magic," he says. "I believe in 'supernormal' magic, meaning that when certain frequencies are sent out into the ether they affect the human subconscious in much the way that certain circus tunes make elephants march." LaVey then runs through a medley of "rain songs"—"Singin' in the Rain," "Let a Smile Be Your Umbrella," a dozen more. "Putting this leitmotif together is magical because I'm the only one who knows it. It sets up a Jungian gestalt. It's called magical superimposition. It's like five characters waiting for a play: I provide the play." LaVey then heightens and sharpens secret magical tonal patterns that he believes he has discovered through years of trial and error. "You get a lot of rain songs together, and imagine all the creative energy, amalgamated creative energy, that went into those songs. Combine that with the emotional energy I produce in playing it. If the audience is right, like the other night in the bar, I can do something very magical because of ego-circuitry."

Proof that magic works? Why, LaVey knew Hatfield the Rainmaker! He saw it work! What is magic today will be science tomorrow, he says, when the effect of biochemical energy is finally understood. He sees proof of magic everywhere. Not just in the return of romantic tunes and nostalgic fashions, but in parking spaces conjured up on the street and good tables appearing suddenly at restaurants, not to mention the San Diego McDonald's massacre and the Mexican earthquake that resulted accidentally after LaVey vented some anger on the keys. He is like a faith healer who has seen too many miracles to doubt.

"It's truly frightening," he says.

There is a long silence. What would you have said? Your cause-effect relationships are spurious? Your assumptions are pre-scientific? You've been under the sunlamp too long? You say he's crazy. Crazier than the Maharishi Mahesh Yogi who says Transcendental Meditation sends out frequencies that can shape world decisions? Crazier than actress Shirley MacLaine's reincarnation? Crazier than people who pray to God? Or people who pray to saints?

"I started out like Edward G. Robinson in *Night Has a Thousand Eyes*," LaVey says. "A carny mental act, a fraud. I believed everything was fixed, gaffed. Then, like Robinson, you start to get real flashes. Only if you know the tricks can you see the reality. Only if your life isn't full of miracles can you recognize the real miracle. Why are you here? Why you, who liked the obscure satanic movie, *The Ruling Class*? What part of this little Jungian fugue do you have?" And with that, Anton Szandor LaVey, the atheist, the unbeliever, has come a long way from twenty years ago when he set out to parody Christianity. He is today a believer. Religious providence has been replaced with magical providence. He says, "Nothing happens without a reason."

"If you wear a mask long enough, it starts to stick to your face," says LaVey's friend, Eastern Michigan University sociologist Marcello Truzzi. "Then it becomes your face."

It's opera night and downtown San Francisco is packed. LaVey says he will conjure up a parking spot and, yes, we park a single car away from the front door to a crowded Max's Opera Cafe, where, yes, a table opens up a few feet from the piano where they are singing "Hello, Bluebird" and "Time After Time." Magical songs.

"Sometimes I get so tired," says LaVey, perhaps made introspective by the music. "Like old man river."

For two decades Anton LaVey has thumbed his nose at all things sacred and respectable. But getting older, he now craves begrudging respect from the Establishment he has flaunted. "Let's give credit where credit is due," he says. The satanic rock lyrics, the satanic movies, even the satanic murders, he says, all grew from the Church of Satan. "Let's give me a little credit for having moved society—up or down—but for at least having moved it."

Suddenly, the passage LaVey read the other night from *The Circus of Dr. Lao* comes to mind: "And for all the good or evil, creation or destruction, that your living might have accomplished, you might just as well never have lived at all." Now it is clear. It is this egotist's nightmare that haunts LaVey: Did *I* matter, did *I* call the tune, was *I* the ringmaster? In pursuit of proof that he mattered, that he lived, LaVey created a mirrored reality, a Den of Iniquity world around himself, an upside-down carnival reality where all freaks are heroic and all good burghers are nitwits, a reality that from every vantage reflected only his own ego, a true satanic feat.

LaVey smiles. "You are really beginning to understand me."

But what about Blanche and Terry in their mawkish clothes and makeup? he is asked. Aren't they props for your selfishness?

LaVey laughs and quotes Dracula: "If you will fall down and worship me—consider, practice, allow yourself to be a reflection of my needs, decide to choose me as your master—it will literally free you to go out into the world and be free yourself."

And your glorification of hatred for people you don't even know, two-dimensional images in your picture books?

"You can't blame me," LaVey snaps. "How can you respect people who will throw away a week's pay to win a plastic doll? What do I care what people think? I *despise* them!"

But don't you ever wonder about *evil*, he is asked, about the old saying that the devil's best allies are those who don't believe in him? LaVey is quiet for a long moment.

"Oh, yes, deep down I have my speculation that maybe there is a force I've tapped into, that I can extract. Oh, yes, I have doubts. But I hate to talk about these things. I mean, Jayne Mansfield's death was a strange thing! It was a hell of a coincidence! Time and space all coming together to merge. What ingredients contributed to this? These things are too much for coincidence. But still, I want to believe they are coincidences. I'm basically just a good, decent guy. But when you ask me what if I came to believe there was some malevolent force, would I want to do it differently? The answer is no. It's too late. I wouldn't give them the satisfaction. Not when I see what they have done in the world. There'll be no deathbed confession." Not from Anton LaVey, not from the prideful angel.

FEBRUARY 23, 1986

Washington Post photograph.

JERRY FALWELL
Respectability Comes to the Renegade Prince

*H*e was never a great preacher, not as fundamentalist preachers go. He didn't have the spit and fire of, say, Jack Hyles out of First Baptist in Hammond, Indiana, or the haunting, poetic grace of W. A. Criswell out of First Baptist in Dallas, or the suffering and sweat of old Oliver Greene out of the southern tent circuit of the fifties. He certainly didn't have the magnetism of Billy Graham. After you heard these men preach, as the fundamentalists said, you knew you'd been preached to. The young Jerry Falwell, on the other hand, could leave a man wondering: *Was that good preaching, or not?* No lurid visions of Hell, no prancing about the pulpit, no loosened necktie or cast-aside jacket and rolled-up sleeves, no moaning, no groaning. By fundamentalist standards, he sweated very little.

Falwell was dignified and tutorial, schoolmarmy, but with a way of touching people where they lived. Perhaps it was the lilting Virginia accent, or the resonant voice, or the liquid eyes that seemed to stop and focus for an instant on individuals in the crowd. It seemed odd that people felt this warmth in the young Falwell, because on the pulpit he often played professor to his congregation classroom. Jerry, his wife Macel (pronounced MAY-sel) would say, tell more stories, dear, parables, Jesus spoke in parables. Falwell did, and over the years his preaching got more folksy and conversational. But a man can learn only so many things that are deeply foreign to him. And parables were subtle, even inscrutable, their lessons ambiguous and meant to be pondered. Jerry Falwell was not a man of subtleties or ambiguities, not a man who pondered. His message was single-minded and relentless: *Come to know Christ—just you and Christ, child and father, friend and confidant—or be damned!*

End of story.

For preacher or priest, this is the heart of Christianity: God loves everyone, but He also loves YOU, alone, as a person, and you can come to know Him as you would a friend. Falwell's knack—call it a gift—for sharing this message of individual reunion with Christ allowed him to reach into an audience of 200 or 2,000 or 2 million and make it seem as if he, too, Jerry Falwell, were talking not to everyone but to YOU, only you. He and generations of Christian evangelizers knew this appeal worked in a mathematical, if imprecise, formula: Look into the eyes of a hundred people with this story of salvation, and some number of them, one or five or fifteen, will suddenly hear what you have said, as if for the first time, and they will be saved. This is the $E = mc^2$ of evangelization.

But Jerry Falwell went on to become the Jerry Falwell of American lore not because of his instinctive warmth or his knowledge of evangelizing mathematics. No, he became Jerry Falwell by marrying these things to a dominating trait of his character: a calm, eerie, absolute certainty that he, Jerry Falwell, knows the Truth—of life, death, existence, aftermath. No doubts, no waffling. Not a blink. It was always so.

As a twenty-year-old man, Falwell was in a hospital bed in Lynchburg, Virginia, his hometown and today home to his church and direct-mail conglomerate. A minister who taught at Lynchburg College was making hospital rounds that night, and he visited young Falwell. "Lynchburg College," Falwell said gruffly. "I used to go there. But I quit going there. They don't teach *the Truth!*" So certain was he. Three decades later, Jerry Falwell has changed a great deal, and not at all. "He is driven by his desire to control and to not be controlled," says a man who worked closely with Falwell for years and still admires him today. This drive—is it providence or ego at work?—has allowed Falwell to modernize fundamentalism, take it into the American mainstream, and earn it a power, respect, and respectability he and his people had long craved. It's not hype to say that only Falwell could have done this. Yet to win that respectability, Falwell has also let loose forces that may be beyond even his control.

Over the years, Falwell has changed his bumpkin clothes, his Jerry Lee Lewis greased-back hair, his hoariest rhetoric. He has changed his mind about pants on women. He has decided that God isn't a segregationist. He has changed his mind about attending parties where booze is served, about sharing the stage with Catholics or Jews or people who speak in tongues. He now says God answers the prayers of all people, no matter their faith. For this, hardened fundamentalists have attacked him. He has even changed his mind about who can go to Heaven—with not only fundamentalists but Catholics and other Christians of all faiths now having a chance.

This is the new, prime-time Jerry Falwell.

What hasn't changed is Falwell's certainty about the Truth. David Frost once asked Falwell what he'd do if God met him in Heaven, thanked him for his ministry, but then asked, *Jerry, why did you ever mix My Word up with right-wingers, racists, and the money changers I threw out of the Temple, the people who want to censor Shakespeare because the relationship between Hamlet and his mother isn't pro-family? Why didn't you stick to the Gospel, Jerry?*

Falwell didn't miss a beat: "I would believe it wasn't Him I was talking to." Jerry Falwell wouldn't fall on his knees and beg and cry for forgiveness, for being exactly what all men are supposed to be in God's eyes—flawed and weak, arrogant and proud, supremely proud. Not Falwell. He'd look God in the eye and say, *You are an impostor.* As ever, Jerry Falwell is without self-doubt. He is supremely confident that he knows his God, that he knows the Truth—and that he is saved. Since January 20, 1952, he is saved. Of this, he is certain—even more certain than he once was about the evils of pants on women, about who can go to Heaven, about the simple God-willed beauty and justice of segregation in America.

The gritty photograph shows not a hint of the future: Jerry Falwell in 1958 as a new preacher hosting a picnic at his Thomas Road Baptist Church in Lynchburg, Virginia—his tie awkwardly short, his body all sharp angles compared with the soft, heavy curves of today, his face skinny and framed by a mountainous nose and fly-away ears. The camera seems to have caught him off-guard, his right hand stuffing a piece of chicken into his mouth. But a closer look reveals that Falwell's body is stiff, his shoulders thrown back, and that he is more likely hamming it up, holding the pose, looking straight into the lens. Even as he chomps on his chicken, he's smiling. Honestly, he looks every bit the hick, and you can't help wondering how the man in that picture got from there to here.

The young Jerry Falwell was the prince of Lynchburg's skunk hollow. As a boy, he'd always had a vague sense that there was greatness in him. He imagined that he would be a journalist or an engineer someday. He imagined that he would enter politics. He believed he would be a leader. Very early on, he knew he didn't so much crave respect as enjoy the feeling he got when he did things that people respected him for. The difference is subtle—the difference between fear and confidence, and Jerry Falwell wasn't ever afraid of anything or anybody, except maybe his father, and that was more respect than fear.

The Falwell homeplace, as it's still called, was near the roughest neighborhood in Lynchburg, the millworker section of Fairview Heights. Tales of street-gang fights with knives and bloody visits to the hospital weren't exaggerations. Good girls stayed away, and if a boy from a better neighborhood dated a Fairview girl, he risked being beaten up by the class-conscious boys of Fairview. They would get respect, one way or another. As their prince, Jerry Falwell breathed his people's resentment like air.

Yet in the Depression, when many of Lynchburg's respectable elite were selling the china, the Falwells were rich. They drove new cars. A chauffeur took Jerry and his brother, Gene, to public grade school in the morning and home in the afternoon—not home to a crowded little millworker's shanty house, but to the big white house atop Candler's Mountain. In a bald commentary about how money and social status don't always coincide, that house had been hauled board by board to Candler's Mountain from Lynchburg's exclusive Rivermont neighborhood.

This was thanks to the king himself—Jerry's father, Carey. He'd only gotten to sixth grade, but before he was forty, Carey Falwell owned a bus line, gas stations, a fuel oil and gasoline company, a nightclub, a restaurant, a motel. Not exactly a Kiwanis Club guy, he ran bootleg liquor during Prohibition, and, as if that weren't enough to ensure his notoriety, he also shot and killed his brother in self-defense in 1931. Nobody messed with Carey Falwell.

His swaggering confidence rubbed off on Jerry and Gene, who acted as if they were beyond the laws of man and nature. The boys hung ropes from the ties of a huge hundred-foot-high railroad trestle south of the homeplace and then swung from rope to rope. The railroad company couldn't keep the water tank beside the rails patched as fast as Gene and Jerry could shoot it out with their .22 rifles. Carey Falwell was a brutal practical joker—once he shot a hole in the kitchen floor to scare the bejesus out of one of Jerry's boyhood friends—and Jerry acquired his father's domineering humor. Even today, he enjoys pulling practical jokes, spinning his tires to spray snow on people or tossing firecrackers. He always played the tune that others danced to.

But young Jerry was so smart, so far ahead in school, so cute and witty that the rat in the teacher's cookie drawer or the phys-ed teacher stripped of his pants and left stranded in the gym was exasperating but not, well, not antisocial. Besides, he was Carey Falwell's boy.

As a teen, Jerry hung with a Fairview gang at "the wall," a concrete fence across from the Pickeral Cafe, from which the gang was evicted regularly. In 1950, they were guys who saw few choices before them. That America's economy was about to boom and sweep millions of blue-collar sons and daughters into the solid middle class—forever changing their lives and values and the lives and values of their children—was not yet a blip on their screens. They expected to get out of high school, go to the mills. That was that. But Jerry had other ideas. He graduated as valedictorian and headed for Lynchburg College, the first in his family to get past high school.

All this time, Falwell says today, he had little use for religion—until his mother planted the seeds of his rebirth. Helen Falwell, a deeply religious woman, would go to Sunday services and leave fundamentalist Charles E. Fuller's then-popular "Old Fashioned Revival Hour" playing loudly on the radio, knowing that Jerry would be too lazy to get out of bed to shut it off. Falwell always tells this story to justify his own mass-media ministry, saying it was Fuller's distant voice on the radio that saved him. Truth is, a lot more than radio preaching saved Jerry Falwell.

Like much of the South, Lynchburg before World War II was a place turned inward upon itself by time and history. Unlike the North, transformed in ethnicity and attitude by the great migrations, the South remained amazingly homogeneous. Religion was part cause, part symbol of this uniformity in the South, where large percentages of adults declared formal church membership. Respectability demanded it. Southerners knew that the rabble to the north often saw them as racist, backward, and benighted, but God-fearing white southerners saw their way of life as superior—as God's last best hope for America.

So this was the setting of young Falwell's life: He lived in a region looked down upon by the larger culture of the nation; within a neighborhood looked down upon by the larger city; within a dynamic, achieving family looked down upon by anyone who claimed status by virtue of old money or education or manners and etiquette. This included not only Lynchburg's Rivermont elite, but even the established blue-collar folk of the city, for whom proper furnishings and curtains, courtship protocols, neat dress, teetotaling, and, of course, church membership helped establish their own respectability. It was in this stratum—a class with more manners than money—that Falwell found his future wife, Macel Pate, whose father built houses one at a time.

Though Falwell claims he had little interest in religion before Fuller's radio preaching saved him, his childhood was imbued with religion, fundamentalist style. His mother took him to a fundamental church as a young boy, and in public elementary school he learned prayers and hymns. As a child and as a teen he prayed privately. He never questioned the existence of God, and his conversion was one of form and depth, not substance. In Falwell's world, religion, like class indignation, also was breathed like air.

Beneath it all was a quiet battle that had raged for years between Falwell's gentle, religious mother and his tough, worldly, agnostic father. The silent tension between so deep a believer and so deep a disbeliever was always present. And when Carey Falwell—to the amazement of fifteen-year-old Jerry—converted to Christianity on his deathbed, the moment was monumental. Carey was by then a broken man, a fifty-five-year-old alcoholic dying painfully. Family folklore has it that from the instant of his conversion and for the last weeks of his life, Carey was finally a peaceful man—a difference, it is said, that only Christ in his heart can explain. So when Falwell confidently tells a prominent atheist that all atheists find God on their deathbeds, he is speaking from a deep well of experience that may be understood through the mysterious workings of God or the mysterious insights of Freud. Either way, it's as if Falwell is saying: *You, my atheist friend, aren't half the man Daddy was, and if he was humbled before God, you will be too.*

After two years at Lynchburg College, Jerry planned to blow town. But as the day neared for him to apply to Virginia Tech or Notre Dame, the young earthshaker began to have doubts. The bright boy who never spent much time thinking deep thoughts suddenly found himself at "the wall" with his buddies, thinking, "My days are numbered." His friends, dear friends, and Mama, Gene, all the Falwells, the homeplace, his status as the renegade prince would be behind him. The realization made him nervous. The ambitious Falwell, who had always felt he would someday be a leader of men, discovered he was a victim of his own limited horizons. He wanted to be a journalist or an engineer, but had no idea what they actually did. He felt confused and lost. Looking back, Falwell recalls this as a time of searching. It is a sentiment often reported by people about to be "born again."

All these things had come before that Sunday morning Falwell listened one more time to Fuller's "Old Fashioned Revival Hour" and decided he'd go to church. He settled on a church known for its pretty girls, one of whom turned out to be Macel Pate. And that night, Jerry Falwell—to his own astonishment and that of his rowdy friends—found himself walking to the front of Park Avenue Baptist Church, where he made his own confession of faith and was born again. As ever, Jerry played the tune others danced to—he immediately returned to "the wall" and set about successfully converting his delinquent pals.

Falwell's career angst was over. Soon, he was off to college—not Notre Dame, but Baptist Bible College in Springfield, Missouri, a radically fundamentalist, unaccredited school recommended by a local preacher. After graduation, Falwell was back in Lynchburg, supposedly en route to open a church in Macon, Georgia, when a group of thirty-five families (including Macel Pate's parents) asked Falwell to pastor a new church they hoped to start. The Baptist Bible Fellowship—the organizing body of Baptist Bible College and 4,000 Baptist churches in America—ordered him not to take the job because the families were bolting from a Fellowship church. If Falwell did, he was told, he could never send students to Baptist Bible College, and he'd be banned from the Fellowship. The story goes that Falwell prayed hard. Finally, he decided he'd do it, start a little church named Thomas Road and be banished forever. Was this the hand of God at work?

That's how Falwell sees it. God wanted him cast out of the Fellowship so he'd be free to follow his heart in creating a new fundamentalism that would appeal not only to country folk and mill-workers but to the solid middle class, a fundamentalism that would abandon the sad, storefront churches and the know-nothing preachers who'd made the faith a laughingstock. God wanted Falwell in Lynchburg because He always uses the unlikely and the humble to send His message, so He can prove His glory. And what more unlikely and humble place than Lynchburg to build Falwell's massive church, his Liberty University with 7,000 students, and his $100-million-a-year TV ministry?

But the hand of God aside, what were the chances of Falwell ever leaving the cradle of Lynchburg, especially when some churchly voice of authority was trying to tell Carey Falwell's boy what to do, especially after he'd fallen in love with Macel Pate? "It would have been very hard," Falwell says today. And the hand of God aside, who was better poised to take fundamentalism into the American mainstream than the prince of skunk hollow? He knew his people's fears, their class resentments. He knew they were as smart as anyone from Rivermont or Atlanta or New York, though they themselves sometimes wondered. He also was armed—with a pugnacious confidence gained from his oddly privileged background, the burning ambition and entrepreneurial bent of his father, and brains that could compete with Lynchburg's affluent sons and daughters. Besides, even a born leader needed people to lead.

Falwell would become his people's preacher and their worldly teacher. He would teach them about God. But he would also teach them that they would respect themselves more if others respected them more, that respect follows respectability. He would teach them to stop wearing black shoes with brown suits, to say "he doesn't" instead of "he don't," to change their hairstyles and to overcome their fear of outsiders, prosperity, and success. Falwell would teach them all these things, in time.

First he had to teach himself.

When Jerry Falwell launched his career at twenty-two, he was an ignorant man. He doesn't say it just that way because he does not admit weakness, but he makes harsh jokes about the old It-Was-Good-Enough-for-Moses fundamentalists, the pop-eyed preachers who sanctified their ignorance by saying that when they opened their mouths, God gave them the words, who imagined that fashionable dress and Billy Graham were demonic, who thought that anyone who associated with anyone who associated with nonfundamentalists was a sinner.

Falwell had bought the fundamentalist line in Bible college, all the "dos and don'ts"—men should always wear short hair; women should never wear pants. He also believed that fundamentalists shouldn't associate with liberal Christians or Pentecostal Christians who speak in tongues, that only fundamentalists were saved, and that the Bible said God meant blacks to be servants to whites. In 1958, Falwell even gave a sermon on segregation that is painful to read thirty years later. It sounds so ignorant, and it shocks, not because Falwell was a segregationist but because of the smug, self-righteous way he used the Bible to rationalize his view.

"In this message," Falwell intoned pompously, "I want to use the Bible alone as our guide. It is never worthwhile to give man's opinion. . . . The answer to the whole subject can be found in Genesis 9:18–27." Falwell went on to explain that Ham, the son of Noah, had seen Noah naked one day. When Noah discovered this, he cursed Ham's son, Canaan: "A servant of servants shall he be unto his brethren." Falwell explained that Ham later became the progenitor of the African race.

He rambled on, still using "the Bible alone" as his guide: "The true Negro does not want integration. . . . He realizes his potential is far better among his own race. . . . We see the hand of Moscow in the background. . . . We see the Devil himself behind it. . . . It will destroy our race eventually. . . . In one northern city, a pastor friend of mine tells me that a couple of opposite race live next door to his church as man and wife. . . . It boils down to whether we are going to take God's Word as final." Oblivious to the hatefulness of his sermon, Falwell concluded: ". . . If we live in constant fellowship with the Lord, He can enable us to live Christ-like before others."

Today, after portions of the sermon are read to him, Falwell says he was wrong, that he had distorted the Bible's message, that he knew in his heart segregation was wrong, but that he was influenced by his Bible college teachers. "You don't know how hard it is to purge yourself of these things," he says. "Unless you've been there, you just don't know. It's the strongest grip."

That grip has always been rooted in fundamentalism's certitude that all life's questions are answered in the Bible. Since the nineteenth century, its cause célèbre has been its battle with the modern view that the Bible is not literally true—that historical, archaeological, and semantic research have revealed many factual mistakes. Most Christians to this day take much of the Bible literally, accepting its miracles or the virgin birth or Christ's ascension into Heaven as real events. But that has never been enough for fundamentalists. For them, every word, date, phrase, description in the Bible has to be true—or none is true. It begins with simple, if circular, logic: God is perfect. If His Book is not perfect, then it can't be His Book. And since it is His Book, it must be perfect.

After World War II, a group of respected fundamentalist scholars finally left the ranks and launched a movement dubbed "neoevangelicalism," which in the following decades became a respected, mainline branch of American Protestantism symbolized by evangelist Billy Graham. Evangelicalism—a name chosen over the increasingly disreputable tag of fundamentalism—encouraged ecumenicism with other faiths and played down the extreme view that fundamentalists must separate themselves from nonfundamentalists. In their war against all things secular, modern, and materialistic, fundamentalists saw evangelicals taking the first steps down the "slippery slope" of accommodation, and they dug in deeper. Jerry Falwell, thank you, stuck with that Old Time Religion.

It was August of 1956, two months after Jerry Falwell had launched Thomas Road Baptist Church in Lynchburg's old Donald Duck Cola building, when Falwell and Harold Knowles, the nineteen-year-old son of a Thomas Road congregant, visited Chattanooga's Highland Park Baptist Church—with its beautiful sanctuary seating thousands and its large college, Tennessee Temple, a dominant institution among unaccredited fundamentalist schools. The young men from a new, poor church were overwhelmed. Halfway up the aisle, Falwell suddenly stopped and said, "Someday, if God allows me, I'll have all this in Lynchburg." It was a weird remark, even to the young, admiring Knowles. "Here's this twenty-three-year-old kid with a two-month-old church in the Donald Duck building, and he says this," Knowles recalls. "I figured he was dreamin'."

But back home Falwell doggedly set about unleashing the $E=mc^2$ of evangelization on Lynchburg. Every morning, he headed out to knock on one hundred doors, sometimes from 9:00 A.M. to 10:00 P.M. He trained his Thomas Road congregants to do the same, using methods more common to politics than to redemption.

Folks answered their doors, and Falwell simply told them he'd started a new church. He then invited them to attend the next Sunday evening service. He didn't say Sunday morning service because local preachers were already angry that he was evangelizing their people, and Falwell figured that by inviting folks to Sunday evening service, he implied they could attend their own church in the morning, though this was not his long-term intent. Falwell was friendly and relaxed, no pressure, but in a few minutes he had name, name of spouse, names of children and their ages, and the name of the family's church, if any. He quickly discovered that people in Lynchburg never admitted that they didn't go to church, so he took to casually asking the name of their minister. If they hesitated in a way Falwell came to recognize, he knew they were, to use evangelizing lingo, "unchurched." Outside, he wrote it all down.

The info went to Thomas Road people who then phoned the homes later in the week, inviting each family to church again. A Thomas Road newsletter also went out—meaning each home was contacted three times before Sunday. People who came to church were called on Monday and thanked for attending. Later, as if to close the deal, a church member dropped by the house. It was a sweet package, because Falwell instinctively understood a sociological truism of conversion: People aren't usually attracted to a church by its beliefs, but because they come to know and like its people. The beliefs come later.

In his first few years, Falwell also launched local radio and TV Bible commentaries, during which he plugged Thomas Road. He now portrays himself as a pioneer in mass-media evangelism, but Falwell was really following in a long tradition of fundamentalists using the mass media—something mainline churches were reluctant to do, fearing it smacked of Elmer Gantryism. This gentility never burdened fundamentalists. The faith's emphasis on evangelizing the "unchurched" always made it easy to justify—even glorify—what outsiders often consider worldly empire building.

Jerry Falwell was no innovator. He was a consolidator, a man who took tried-and-true methods and organized them better, more efficiently, more technocratically than the inventors themselves. Later, this skill and the computer—with its segmented mailing lists, personalized form letters, and ZIP Code precision—would make an empire possible. The Falwell Formula worked: Thomas Road grew from 35 families to 1,000 members in a year, to 10,000 in a decade, to 22,000 today.

Macel Falwell has a red tie with yellow polka-dots that she has kept for thirty years to show how Jerry once dressed. She shows it to audiences, and it always gets a good laugh, as it also humanizes a man who has now become the kind of superstar only television can create. Macel, a proper woman whose mother emphasized manners, dress, and respectability, had Jerry out of polyester very early. He still wore brown suits, though, and it was many years before Macel could get him out of those black ankle-high shoes. But Falwell learned quickly. A friend of his recalls Falwell coming home from a trip to the Middle East and mentioning casually that the Arab leaders always wore dark blue business suits. Soon after, the friend says, Falwell made a joke from the pulpit about leisure suits—and leisure suits disappeared at Thomas Road. Today, Jerry wears dark blues. It was vintage Falwell.

Long ago, he'd recognized that fundamentalists had two choices: do what evangelicals had done and abandon the name *fundamentalism* or retool its popular meaning and image. He opted for retooling, publicly distancing himself from "the idiots" and "snake-handlers" of his faith even in the fifties and moving quickly to plan for the construction of his magnificent church, with its antebellum pillars and its aura of prosperity and permanence. Over the years, Falwell had learned that those with the power to give or take away social respect used even the smallest details as excuses to disregard him and his people—unfashionable dress, poor grammar, beehive hairdos, Vitalis, beat-up cars, dumpy churches, orange shag carpets. These weren't seen as simple differences in taste and class but as proof that fundamentalists were stupid, not deserving of respect—that they existed at the margins of America.

Yes, Falwell wanted the respect his family had been denied. Yes, he was ambitious. But Falwell also seems to have had a sincere sense of himself as a defender of his people. He mentions that ignorant, uneducated, even bigoted people can still be good people. He says his Bible college teachers were "good men" trapped in a time warp, and not wholly to blame for their ignorance. He is forever correcting the grammar of his people: You may be as smart as any Harvard grad, is the message, but folks won't listen past the first "ain't."

Nothing better captures Falwell's obsession with the appearance of respectability than Liberty University, which he founded as Lynchburg Baptist College in 1971 and which he envisions as the Baptist Notre Dame of tomorrow. From Liberty, which unlike most fundamentalist schools is fully accredited, Falwell wants to send an army of fundamentalist evangelizers also armed with a liberal arts education that allows them to compete in the best jobs and the best graduate schools, something kids from fundamentalist colleges could never do.

What's striking about Liberty students is how normal they look. A decade ago, almost nobody at Liberty knew about Bass Weejuns. Now they're everywhere. Boys then often wore black pants and white shirts—"the preacher-boy look," it was called. Girls wore modest dresses. Today, kids wander about campus in punk-rock attire, jeans, and flashy ties and shirts meant not to match. The rules are still strict—no dancing, gambling, Hollywood movies, booze, tobacco; dresses only two inches above the knees when seated; ties worn to classes; no displays of affection; no rock music. But boys will wear crewneck sweaters to hide absent ties, and girls will wear long skirts with high slits to look more alluring, until the campus enforcers catch them. Rock music can be found, and as of last year boys and girls can even hold hands. Rather than soft-pedal Liberty's new, mainstream feel, Falwell revels in it.

The message: Kids can be fundamental *and* hip!

This is Falwell's path to respectability. He has even adopted the civil rights movement as his model. "We are the last minority," he says. "You can no longer attack a man's color, but right today you can refer to fundamentalists as Bible-bangers." He disagrees with nearly all Jesse Jackson says, but Falwell is fascinated with Jackson's journey from the fringes of respectability to the heart of it. Falwell knows that his congregants and his national following get a charge from hearing his stories about visiting Anwar Sadat or the president, or seeing him on "Nightline" or "Donahue" or "Larry King Live." Like Jesse Jackson, Falwell has crashed the gate—and symbolically taken his people with him.

"Why shouldn't we have the best church?" a Thomas Road congregant recalls Falwell saying repeatedly over the years. "Why shouldn't our preachers have a nice house and a nice car? Why shouldn't we have the best?"

There are so many things being said here. Falwell has lambasted the "prosperity theology" of Jim Bakker's TV preaching—the idea that being rich means God has blessed you. Falwell isn't so crass. But he has preached his own brand of prosperity theology—one rooted in his people's rise from the back streets and backwoods to the suburban homes of Lynchburg and America.

Falwell himself lives in a beautiful antebellum mansion with a swimming pool and high fence. His twenty-one-year-old son drives a BMW. Last year, Falwell earned $432,000, most of it in book royalties and advances, though he says he gave more than 30 percent of that to his church. Falwell does not apologize for his wealth, and for good reason. One of the implicit messages of his ministry is that fundamentalists can have it all—keep their faith and climb the ladder.

It was not always so easy. When fundamentalists rose in society, they often jettisoned their faith for mainline denominations, not only to win respectability, but also because fundamentalism was a tough faith for successful people. It was tough to be, say, a lawyer or corporate executive and never go to a party where booze was served. It was tough to oppose fashionable dress so fiercely that you had to taper your own slacks because bell-bottoms were all you could find in the stores. And it was tough for a woman to wear "modest"— translate this as "drab"—clothes if she worked in an office where performance was subtly graded on tasteful dress. Falwell argued that if fundamentalists were to be an army infiltrating and evangelizing America, its soldiers for Christ had to look, dress, talk in ways that allowed people to listen.

Hardened fundamentalists saw Falwell leading a generation down the "slippery slope"—selling out, accommodating to win power, glory, and respect from the unsaved. The fundamentalist newspaper *The Sword of the Lord* criticizes Falwell regularly. Prominent fundamentalist preacher Bob Jones, Jr., who once preached at Falwell's church, has called him "the most dangerous man in America." The president of the Fundamental Baptist Fellowship of America has attacked him for mingling with Christians who take the unfundamentalist view that speaking in tongues is biblically mandated.

Falwell now pays little attention to his far-fundamentalist critics, but even he acknowledges they are correct about one thing: His is a dangerous path. He says it will be two generations before it will be clear whether his brand of fundamentalism will remain distinctly fundamental or become a watered-down, mainline Protestantism. But, he says, there was no choice. It was modernize fundamentalism or watch it die.

Out with the old and in with the new . . .

The Old Falwell: once joked cavalierly that American Communists should be registered, stamped on their foreheads, and sent to Russia. He once said, after a top *Playboy* magazine editor was killed with 274 other people in a plane crash, that God had passed His judgment against pornography. He once said some homosexuals would "rather kill you than look at you." He once said there are "almost as many alcoholics as there are Negroes." He once called the feminist movement "a satanic attack on the home."

The New Falwell: talks of love and forgiveness and giving a counselor's helping hand to homosexuals and women who have had abortions. He talks about the beauty of pluralism in America, about the parochialism of Lynchburg years ago and how his travels have made him appreciate diversity. He talks about how wrong he was on race and how he once spent too much time condemning sinners, not enough condemning sin.

The New, Old Falwell: talks about a thoughtful, in-depth article written about him and, with a kindly smile, says he didn't like it, but that it's hard to be objective about himself. Then, out of the blue, Falwell flashes the same smile and says he has since discovered that the article's author is a homosexual. This, it seems, is supposed to mean something. Perhaps it means, in that old fundamentalist way, that Falwell can still be hateful toward those he doesn't understand.

So is there a new, transformed Jerry Falwell? Or does his change of heart grow from a boundless need to control and to not be controlled? Or his need to reach into middle America to meet his goal of 50,000 Liberty students a year? (Falwell already has taken the word *Baptist* from the name of his college to broaden its appeal.) Or has he changed because of the way his burgeoning Christian empire sucks up money and demands wider sources of income in the face of a narrowing market for TV preaching? Money is tight after televangelism's scandals, and Falwell's fund-raising was down $6 million last year. With much fanfare, he pulled back from his handling of Jim Bakker's PTL scandal and from his day-to-day running of the Moral Majority, the conservative lobbying group he founded in 1979. He went home.

In Lynchburg, Falwell had already launched a profit-making TV network, Family Net, and a new videocassette, at-home college degree program that is highly profitable. He began a TV talk show called "The Pastor's Study," much of which is a money-raising appeal for, say, his videocassette college or his upcoming Christian Cruise vacation. In the works are TV shows aimed at mainstream audiences. They carry a light-'n'-easy fundamental message and deal with secular issues such as pop music, abortion, and interracial marriage. They are meant to be hot—and to soft-sell fundamentalism in order to evangelize more people. But they also are meant to make money because Falwell is planning for the day that his TV fund-raising falters even more or the day that he dies. The shows will certainly anger Falwell's far-fundamentalist critics—and harden his image as a man moving to the middle about as fast as feet can carry.

But this is no revelation. It's a predictable finale to a life lived in pursuit of respectability. Call it a slippery slope, call it learning from experience, call it a cynical marketing ploy. The result is the same: Falwell's brand of fundamentalism has lost its strident separatism. This is what evangelicals called for decades ago. It's what Falwell once abhorred. It's what he now glorifies as an effort to evangelize America. This is the preacher-pragmatist, the politician, in Falwell, and it is a politician he cites to make his point—conservative North Carolina Republican Jesse Helms. He's right for God and America on 98 percent of the issues, Falwell says, but Helms is from a tobacco state, and he can't back strong restrictions on smoking—although 320,000 Americans die yearly from diseases linked to the habit. "It hurts him with our camp," Falwell says. "'Why don't you come down on that tobacco lobby?' I've never talked with Jesse about this. I don't want him to have to tell me. I know what he's doing. He's trying to stay alive so he can fight for all the other issues."

Jerry Falwell has accepted a very worldly reality: God's truth may be absolute, but man's truth must be negotiated.

The preacher thinks more about dying these days. He turns fifty-five next month, the age at which his father died. His original Thomas Road Baptist Church members have begun dying of old age, and Falwell has been deeply saddened by their deaths. He mentions how odd it is when a young person doesn't recognize the name of baseball great Ted Williams. Or how strange it is that few people remember the influential 1950s TV preacher Rex Humbard. He laughs and says that decades from now the kids at Liberty University will say, "Yeah, we remember Falwell. He helped us get going." He laughs again.

There is a Liberty professor, Falwell says, who believes the Falwell ministry is a movement that will someday be an institutionalized denomination with Liberty as its Rome, with the school producing seminarians who will plant 10,000 churches in America. The professor, Falwell says, believes all denominations begin with a great leader—John Calvin and John Wesley, for instance—and end with an organized denomination. No, Falwell says, he doesn't think of himself as a Calvin or a Wesley. He is only saying what the professor says. Still, Falwell is pondering his legacy.

Falwell never talks about his private feelings or fears or his own struggles with sin. "We're all sinners," he says, and leaves it at that, although he does mention the sin of pride several times in casual conversation. Asked if he has struggled with his own pride, Falwell shrugs off the question. He believes it does the faith no good for preachers to be running around confessing their sins. He couldn't stand it when TV evangelist James Robison stood up and said he had lusted after women in his heart, but that God had healed him. People don't need to hear that—they need certainty!

There's an old story about a preacher who converts an atheist by telling the atheist he has nothing to lose by believing in God, because if there is a God, his belief will earn him salvation, and if there isn't a God, he will still be just as dead. Falwell doesn't like that story. It implies that the preacher allows for the possibility that there is no God—and that must never be. If the unsaved see only absolute, certain faith, they'll become curious about how a person can believe in God so wholeheartedly, especially in this secular age. They will then seek out the answer, Falwell says, and be converted.

It seems inescapable: Falwell's vaunted certainty isn't only a state of mind, but an evangelizing stance—a kind of PR posture for God. Even if Jerry Falwell doubted himself or his faith or his God, he would never admit it. Maybe that helps explain how he can claim absolute certainty in his religious beliefs at the same time that he has changed his mind about so many things, from rejecting the old "dos and don'ts," to changing his opinion of what "the Bible alone" says about segregation, to changing his view that people in any Christian denomination can be born again, even if they don't describe the experience of Christ entering their hearts as a fundamentalist would. None of these things, Falwell insists, are at the heart of fundamentalism.

This is what a person must believe to enter Heaven: He must believe that Christ was the son of God born to a virgin, that he died for each person's sins, that he rose from the dead and ascended bodily into Heaven. He must acknowledge that he is a hopeless sinner and give himself over to God's will—be born again—and enter into a deep, personal relationship with God. Then, no matter his sins, a sincere believer is saved.

Take note: Falwell doesn't include in his list a belief that the Bible is wholly without error, though this has been the battle cry of fundamentalism for a century. Only a decade ago, Falwell himself said anyone who didn't believe in the "absolute infallibility" of the Bible "is in the spirit of the anti-Christ." Falwell still believes the Bible is without error and that any sincere Bible student will conclude this. It's key to calling yourself a fundamentalist, he says, but a Christian need not believe in a Bible without error to enter Heaven. Jerry Falwell has gone ecumenical. What still gives his fundamentalism a taste of the self-righteous Old Time Religion is his belief that only born-again Christians can enter Heaven—all the rest are damned. Liberal Catholic and Protestant theologians believe God provides avenues of salvation for good-hearted people of all faiths and even atheists. Not Falwell.

Anne Frank is in Hell? he is asked.

"Christ is the only way," Falwell says, meaning, yes, the little girl is in Hell—a real place to Falwell, with flames and pain and eternal suffering.

Buddha, Mohammed, Gandhi, they are all in Hell, too?

Falwell's answer is yes.

This is still fundamental.

"What we are doing has never been done before," Falwell says.

He means that trying to modernize a faith without losing its distinctive flavor, without watering it down, is a dangerous tack. Mingling with nonfundamentalists, flirting with the adornments of modernism—big houses, BMWs, skirts with high slits—eliminating the "dos and the don'ts" that once defined membership and behavior is indeed a slippery slope. Falwell is trying to barricade against this. He plans to pack the Liberty University board with preachers so that intellectual curiosity can go only so far. He has bragged that if Liberty ever got too liberal, his "Old Time Gospel Hour" TV show, which owns the campus and gave the school $10 million last year, would shut off the spigot. Maybe this will work. But there are other, more subtle threats to fundamental doctrine that even Falwell's need to control cannot control. As he says, the passing of belief from one generation to the next is the final test.

Consider Falwell's oldest son, Jerry, Jr. He is twenty-six. He made his first profession of faith as a young child. He was always very smart, very thoughtful. He graduated from Liberty, went to summer school at Yale, got a law degree at the University of Virginia. He was offered jobs with law firms in Richmond and New York before starting his own firm in Lynchburg. His wife owns a tony dress shop in the city's Rivermont neighborhood—the other side of the tracks from Jerry Falwell's boyhood. Jerry, Jr., has made the leap from skunk hollow to respectability. He is shy and dislikes the limelight. He is very decent. He considers himself a fundamentalist.

He is asked, Do you believe Gandhi had to go to Hell because he was not a Christian?

He answers, "I don't believe that."

You don't believe that? he is asked.

"No," Jerry, Jr., says, firmly disagreeing with his father's bedrock religious belief.

No doubts, no waffling. Not a blink.

He is the next generation.

JULY 24, 1988

GARY POE
Just Like Us, Only Retarded

*B*R-I-C-K-S.

Gary Poe used to know that word. He's sure of it. He hasn't studied in three years, though, and this is payment. He blames himself. "Brrriiicks," he says hesitantly, his head leaning forward over the dining room table as if to coax the word from memory. He smiles broadly. If only he could remember things, Gary Poe believes, he would be flying airplanes or running an office somewhere. He'd never again wash a plate or clean a urinal or bathe a dog. The army of counselors would harass someone else. He'd be driving a car and carrying a Ward's credit card. He'd figure his change from a $20 bill without a calculator, tell his left hand from his right without looking to see which arm his watch is on. There wouldn't have been a vasectomy. He'd read every item on the menu at the Howard Johnson's, instead of always ordering the Big Breakfast No. 1. Women would never again take that tone and call him "darling." And once he knew that 9×9 equals 81, he would know it, instead of adding the number 9 on the calculator nine times. He'd just reach back past the tip of his tongue, think for an instant, and . . . remember!

But Gary Poe isn't smart—at least not about 9×9. He sits in his apartment hunched over a third-grade reader two nights a week, a thirty-two-year-old man smoking a Benson & Hedges cigarette and determinedly working his way through the u-sounding words: *mother, brother, some, from.* He sits prayerfully below a single hanging lamp, his good hand and his bad right hand resting gently on his knees, which knock permanently from cerebral palsy. As always, the words scramble in transmission from symbol to meaning.

"This is Buck . . ." There is a long pause. "This is *Bud* Buck . . . Mr. Buck is Ed's uncle . . . Uncle Buck—Uncle *Buck?*—Uncle *Bud* comes from the city in his truck." This is Workbook 2. Years ago, Gary Poe was through Workbook 3 and ready to start Workbook 4. Then he moved, couldn't keep a job, got married, and got lazy about his studies. When he started up again, he was in Workbook 1.

"It gets you discouraged," he says. "You shouldn't have forgot."

Photograph by Tom Wolff.

A century ago, Gary Poe might have been called "feeble-minded." Before World War II, he might have been called a "mental defective," many of whom were forcibly sterilized. By the fifties, he might have been seen as a sad, "mentally retarded" creature deserving of sympathy, but doomed to perpetual childhood. The fifties wisdom often called for virtual imprisonment, and it was only the insistence of his father that kept Gary Poe from Maryland's infamous Rosewood Center for the retarded.

Much has changed since then. The knowledge that intelligence isn't fixed, but shaped by experience and education, among smart people or dumb, took root. The common wisdom today is that retarded people need not be incompetent—especially the 95 percent of America's 6 million retarded citizens who, like Gary, are only slightly retarded. Even the label *retarded* became a stigma, and the words *slow* or *disabled* came into vogue.

The Gary Poes of the world do grow up, although it is often a battle. Gary is every father's favorite son. At Maryland's Montgomery County job training center for the handicapped, just outside Washington, D.C., he was seen as a model for the 240 adults there. He will work until he drops, he is neat and well-spoken, he knows which fork is which, he is always on time, his humor is wry and self-deprecating. Gary wants only to be "normal"—free of handouts, social workers, and sympathy. "You take one day at a time," he says. "And even if things don't seem very funny, you laugh anyway. . . . You just don't give up. You prove to yourself that you *can do something*."

Yet Gary is out of work again. He is, after all, slow—clinically slow, his measured intelligence falling in the bottom few percent of all Americans. So he fights not only his limitations, but also the fears of his father and in-laws, the cynicism of embittered friends who are themselves slow, the prejudice of bosses, the guaranteed federal disability paycheck that can sap ambition, and, sometimes, even the attitudes of the counselors and teachers assigned to help him. Through fear and good intention, they conspire to keep Gary a child forever. The catch is that Gary *does* need help. He resists, however, when the price is his dignity. About that, he is very smart.

The woman listens, but she doesn't hear.

"It is absolutely important that you tell the truth," she says, as Gary Poe and two other slow men sit before the blackboard in their weekly "job club" meetings at Montgomery County's Centers for the Handicapped. Gary considers it a step backward to be here, but he has no choice. Without the help of the Centers' job counselors, no one would hire him when he moved to Montgomery from a nearby Maryland county five years ago.

They'd look at him, Gary says, and say, " 'You don't look like you really have the qualifications'—for a dishwashing job you know you've done for seven years!" Gary was kept at the Centers, at a cost of about $5,500 a year, for two years—complaining constantly that he was ready for the outside. When he lost his most recent dishwashing job, however, Gary returned to the Centers—not to learn, but to plug into the county's bureaucratic job pipeline for the disabled.

Gary sits stiffly, open black binder on his lap, head cocked back, his direct brown eyes intent on the woman at the blackboard, the hint of a smile on his face. The cerebral palsy gives Gary an ostrich-like strut when he walks, but his more subtle movements are not jagged, but deliberate. When he rubs his hair with his left hand, the motion is only vaguely robotic. He wears dark blue casual slacks, black wing tips, and a light blue shirt with a sheen. Its top button is hooked, and the shirt pulls across lean and muscular shoulders and arms. He sips his coffee and the slurp is delicate but audible. The woman leading the session asks Gary to read a question from his application for a dishwasher's job at Farrell's Ice Cream Parlour Restaurant. He reads clearly, though as usual his speech is slow and monotonal: "When did you last see a doctor? Why?" Gary's confusing answer: "No." Gary had been to a doctor late last year after repeated dizzy spells. The doctor feared he was suffering seizures and prescribed a seizure medication. Gary, who had never had seizures, believed his trouble was exhaustion. When tests failed to confirm seizures, he immediately asked to stop the drugs. His doctor agreed—meaning Gary takes *no* regular drugs.

"Weren't you having a problem with your medication?" the woman at the blackboard asks. She suggests that Gary say he had last seen the doctor for a "change in medication." Sitting a few feet away, Gary says he takes *no* medication. But his words are lost. What if you were having problems with "the new medication" and your employer found out? the woman asks. "You don't have to tell everything you know," she says, "but you do have to tell the truth."

Gary says nothing. He has been ignored, talked down to, gawked at, or belittled so often that practicality, not pride, usually governs his reaction. "I started to speak up and say, 'I don't think you understand me,'" Gary says, but the woman's point about telling the truth was a good one. Besides, he's known a lot worse: one Centers instructor, angry at a remark from Gary, once stooped to one-upmanship. "What college did *you* go to?" asked the instructor. No, an accidental snub from the woman at the blackboard, a woman Gary knows and likes, just isn't worth worrying about. He is here for a job.

"Why did you select Farrell's," asks Earle Goss, Gary's job counselor, when he joins the group.

"It's a dishwashing job, and it's close to home."

"Do they have glass dishes?"

"Mostly glass dishes."

Then out of the blue: "Unbutton your top button there, Gary, you can talk better." Startled, Gary straightens up and touches his collar. The exchange has nothing to do with talking better: Earle Goss has told Gary repeatedly that he looks "weird" with his top button hooked. Gary unbuttons his button. He appreciates the reminder. Earle asks, Are the dirty dishes pushed on carts or carried on trays?

With a shy grin and deadpan delivery, Gary says, "With my condition it would be better with wheels, for their benefit—and for mine." The list of such arcane considerations is long: Does the restaurant run out of dishes during its rush times? *Gary cannot always keep up during peak periods.* Would he do more than wash dishes, perhaps take out trash, mop the floor, clean the kitchen? *Too many tasks can make Gary forgetful.* Has he ever run this type of dishwashing machine? Would he need to read written instructions? What was the expression on the manager's face when Gary first walked in? For Gary Poe, everything from the physical dynamics of the task to kitchen design to intuitive vibrations separates another two-week stand from a job with tenure.

"I'll add it to the 160 others in your file," Earle jokes.

In the next few days Earle Goss will talk to Farrell's and type a "clean" application (Gary's is barely legible), adding Gary's work history. It is an impressive record: first job at sixteen; seven years washing dishes at Joe Theismann's restaurant; a year bathing cats and dogs at an animal hospital. Unlike most slow adults, Gary has spent much of his life living and working among, as Gary calls them, "straight people," and that too is a strong selling point.

"I believe I can work my speed up to theirs," he says. "And then I would be classified as seminormal."

Gary Poe's psychological profiles confirm what anyone who spends a few hours with him knows: He is emotionally stable, confident, and without anger or bitterness about his disabilities. He has achieved the great dream of disabled adults. He faces the world— and all its painful rebuffs—with humor, dignity, and determination, trying to force straight people to see him not as disabled, but as an individual with strengths and failings. It wasn't even until he was out of work and forced to seek help at the Centers for the Handicapped that he really began to *feel* disabled. All his life, he had fended for himself. "Gary had it rough as a kid," says Ray Jenkins, an old, straight friend of Gary's. "But in the long run it may have done him some good."

Gary Poe was twelve when they told him he was mentally retarded. "I thought they didn't know what they were talking about," he says. Sure, he'd gone to special schools. He'd spent a lifetime in hospitals. It took him longer than other kids to pick up on things. But somehow that always seemed connected to his cerebral palsy. To *his body, not his brain.*

"I always thought I could catch up with them," he says. "I just thought I had to try a little harder."

Gary was three months old when his father, headed out the door for work, stopped at his crib. The child looked dead! For the next six weeks, he lay in a coma. His father remembers no cause, though malaria was mentioned. When he awoke, they said the brain damage meant Gary would never walk or talk or feed himself. In the naked language of the day, he was a "vegetable."

"It was just something that happened," says Gary's father. Gary was the family's third child. His dad, a laborer, was going from job to job then, and keeping a baby with so many serious medical problems seemed impossible. The doctors suggested the infamous Rosewood Center. "It had a pretty bad reputation even then," recalls Gary's father, and he refused. The boy went to a foster home. The wisdom of the day held that it was best for Gary not to see his real parents, and it was only a few years ago that father and son were reunited. His mother is long dead.

The doctors, so often wrong about the retarded in those days, were wrong about Gary, too. Gary's foster mother, who died a few years ago, spent hours massaging and doing special exercises with his legs. His earliest memories are of the ropes hung from tree to tree around the yard. They were his highway. With braces up to his thighs until age seven, Gary learned to walk by dragging himself along those ropes. A wheelbarrow eventually became his walker.

"I'd smack the ground," he says, laughing.

He remembers few friends. The kids called him "retard," and he was often nixed from games such as basketball. The words became a refrain: "You would just slow us down!" Gary became stubborn, insisting that he try everything. But he was angry at the world. "Why me?" he'd scream. Sometimes, he would try to plead disability: "No way!" his foster mother would say. "If your room's a mess, you clean it up."

Self-pity eventually became self-esteem, however, as Gary transformed his disability into a badge of honor. Each accomplishment was a sweet victory—a dishwashing job, an apartment of his own, learning to ride a moped. "I wasn't supposed to walk or talk!" he says. Disabled people, Gary explains, can be "better" than straight people, because straight people can coast through life. For Gary, just getting dressed is a challenge. The result: "You can care more about yourself." Gary became a local character in his suburban neighborhood, where people took a benign attitude toward the image of him wobbling down busy streets on his bicycle. By his early twenties he was pretty much on his own. He shared a $400-a-month apartment with a succession of roommates. He remembers being stuck for the rent regularly. "One was supposedly normal," Gary says. "But he wouldn't work."

Gary took whatever job he could get, and over the years he washed dishes or cleaned up at the Port of Italy Inn, Jack's, Bob's Big Boy, and Joe Theismann's, where he worked for nearly a decade. One year his straight friends threw a birthday bash for Gary and he danced simultaneously with five women to the tune "Macho Man" and, as a finale, tore open the buttons on his shirt to expose his chest. It was a good party—and it was a good time in Gary's life. Even then, he had trouble keeping up with the rush-hour flow of dishes. But at Theismann's someone from the kitchen might pitch in for a few minutes. A waitress might take an instant to remind Gary that the silverware was running low. People liked Gary. He was a person, not a disability.

"That was my territory," he says proudly.

It was during these years that Gary hooked up with Ray Jenkins, a house painter and a friend of Gary's brother. Gary started dropping by Ray's house. They'd go fishing. ("I'd have to bait up his hook and throw it out," Ray says, "but I have to do that for half the people I go fishing with.") Or they'd go out for a beer or maybe watch TV. When Gary couldn't find a decent place to live, Ray invited him to move in. It was the beginning of an unusual friendship. Researchers know that retarded people often name normal people as friends, but those normal people, asked to do the same, often list the retarded as only acquaintances. Gary, on the other hand, was about to get a crash course in straight friendship.

"He didn't have dreams when I met him," says Ray Jenkins. "He started to dream about things getting better."

Gary looked and acted differently in those days. He often wore clothes that neither fit nor matched—wrinkled high-water plaid pants and a striped shirt. The whitewalls over his ears had for years been cut too high. In those days, Gary might stare at a woman's legs with embarrassing obviousness. Ray rarely gave advice. And Gary was duped more that a few times—a girlfriend would lift money from his wallet, for instance. (Gary knew it, but figured this girlfriend was better than none. So he'd hide his wallet under the sofa when she came over.) "He gave me a place to stay and didn't treat me like I was handicapped," Gary says of Ray Jenkins. "He'd say, 'Get your crippled self out of bed!' I'd say, 'There's snow out there!' He'd say, 'If I have to go in, so do you.' "

The two men became "running mates," tooling around in Ray's T-top Corvette (a "girl-catcher," Gary called it), and hitting the night spots. The men came home so looped one night that Gary passed out in the rosebushes. Ray went to bed, got up at dawn, and dragged Gary in the house—before Gary even knew he'd slept outside. Gary began to change. He'd watch Ray get dressed for dates, and pretty soon Gary's clothes matched. Ray told him that after a day's work, it was smart to take a second shower and change his socks and his underwear before going out. Gary expropriated Ray's cologne—his "smellgood," as Gary called it— and eventually learned about too much of a good thing. Finally, an exhilarated Gary burst into the house: "Man, I've got a date! I've got a date! Everybody clear out!"

Gary's secret goal then was to date straight women, and occasionally he did, though more often they were women with disabilities. Moving from friendship to romance was always hard for Gary, but he became a ladies' man in his own way. He could do his laundry, fold and crease his clothes perfectly, Ray recalls, but Gary would inevitably flash his "dog-eyed look" and "Cool Hand Luke smile" at some woman in the laundromat. Soon enough, she'd be laughing and joking with Gary—and folding his laundry. "He'd call me at three in the morning and say, 'I've got a hot one here! I need your car,'" Ray remembers. "So I'd get up and take him to an all-night café and they'd drink coffee and talk." The help was mutual: Ray would always bring his dates to meet Gary—after the two men realized that women always seemed to think Ray was a rare and sensitive man to have a disabled friend.

"We were really the odd couple," laughs Ray.

During the years they shared a house, Ray found himself abandoning bias after bias. He saw that people often stared at Gary, but that Gary seemed oblivious. Ray noticed, however, that when kids gawked, Gary responded—he'd walk over, pat them on the head, smile, and make a joke. He'd known all along. Gary once volunteered to paint the garage, but Ray figured he couldn't. He did, perfectly. Ray was certain Gary would never master Washington's Metro rail service. He did. And when one of Gary's sisters gave Gary a moped, Ray doubted he could drive it. He did—complete with characteristic smoking pipe poking from his helmet.

The time eventually came for Gary to go out on his own. He moved to a federally subsidized apartment building for the disabled—and left his job at Theismann's because it was too far away. The apartment's price was right, but Gary despised living in a ghetto for the disabled—and he missed Ray terribly. He adjusted. And when Gary married Maureen, a thirty-two-year-old slow woman with cerebral palsy and mild epilepsy, Ray Jenkins was the best man. Even years later, as Ray lay in a hospital bed—his legs temporarily paralyzed from treatment for cancer he successfully fought—it was a visit from Gary and Maureen that buoyed Ray the most. The couple came by bus—and managed to find his thirteenth-floor room among the fifty-nine buildings on the massive National Institutes of Health campus in Bethesda, Maryland. Gary loaded Ray into a wheelchair, and the three of them, guffawing all the way, headed for the cafeteria—Gary steering erratically ("those gimpy legs," laughs Ray), as the wheelchair bounced off walls and doors all along the way.

Says Ray Jenkins: "Gary Poe is my best friend."

Maureen MacCallum and Gary Poe married and another taboo shattered: Slow people rarely marry. But then, they seemed a perfect match. He wanted someone to take care of, because that is what normal men do. She wanted to be taken care of, because she always had been—and she badly wanted to marry before her younger sister. Gary is calm, articulate, and something of a loner. Maureen is frenetic, easily lost in her words, and a social butterfly. He can barely read and easily forgets. She reads at an eighth-grade level and rattles off the phone numbers of people she hasn't seen in years. His disabilities left him tough. Her disabilities left her vulnerable. He is obsessed with making it in the outside world. She would just as soon ignore it. That has not been so easy since marrying Gary Poe.

"I married into it!" she says with a wild, piercing laugh.

Maureen Poe was almost two years old before her mother realized she was dragging her left foot. The pediatrician gave a blunt diagnosis: Maureen had cerebral palsy and, they later learned, slight mental retardation—probably due to lack of oxygen during birth. The doctors said she would never make her own way in the world. "The idea was to keep them in the closet," says Eleanor MacCallum, Maureen's mother. Maureen, too, went to special schools. She lived in Washington's Maryland suburbs with her mother, sister, brother, and father, a career military officer. She was, says her mother, pampered. She did her chores so slowly, Eleanor MacCallum recalls, that it was often easier to do them for her. Maureen—warm, friendly, and bright for a slow child—became expert at manipulating her disability: "My hand doesn't work so I don't have to do that—I'm handicapped," she often told her younger brother and sister.

Unlike Gary, the childhood taunts of "retard" and "idiot" didn't toughen Maureen; they frightened her. And one evening, as Gary talks about the "outside" world, Maureen interrupts with this story: When she was a girl Maureen had a bicycle with training wheels and she happily rode it everywhere. Think of the bike as retarded, she says, because it had training wheels. One day her father removed the training wheels—making the bike "normal." At first she couldn't ride it. She fell so many times that it seemed her entire body was scraped and bruised, but she finally mastered it. "But," Maureen concludes, "I feel my banging-up days are over."

Yet as Gary changed after he moved in with Ray Jenkins, Maureen also changed after moving in with Gary. Maureen always knew the little rules of getting along—dressing nicely, acting mannerly. But a couple of years ago, if she didn't get her way, she might pound her fist on the table. If she missed the bus and was late to the Centers, where she has been in job training for six years, it wasn't her fault. After all, it was "not fair" that she had to take the bus, while others drove cars. Today, Maureen seldom loses control. Late returning from lunch one day, she tells her instructor: "It's my fault. I lost track of the time." While visiting home a while back she gave her stunned mother a point-by-point rundown of why she and Gary had voted for Walter Mondale over Ronald Reagan. Slightly overweight, she went on a diet and lost twenty pounds. She has even begun to talk about what it would be like to someday have a job on the outside.

"I used to be against him going into the outside world and fighting it out," Maureen says of Gary. "Just settle for handouts, because people take you in like they care and then they just drop you. You're like a yo-yo on a string! I don't feel that way anymore."

This is Gary Poe's dream.

He starts his new job at $3.35 an hour, and over the years it rises to $7 or $8, the ideal is $10. The $351 in monthly disability payments stops. He and Maureen go off Medicaid. Visa, MasterCard, and Ward's credit cards are granted. Maureen gets a job. He gets a driver's license. They buy a car. They move out of the apartment building for the handicapped. The caseworker comes only when Gary calls. They save their money. They buy a house. They take a vacation. It is a modest dream for most. It is pie in the sky for Gary.

"He'll get in a dream world and want a house or a car," says his father. "I tell him, 'Dream about it, but forget it!' He'll agree with me but a couple months later he'll get back in that dream world again. . . . He may luck into a job like Theismann's someday, but there'll be ten handicapped people who won't—and there's nothin' that says he will either. . . . It's just something you got to face." The father fears failure for the son.

Yet driving is a practical dream, because leading a normal life, even holding a job, is tough without a car. But Gary Poe, as ever, is a special case. Gary's father said absolutely no—it would be too dangerous. Maureen's mother first said good luck, but later changed her mind. Gary isn't physically capable of driving, she now says. His reaction time is too slow, and he can't see well enough to read traffic signs. Gary's caseworker, in the style of caseworkers, didn't say yes or no, but asked whether Gary could afford a car, insurance, and car maintenance. If not, why get a license? Only Ray Jenkins saw Gary as no special case. "I don't think it would be too safe for him to drive, but he's got every right to try." If the state of Maryland gives Gary a license, Ray says, he'll be the first to let him drive his car. But what of Gary's terrible disappointment if he fails? Says Ray, "He told me he'd try to get his license this time and then if he can't, he'll forget about it."

But the dream of a good job—the path to self-esteem for the straight and the slow—cannot be so quickly forgotten. Gary's last job was cleaning cages and bathing animals at a veterinary hospital. He'd wash down six large animal runs each day, clean out about thirty occupied cages, bathe and dip pets in various medicinal treatments, and then put them in and remove them from the air dryer. It sounded simple—except for the arcane considerations. Earle Goss, Gary's job counselor, rolled up his sleeves and taught Gary how to wash a dog. Gary had trouble matching the animals' names on the daily bath list to the names on their cages. Earle devised a system of tags. Gary had trouble remembering which chemicals were used for which treatments. Earle came up with a color-coded system. Gary had trouble seeing when the animals were completely rinsed. Earle devised a step-by-step checkoff list to ensure his close attention. But worst of all, Gary had trouble doing everything at once. Finally, he forgot a dog in the dryer: It was found sprawled out and panting, but, fortunately, unhurt.

At the same time, Gary was struggling with the arcane considerations of daily life. He sprayed a whole can of Mr. Muscle oven cleaner in the oven and it caught fire. He realized that he could no longer read the product labels at the supermarket and he started reading lessons again. His new dog, Brownie, was backsliding on her housebreaking. Maureen was having frequent seizures in the middle of the night—and Gary was up taking her to the hospital. It also was an hour bus ride to the animal hospital, and, as ever, Gary was there fifteen minutes early. Because the cerebral palsy leaves his body muscles knotted and aching in the morning, Gary must take a long steam bath to relax. So to be at work by 7:00 A.M., he was up at 4:30. He never missed a day. It was then that his exhaustion began. After a year, Gary finally quit. Said his boss at the animal hospital: "I wish I had a thousand like you."

The man at Farrell's Ice Cream Parlour hasn't called, and Gary Poe is fidgety. He has applications in at Howard Johnson's and the Hot

Shoppes. He has got interviews at two nursing homes. He even called the animal hospital about a job, and Earle Goss is talking to some "bigwig" at Marriott about a job for Gary. Now that's the clout he figures he needs! "I've had people ask me, 'Why do you want to work when you can have taxpayers pay?'" Gary says. "I hear it so much I turn and walk away. I know different. Even if you are making just minimum wage, you feel better about yourself. I want to own my own place someday!"

Yes, he gets depressed, wonders whether everyone isn't right: Maybe the future won't get brighter. "I'm probably not worth minimum wage," he says in a rare moment of self-pity. But then, he still wishes that guy from Farrell's would call. If he doesn't call soon, Gary decides, he will call him instead. "I don't care if he does give me a job or he doesn't give me a job," he says. "I just want him to call. So I can move ahead."

Finally, Gary calls—and the man hires him, but only part-time. Gary starts working on Sunday. On Monday, after work, he begins looking for a full-time job.

MARCH 3, 1985

Washington Post photograph.

GEORGE BUSH
Born to Run, Born to Rule

*I*t's a twenty-five-minute ride at a good clip on a rough ocean to the Saco River, where George Bush has heard the bluefish are biting. Along the way, he gives the nickel tour—how to read the wind in the whitecaps, the island where he picnicked as a boy, the boulders hidden beneath the rising tide. Bush knows every rock along this Maine coast. He has come here sixty-one of his sixty-two summers. Only getting shot down in the Pacific kept him away in 1944. Soon he is trolling the Saco breakwater, fighting tangled lines and backlashed reels beneath cawing sea gulls swirling against a gunmetal sky. Bush leans comfortably against the captain's chair of his twenty-eight-foot Cigarette boat, the *Fidelity*, one hand on the wheel, the other holding his fishing rod off the starboard side. He wears old blue cotton pants, a ratty navy-blue pullover sweater, a camouflage cap, and dirty Reeboks. And he tells his fisherman's tale: He caught three big blues a while back over at Wood Island Light.

Uh-huh, sure.

No, really.

George Bush—in the middle of his second term as vice president—is a political phenom in reverse. He has made a life of mythic proportions seem somehow trivial, and he cannot understand why. He was the most lovable boy, always. President of his class at prep, president of everything else, too. Never a bad word about him. A war hero—not like John Kennedy, but an *undisputed* war hero. Skull and Bones, Phi Beta Kappa at Yale. Cushy job offers up the ying-yang. George said no. He packed his wife and infant son into his red Studebaker and hit the road for god-awful, roughnecking West Texas—and drilled a fortune in black gold. Then Congress, the United Nations, China, the CIA, Saint Reagan's veep. So why the mean quips? "There's no there there." Why the David Letterman gag lines? Why the "Doonesbury" attack on his manhood?

How did it ever come to this: George Herbert Walker Bush reviled as a whiny, waffling, bootlicking wimp?

What I knew of George Bush a few months ago is what you know of him now—a grainy blur of telegenic biases: competent but boring, sometimes shrill, sometimes goofy, speaks high when low will do, Eastern scion hiding out in Texas, a moderate doing a Rose Mary Woods stretch to the Right. But this is TV knowledge, something akin to heat rising off a summer highway. The idea was to toss out all these vague impressions and start from scratch. What makes George run? Bush, jealous of his privacy, had his doubts. But his aides saw a chance to humanize his image, and they prevailed on him.

The door swung open for interviews with his brothers and sister, children, wife, mother, boyhood buddies, business partners, and political cronies. There was a visit to his Waspy hometown of Greenwich, Connecticut, a tour of the elegant Victorian where Bush grew up, walks along the streets of Midland, Texas, where he got rich. Finally, I was invited to Walker's Point, the Bush family compound in Maine, where Bush, his wife, and their children and families were vacationing. They worshiped at St. Ann's Episcopal Church, ate hot dogs on the deck at Walker's Point, sang "Happy Birthday" to a Bush grandson.

But George Bush and I also sat in the old caretaker's cottage and talked about what I had learned of his life and its two recurring themes—great ability and great privilege. Bush is magical—smart, funny, charming—and I found myself wanting him to like me. Intimacy is his gift. But let's face it: Bush was handed opportunity after opportunity because of his family's wealth and influence, making him also a child of a lasting American inequality. As a boy, Bush wanted to be president, and his rare mix of ability and privilege has given him a shot.

Let me tell you, the vice president of the United States is very tired of hearing this. When I return to Walker's Point later that day for a fishing trip, Bush's wife, Barbara, pulls me aside. George had come back from the caretaker's cottage and said Barbara shouldn't be surprised if the boat returned one person lighter. I'm sure he was joking. But imagine his distress. One more story calling him just another rich man's kid. This story doesn't say that, but Bush couldn't have known that then. And as George Bush, his forty-year-old son George, Jr., and I bob lazily on the Saco River, the vice president becomes suddenly reflective.

"I think you think 'class' is more important than I do," he says.

I suggest—I'm smiling when I say this—that people at the bottom of society often think social class is more important than do people at the top. But Bush will not be deterred. What did I mean when I said he was a product of America's upper class? Bush believes "class" is the snottiness and arrogance found in some rich people, those who think they are "better" than the less well-off. He says he has never felt that way. Exactly what does the word *class* mean to me?

This is an uncomfortable turning of the reportorial tables, and I am less than eloquent. But in fits and starts I say that "social class" is all about family connections and money and expectations and training, and what those can mean. I say the sons of fathers in high-level jobs end up in high-level jobs about half the time, while the sons of manual workers end up in high-level jobs about 20 percent of the time. I say that social class shapes everything from our self-esteem to our child-rearing to our sense of control over our lives. I say that education is the great American leveler—but that rich kids get more of it. And that families like the Bushes often send their kids to expensive private schools to ensure their leg up.

This sounds, well, un-*American* to George, Jr., and he rages that it is crap from the sixties. Nobody thinks that way anymore! But his father cuts him off. "No, I want to understand what he's saying." He seems genuinely interested—and relieved that I don't plan to call him snotty. But the amazing thing is that Bush finds these ideas so novel. He seems baffled that I could see America in this way. People who work the hardest—even though some have a head start—will usually get ahead, he says. To see it otherwise is divisive.

I confess: I think a lot of Americans see it otherwise.

No matter, the secret to what makes George Bush tick is not philosophical. It is somewhere here at Walker's Point, a boot of rocky land jutting austerely into the Atlantic. The place has been in the family since 1899, and it's home to the Bush family values. The Bushes are big on values. They exude them, impose them on each other and themselves, use them to judge friend and foe. And in his grandfatherly role, George Bush has become the keeper of these values. A few years ago, for instance, he wrote a letter to his oldest grandson, George Prescott, who was then six. It is a surprising letter, surprising for its warmth and for its nostalgic recall—traits not associated with Bush's sometimes graceless persona. Yet the letter also evokes the Bush family expectations for the next generation, the generation in training. The letter consciously binds young George Prescott's very senses to the family, past and present, and to the objects that surround him at Walker's Point, as they did his father, his grandfather, his great-grandfather. It transforms these objects—a rock, a boat, a great-grandparent—into talismans for the family values of tradition, empathy, and loyalty. It's not a letter meant for a boy, but a letter meant to be read again and again as the boy becomes a man.

"Dear 'P'," the letter begins, to distinguish the young George Prescott from the vice president and George, Jr. (In the Bush family, everyone seems to be named after everyone else in the family.) "I've been thinking a lot about this summer. I had a very good time. . . . It was fun going out in the Fidelity—remember the day we caught all those greasy pollock. . . . That was a good day. . . . You and Noelle liked the Beach a lot, but I don't like going there. Now I am too old for that. If I get cold I get all stiff, just like my own Dad used to do. . . . This year for the first time I felt a little that way. . . . Another thing that was fun for me but wasn't too much fun for you and Noelle. It was when we went over to see My Mother—'Ganny to your Dad and Mom, Great Ganny to you.' I loved checking up on her—wasn't she nice? She always cares how the other guy feels.

"But, 'P', I've been thinking about it a lot—the most fun was the big rock boat, climbing out on it. . . . Watching you and Noelle playing on it. Near the end of the summer when the moon was full the tides were higher, and there was that special day at high tide when it almost seemed like the boat was real. . . .

"No, I think the most fun was that rock boat. . . . Don't ask me why this was the most fun. Maybe it's 'cause just at that moment I turned a corner in my life. I could see down the road with no fear and I suddenly had great happiness because I felt that in 50 years or so, you'd be there out on that rock boat—loving the ocean as I do, surrounded by family love—aching a little bit when it gets cold. I can't wait til next summer—Love, Gampy."

That is what makes George run. It was bred in his bones.

"It was a, uh, very enjoyable, a very unnoteworthy existence. We were very lucky."

—George Bush, on his childhood

The house on Grove Lane had no number when George Bush was a boy. People just called it the Bush house, and everyone in Greenwich knew. The town, about forty-five minutes from Manhattan via the New Haven train line, was among the wealthiest communities in America. With its endless miles of stone fences and homes visible from the road only when the leaves were off the trees, Greenwich was the proverbial world apart. Its great summer estates, those of the Rockefellers and the Milbanks, had been subdivided by the thirties, but the bankers, brokers, and businessmen who bought Greenwich's new miniature estates assured its affluence. The Great Depression raged, but the children of Greenwich would grow up without even a memory of it.

"Did you talk about the issues of privilege versus underprivilege, the haves and the have-nots?" George Bush's younger brother Jonathan is asked.

"No, no, no," he answers.

George Bush attended the private Greenwich Country Day School in his elementary years. It was the kind of place where students could joke about how their chauffeurs had gotten them to school on time during even the worst of blizzards. The Bush chauffeur, Alec, was among the best. At home, there were maids and a cook, golf and tennis lessons, the whole nine yards. Christmases were spent in South Carolina, where Mrs. Bush's father, George Herbert Walker, owned a plantation named Duncannon. On their visits, the children awoke in the freezing mornings to the sound of the black servants building crackling pine fires in their bedrooms.

With the hot months of summer, the Bushes left Greenwich for Maine, where Grandfather Walker also owned Walker's Point. The Walker family, in the dry-goods business in St. Louis, had bought the place to escape the summer polio epidemics of the city. George's father, Prescott Bush, a New York financier, would arrive in Maine by sleeper car on Saturday mornings and return Sunday nights. The children had a small motorboat, and the neighbor kids always marveled that George and his older brother, Pressy, were allowed to take it out alone.

"There wasn't much 'heavy weather' in those days," recalls Fitz-Gerald Bemiss, an old George Bush friend from the years their families summered together in Maine. George and his friends—the children of other white, rich, and successful fathers—fished and swam and heaved ripe rose hips at each other along the rocky waterfront. And at night, George and Pressy climbed into their bunk beds on the screened-in porch and fell asleep to the sound of the pounding surf.

If all this sounds a little Old Worldly, it was. George's mother, Dorothy Walker Bush, eighty-five and still living in Greenwich, chuckles self-consciously at the memory, especially the thought of George and Pressy being driven to school by Alec the chauffeur. "It seems unbelievable now," she laughs.

Yet all this gentility harbored a fierce competitiveness. Grandfather Walker, after whom George Bush is named, was a champion polo player and the donor of golf's Walker Cup British-American amateur competition. Grandfather Bush was a fine golfer, and George's father was the Yale baseball team captain and Ohio's amateur golf champion. Mrs. Bush's brother, Herbert, called Uncle Herbie in the family, was an avid golfer and a Yale letterman in baseball. Prescott and Herbie, the reigning family patriarchs, were fierce competitors, and a guest on the golf course was once shocked to see a virulent argument break out between them when the guest declared a ten-inch Prescott putt a "gimmie."

"You can't give him that putt!" Herbie fumed. The guest didn't.

George's mother was competitive, too, but delightfully so. A superb golfer and tennis player, she never lost her temper at a bad shot or a muffed putt or criticized poor play in others. Her young sons might be storming around the court, throwing tennis rackets, kicking the net, but she would ignore them, and calmly call out the score. Dorothy Bush was a lithe, beautiful, vivacious woman with a marvelous sense of humor. A devout Episcopalian, she seemed to live by the Bible's pieties effortlessly. "I didn't ever say anything disagreeable about anyone in front of her," recalls FitzGerald Bemiss. Behind her gentleness, though, Mrs. Bush also took her games seriously. Visitors discovered, for instance, that she wouldn't pair them with their spouses at say, tennis, unless the couple was well matched. Feckless adult athletes found themselves playing children.

The Bushes competed at everything—golf, tennis, tiddlywinks, backgammon, blackjack, bridge, anagrams. Anything that measured one person against another. When George was a young man, his teenage brother, nicknamed Bucky, was given a new ball-in-a-laby-rinth game and beat George handily. Bucky went to bed proud and awoke to George's casual challenge to a rematch. George won with a perfect score. Family members, in on the joke, howled with laughter: George had stayed up late perfecting his game to ambush Bucky.

Yet the competitiveness remained good-natured. The concept of "family" was so powerful that it sometimes seemed to friends that the Bush children functioned as a single mind rather than as five kids fighting for parental affection. No doubt some of that grew from a unique quirk of Mrs. Bush's, who tempered her children's hell-bent, prideful pursuit of victory with this ironclad rule: *No one could brag!* "I just couldn't bear braggadocio," she says.

The Bush kids did not automatically get respect; they earned it. George Bush's thirty-three-year-old son Jeb would later say that he and his siblings believed they "weren't crap" until they'd gone out and proven themselves on their own. Says George Bush, "That's exactly the way I felt forty years ago." Bush is terrible at recalling childhood stories, but one sticks clearly in his mind. At eight years old he came home from tennis and told his mom he'd been "off his game." With uncharacteristic anger, she snapped, "You don't have a game! Get out and work harder and maybe someday you will."

"You just didn't talk about yourself," recalls Jonathan Bush. "Bad taste."

Aimed at shaping humility in proud, rich children who could easily come to think they were "better" than others, this attitude kept the Bush kids from acting self-important. Yet there's also a tension between craving recognition and enforced humility. "These people regarded themselves as 'better,'" Nicholas King, author of a sympathetic 1980 Bush biography, says of New England's patrician class. "Bush has neutralized this. But at one time he would have had to be this way." Indeed, Bush's inbred reluctance to "blow on" about himself now seems constantly at war with his prideful craving for admiration.

"You could never come home and say you played well in a game," Jonathan Bush says. "I think it was a mistake, frankly. . . . You're really suppressing your joy in achievement." The result: Pressy could brag that George had played well or George could brag that Pressy had played well. A child could bask in success only through the eyes of admirers. At this, George became the master. All the Bushes liked the limelight, says Bush's boyhood friend George de B. Bell, whose family also summered in Maine, but George liked it the most. "He wanted to be the Number 1 guy," Bell says. "It was in his makeup." With George's father around, that was difficult. He was an imposing six feet four inches tall, a stiff, stern man, gracious and friendly, but formal even with his children. "At one point I said I never heard him fart," says Jonathan Bush, laughing. You'd never find Prescott on his knees giving horseyback rides or putting together a toy train set. He rarely joined the family games, which seemed to swirl around him. And he was very sparing in his praise.

"You might get a note at school," George Bush recalls.

"And what would he say?"

"'I was very proud to see that you were elected captain of the team.'"

"How would he sign it?"

"Devotedly, Dad."

Prescott Bush had gone to private high school in Newport, Rhode Island, then to Yale, where he was inducted into the prestigious secret society Skull and Bones, a direct pipeline to America's Eastern Establishment. At Yale, Prescott became friends with E. Roland Harriman. A few years out of college, Prescott married Dorothy Walker, whose father had left his finance firm in St. Louis to head a Wall Street investment firm being started by Roland Harriman's brother, Averell, who eventually became the quintessential member of the Eastern Establishment—financier, ambassador, and adviser to presidents. Prescott Bush followed his father-in-law to the firm that eventually became Brown Brothers Harriman.

Despite these powerful connections, Bush family folklore held that Prescott's own father had given him only $300 after college, which meant Prescott was a self-made man. Prescott worked long hours. He was forever taking important calls in his study. He was a Greenwich hospital board member and for twenty years served in the Greenwich government. He was home only a few nights a week. On Saturdays, he played golf.

"We were all terrified of him as boys," says Jonathan Bush.

The kids never knew it, Mrs. Bush says, but Prescott wanted to enter politics as a young man. He didn't enjoy business much and rarely talked about it—he talked politics. He believed, however, that he first had to put his five children through their de rigueur private educations, elementary through college—costing literally hundreds of thousands of dollars even then. So he was fifty-seven before he became a U.S. senator; sixty-seven when he retired in failing health. With pride and sadness, Mrs. Bush hints at a failed ambition: "He would have been the president of the United States if he'd gone into politics earlier."

Prescott Bush became the family's idealized image of achievement, propriety, and duty. He talked constantly of the need to "give something back" to the society that had treated him so well. And if the Walker side of the family contributed its fun-loving spirit to the family, it was Prescott who contributed its stoic sense of noblesse oblige.

In personality, though, George took after his ebullient and empathetic mother. He liked pleasing people, and it was often said that he'd someday become a minister. "He was the easiest child to bring up, very obedient," says Mrs. Bush. She and George were great friends, sometimes even getting under the skin of the stiff-necked Prescott. George and his mother often broke into giggles at Sunday service, earning Father's glare. She also told the children that when Prescott joined the Elks, he sat naked on a huge cake of ice as his initiation. The idea of Father naked on a cake of ice put them in stitches—if Father wasn't around. Says Jonathan: "Dad was no laughing matter."

Yet George rarely got in trouble with Dad, skirting the edge of his temper so that Prescott had to chuckle. Even then, George's intuition was sharp, and everyone came to recognize his magic. Young George was like a laboratory clone of his mother's personality and his father's values. He acquired his father's ambition but also his mother's enchantment. He was so kind, always watching out for the fat kid who couldn't keep up. He was the most popular boy with the kids—and with the grown-ups.

"He was earmarked in the family as a tremendous winner," says Uncle Herbie's son, George Herbert Walker III. Uncle Herbie—nineteen years older and a powerful, successful man himself—idolized young George. He believed George could do anything, and later would show that confidence in the form of half a million dollars in investor financing for George, the young oilman.

By the time Bush was ready for high school, his father wanted him out of the stilted atmosphere of Greenwich. He picked Phillips Academy, called Andover after the Massachusetts town where it's located. Old and prestigious, Andover emphasized not only social pedigree but merit. Even then, it admitted a handful of blacks and Jews and had a large number of scholarship students. So despite its securely elitist cast, Andover was a place where kids could learn, as Prescott said, "to mix with everybody." At Andover, George excelled again. His senior yearbook entry lists more activities than do those for any of his classmates—student council secretary, senior class president, captain of the soccer and baseball teams, and twenty others. Bush's grades were mediocre, but he was, if not the most popular boy at Andover, certainly among them. And classmate Walter J. P. Curley voices what was by then a refrain: "George was a star."

At Andover, classmates also began saying something else about George Bush: They began saying he would be president of the United States someday.

"I had a very powerful father . . . Very much of a leader and admired by everybody, and I didn't want to do something on his, I had a kind of a, not a competitive thing with him, but I wanted to go out and do something on my own."

Secretary of War Henry L. Stimson must have made a lot of parents breathe easier when he told the members of the 1942 Andover graduating class they shouldn't enlist in World War II, but go on to college. Most boys listened. Not George Bush.

"Has this changed your idea?" Mrs. Bush asked George as they walked out of Cochran Chapel after Stimson's speech.

"Not a bit!" George responded.

Mrs. Bush had already tried to talk her son out of enlisting, without luck. His father too had wanted him to stay out of the war until he was drafted, but in his stiff-upper-lip manner had said nothing of his fears to George, who enlisted. He became the war's youngest Navy pilot and flew Avenger bombers in the Pacific. His plane was hit. With smoke and flames pouring from his engine, Bush still dropped his 500-pound bombs on an enemy radio station before bailing out into the ocean. His two-man crew was killed. After hours at sea, Bush, sick and vomiting, was saved from Japanese gunboats by a U.S. submarine. He was a bona-fide hero, the recipient of the Distinguished Flying Cross. He would rack up 1,228 hours in the air and fifty-eight combat missions. Yet the question remains: Why did he enlist so soon? Probably because he'd taken to heart the values of loyalty and patriotism taught by his era, his social class, his father, and Andover. But he also had his own reasons.

George lived in awe of his father and wondered whether he could equal his dad's record at Yale, one of Bush's Andover friends, Ernest D. Obermeyer, told Bush biographer Nicholas King. Obermeyer has since died, but King's notes show that Obermeyer believed Bush wanted "out from under" the shadow of his family. By going to war, Bush found a solution—and his way in the world. Over and over, Bush would seek his identity in doing what *wasn't* expected. The road led to the same place—great success. But it got him "out from under"—and assured the glory of his youth: Bush was a star. And stars do more.

"Was it a shock to go off to war from your background?" Bush is asked.

"It was *the* shock."

George Bush still remembers his anxiety as his father put him on the train to war a month after his eighteenth birthday. He worried about what was by then his psychological signature: "I guess I was thinking, 'Will I be accepted?'" Bush says he was apprehensive because he was younger than most of the men. But it's hard to believe he didn't also wonder about a more ageless gap between men, because Bush had never really stepped outside his insular world. Pilot Jack Guy, for instance, was a country boy from Claxton,

Georgia. When Bush once mentioned that he'd gone to Andover, Jack Guy's reply was, "Well, I went to *Claxton!*" As ever, war is the ultimate leveler, a meritocracy where lineage takes a backseat to twenty-twenty vision. Says Bush, "It was a revelation." Bush was knockdown handsome then—tall, wiry, athletic—with a devil-may-care aviator style. Only the white scarf was missing. In photos from those days his angular face, clear eyes, and open smile are like a beacon. "He was a lot of fun, a live wire," recalls Guy. "Everybody wanted to cotton up to him. . . . I don't know anyone who didn't like him for any reason. I don't know how to say it any other way."

Bush was, to use the day's slang, a straight arrow, and engaged to Barbara Pierce, daughter of the Rye, New York, chairman of the McCall's publishing empire. "We'd go out partyin' and raise hell," remembers Guy. "But not George. He had Barbara. Pick up gals? Not George." Bush's brother Jonathan once made this joke about why George was so dedicated to Barbara, although its insight into Bush's personality goes beyond light humor: "She was wild about him. And for George, if anyone wants to be wild about him, it's fine with him."

Though Bush was younger, he seemed more mature than the other men. He was relaxed with superior officers in a way his buddies weren't. And he was more serious. When the war ended, and everybody went out to celebrate, George and Barbara were late—their first VJ Day celebration had been at church.

"If one of us had to be great someday, it would have been George," says Bush war buddy Lou J. Grab. "He had a better education, a little more going for him." And Bush seemed to know clearly what he was fighting for. When the men went home with him on leave, they learned what some of those things were.

"What came across, was when I went by his grandfather's or uncle's apartment in Manhattan," recalls Guy. "It was about the grandest thing I'd ever seen." Pilot Milton Moore, Bush's best friend in those days, was invited to Greenwich for George's wedding in 1945. "I was very impressed," says Moore, whose father owned a laundry. Everybody was friendly, but Moore noticed that the young people at the wedding seemed more self-assured than those he knew. No one in Moore's family had even gone to college, but everyone there seemed to talk about college constantly. When introduced, people's colleges were added like extra last names. But Moore always felt comfortable with George. He visited Bush after the war at Yale, and he visited him later in Texas.

"Everybody liked him," says Grab. "And those qualities endured

over the next ten or even twenty years. Your attitude might have
changed about some people you liked. But George endured."

*"And when we hit that new century, I want the young people just starting out
as we did to still have that same kind of opportunity, the same kind of opportunity that Barbara Bush and I had. And we can see that they get it."*

George Bush will not keep this promise. He can't. The opportunities that came to him do not come to the average man.

After the war, he whizzed through Yale in two and a half years. He
was Phi Beta Kappa, captain of the baseball team, all-around BMOC.
But the greatest hint of Bush's future success came on Yale's April
"tap night," when the school's best and brightest are inducted into
Yale's secret societies. Bush was "the last man tapped." In tapdom's
neo-Masonic world of mysterious chants and psychosexual confessions, the first are last, making Bush the most desirable man in his
class. The selection might not have been a total surprise, since
Bush's father and Averell Harriman were Bonesmen. But it was no
small honor. Besides Prescott Bush and Harriman, Bones alums
include Stimson, William Howard Taft, Henry Luce, and McGeorge
Bundy, to name a few.

After Yale, greatness was assumed for Bush. His cousin, George
Herbert Walker III, predicted to Barbara Bush that George would be
president someday. Jonathan Bush had told his prep school classmates the same thing. By then, it seems that even George had succumbed to this acclamation. Yale classmate Ethan Shepley, Jr.,
remembers hearing at Yale that Bush planned to make money in
business and then enter politics.

Brown Brothers Harriman, where his father worked, waived its
nepotism rule to offer Bush a job, but he said no. He wanted "out
from under." But in Bush's world it was hard to escape the womb of
privilege. One of his father's closest friends, Neil Henry Mallon,
was president of Dresser Industries, an oil conglomerate, and Prescott was on its board. Mallon had no children, and George was like
a surrogate son. (Bush would eventually name a son after Mallon.)
So when Mallon offered him a job selling oil-rig equipment in
Odessa, Texas, Bush took it. Here the official story of Bush's life
gets embossed to fit a more Middle American model: The red Studebaker is packed with wife and baby, and off they trek. The truth is
less prosaic, but in its own way uniquely American. Bill Nelson
was a hardened Texas oil-field worker, and when Bush walked into
the West Texas office of the International Derrick and Equipment

Co. in the summer of 1948, Nelson took one look and figured he'd last a week. Bush was dressed for West Texas all right—wool trousers, white shirt, black shoes, no tie. But his manner gave him away. "He was so different from the ordinary man in West Texas," says the eighty-eight-year-old Nelson, an Ideco supervisor then. "You'd wonder, 'Why did *he* come out here?'"

Nelson had already been told that Bush was a Dresser board member's kid. "That meant put him to work and learn him what I could," he says. That turned out to be easy. Bush asked questions until Nelson was tired of answering them, and he worked constantly. Nelson would go home with a list of things to do atop his desk—and the next day George would already have done them. Over the years Nelson had hundreds of trainees. "George was better than any," he says.

When Bush hit town, West Texas was in the midst of the great Scurry County oil boom. Housing was so scarce in Midland and Odessa, the area's twin towns, that tent cities cropped up. The Bushes lived in Odessa, the blue-collar sister city to the white-collar Midland. Their shotgun apartment on a dirt road shared a bathroom with a whore next door. Their life seemed true-grit American—another young couple "just starting out." But their mind-set was still that of the children of privilege. This foray into the workaday world was, as Barbara Bush said, an adventure. The prostitute might be staying in the shotgun digs in Odessa, but the Bushes would be moving on. It's difficult to overestimate the importance of knowing this: Real power to shape the future breeds optimism, which breeds effort, which breeds success.

"I never thought we'd live on East Seventh Street the rest of our lives," Barbara says. "I mean, trust me. . . . George and I never thought we were poor. We knew we weren't. We knew if something terrible happened to us, we had family. . . . It's a little bit smug to say these things didn't matter."

Bush hadn't set out to make a wildcatter's fortune, but he caught the fever. And he wasn't the only Eastern import who did; they were swarming all over the place. Dubbed the "Ivy Leaguers," these migrants became key players in West Texas oil. The imports weren't all Ivy Leaguers, but one quality distinguished many of them: They too were from well-connected families of wealth and privilege. Even wildcatting wasn't an equal opportunity employer.

Bush arrived at just the right time for his rare blend of ability and privilege. Before World War II, wildcatting was a mom-and-pop store. But rising drilling costs had made financing tougher. Bush and the Ivy Leaguers brought what the natives needed: pipelines to money. "Connections were the whole game," says C. Fred Chambers, a Texas oilman who became Bush's best friend. Independent oilmen are oil-deal promoters who convince landowners to sell a portion of their mineral rights to investors. In return, the promoter gets a free share of the deal. Bush did this successfully, and then with William C. and J. Hugh Liedtke, who would later form Pennzoil, he created Zapata Petroleum. The Liedtkes, whose father was Gulf Oil's chief legal counsel in Tulsa, had gone to private high school and Amherst College. They tapped their Tulsa connections for about half a million dollars, and Bush tapped his Eastern connections for the same—with the help of his admiring Uncle Herbie's investor clients.

Zapata scored: 128 wells without a dry hole.

In oil deals over the years, Bush would hit on his Eastern connections again and again. Fred Chambers, whose connections were modest compared with Bush's, recalls with awe a meeting he and Bush had with Eugene Meyer, a founder of Allied Chemical Corporation, the principal owner of the *Washington Post*, and a friend of Prescott Bush.

"Well, how'd we do on those other deals, George?" Meyer asked.

Pretty well, Bush said.

With that, Meyer invested $50,000. He then offered the young men a ride to the train station, and as they were leaving his limousine, Meyer asked: "Say, do you have any more of that deal?" Bush said yes—and Meyer invested another $25,000. Such was Bush's world. At thirty, he already traveled in circles that hard work, charm, brains, and empathy alone could never have opened.

In Midland, as usual, Bush was being everything to everybody. His wife recalls that so many people depended on him then that she was jealous. He coached boys' baseball, helped found the YMCA and the community theater, and was a director of a new Midland bank. Again, the two threads: "He did represent some outside financial interests from New York and Tulsa," says Midland oilman Earle M. Craig, Jr. "But he wouldn't have been asked if he weren't an outstanding young man."

In 1952, Bush got into politics, opposing the old Robert A. Taft Republicans in Texas in favor of Dwight D. Eisenhower. Back in Connecticut, his father was doing the same as part of a group that talked Ike into running for president. Once a staunch Herbert Hoover man, Prescott Bush was at the heart of the Republican party's shift away from old-line conservatism toward a more nonideological, pragmatic Republicanism that had made its peace with the New Deal. In 1952, he was elected to the U.S. Senate. He mixed well with the beer-hall crowds, but wasn't totally at ease.

"I always thought Pres did a very good job of mingling with the ordinary guy, but he really didn't understand them very well," says John Alsop, a Republican mover in Connecticut for the past forty years. "He'd just never been one."

By the mid-fifties George Bush would tell his closest friend, Fred Chambers, that he hoped to enter politics himself someday. It was a good choice, a way to earn the prideful affirmation and boundless admiration he craved while at the same time being able to humbly "give something back." He also pushed ahead in business, moving to Houston and forming Zapata Off-Shore, one of the nation's first offshore oil-drilling companies. It was a tough business. Zapata prospered modestly; Bush got a bleeding ulcer. Meanwhile, Prescott Bush was having the time of his life in the Senate. He loved politics and believed George would too. Harry Hurt III, writing in *Texas Monthly* magazine, reported this 1961 exchange between Prescott and Houston Republican James A. Bertron:

Prescott: "Jimmy, when are you going to get George involved?"

Bertron: "Senator, I'm trying. We're all trying."

"What I hope people perceive is reasonableness."

George Bush finally did it in 1964—ran for the U.S. Senate in Texas. Most of his business friends were baffled about why he wanted to give up a fortune, sacrifice the privacy, take all the crap. "You know, I just love it!" Bush told a friend. If Bush had ten minutes between campaign speeches, he was out shaking hands. On the road, he was up at 6:00 A.M. delivering coffee to his staffers' rooms. Bush was in his element. "I think he is very uncomfortable without people around," says Chase Untermeyer, a Bush friend and campaign worker from those days. "He craves people." Bush's political philosophy through two races for the U.S. Senate and a single contested race for Congress was, like his father's, a pragmatic, eminently reasonable conservatism. He ran as a Goldwater Republican in 1964, but by Texas standards he was a moderate. He took way-out liberal positions such as opposing repeal of the federal income tax. Yet he was a hawk on Vietnam and an opponent of civil rights legislation. He called Robert F. Kennedy "a left-wing carpetbagger" and Medicare "socialized medicine." He lost.

In 1966, Bush was elected to Congress from a safe, silk-stocking

Republican district in Houston, and his views became more liberal. He voted for civil rights legislation, the eighteen-year-old vote, the abolition of the draft. He backed a call for American withdrawal from Vietnam. According to Americans for Constitutional Action, a conservative ratings group, Bush's voting record fell from 83 percent conservative in 1967 to 58 percent conservative in 1970.

"At that time he told me he regretted having gone that far right and that he'd never do it again," recalls the Reverend John F. Stevens, the former secretary of the Executive Council of the U.S. Episcopal Church. "The implication was he had to do it to get elected."

The pragmatic Bush was a hot political property. His ability was respected in Congress, and as a first-term member he was given the rare honor of a seat on the House Ways and Means Committee. But the other great force was also at work. "His father came to me . . . and wanted him on my committee," recalls Wilbur D. Mills, then Democratic chairman of Ways and Means and an old friend of Prescott Bush. "I said, 'I'm a Democrat and I don't think I can do anything.' He said, could I call Jerry Ford? And so I did." Ford was then Republican leader of the House. "He engineered that," Mills says, as a favor to Prescott Bush. Ford recalls helping Bush win the seat, but as a way to give Texas Republicans "a shot in the arm." He says, however, that Bush wouldn't have gotten the seat if Mills had objected.

But Bush had a higher calling: As a congressman, he told Houston minister Hartsell Gray that after meeting the men who ran Washington, Bush knew he could handle any job in town. "That included the presidency," says Gray.

"It was the same drive to do something on his own that got him down to Texas," Bush friend Ernest Obermeyer told biographer Nicholas King. "A driving sense of accomplishment. Once he has accomplishment, he has a tendency to walk away from it. . . . His attitude was, 'Well, I've done that. And that wasn't so hard. And let's see what I can do next. . . .' He wasn't willing to wait around. He was after the ultimate challenge—first the Senate and then the presidency."

In pursuit of his great ambition, Bush ran for the Senate in 1970 and lost. He stayed in politics by taking an appointment as the U.S. ambassador to the United Nations, then as the U.S. liaison in China, and then as the director of the CIA. In 1980, these jobs would justify Bush's run for the White House. His slogan: "A president we won't have to train." In truth, the years of broad experience were epilogue to a life's ambition.

"When did you decide to run for president?" *New Yorker* magazine reporter Elizabeth Drew asked Bush in 1980.

"Well," Bush replied. "I started thinking a long time ago—I mean, like, hasn't everybody thought about being president for years?"

"It's just plain beautiful. And it's ours. It's our piece of turf."

After four hours of trolling the Saco River, George Bush finally gives up. No vice presidential fish fry tonight. But it has turned out to be a glorious afternoon, the wind about eighteen knots, the sky clearing, the sea beautifully rugged. Bush quotes someone who once said that the time a man spends fishing shouldn't count toward the time God allotted that man on earth. He says this several times, so I figure he wants to be quoted. That's okay. It's a good line. Because in all my hours with Bush these are the first I feel relaxed. Private time with him is indeed magical. It's a nice feeling to have about a man who would be president. But does it really matter?

Well, it matters in one way. They say George Bush doesn't know himself, because he has blown with the political winds: Goldwater conservative to Jerry Ford conservative to Ronald Reagan conservative. This is silly. George Bush knows exactly who he is: He is the son of Senator Prescott Bush, the son of Dorothy Walker Bush. He is a *Bush*, a ragingly proud Bush. He was in a very real sense born to rule. And when you are born to rule, you rule what there is to rule. He didn't come to this ambition by ideology, but by osmosis. Bush wants to be president, always has. And he is a *reasonable* man. He'll change with the times—and change back with them again. He opposed civil rights legislation, then favored it. He backed the Vietnam War, but later wanted American soldiers withdrawn. He opposed a constitutional amendment barring most legal abortions, but now favors such an amendment. He opposed Ronald Reaganism, but now favors it.

Issues don't motivate Bush. People and ambition motivate him. His ardent backers spout not ideology, but faith in his goodness. Wasn't it reasonable to oppose civil rights legislation in 1964, reasonable to favor it in 1968? Remember, Bush's father was a Hoover man who helped draft Ike. Changing with the times, a guiltless pragmatism, is Bush's trademark. He is a living barometer of the middle course.

Bush's personality—his reasonableness, his decency, his empathy—is the glue of his politics. Oddly enough, those traits also explain how so mythic a life can seem somehow trivial. George

Bush has never been immutably tied to the great currents of his time. He's no trailblazer. His political motives aren't linked as much to a special vision of the body politic as they are to his family's dedication to proving itself again and again. The presidency, as Ernest Obermeyer said, is Bush's ultimate challenge, the final affirmation. This isn't a flaw in his character. It is the heart of his character.

A key to understanding Bush is his belief that he can make almost everyone happy. While Bush is on the *Fidelity*, a man flicks him the bird from shore. Barbara is along, and she teases that George should turn around and go talk to the man, win him over. Husband and wife banter and laugh. But deep down, I bet they believe George could win that man over. It is his gift.

But Bush isn't built for TV. He's hot while the medium is cool. He sometimes seems on fire, out of control on TV, his metallic voice screeching like chalk on a blackboard. In person, the uncertain, melodic quiver, the breaks in pitch, the halting sentences, the fragments of thought, aren't grating. In person, his manner evokes a natural intimacy, like the fumbling, boyish eloquence of Jimmy Stewart. On TV, he can seem weak and confused. The natural tension between Bush's enforced humility and his great pride can, under hostile questioning, also surface in flashes of temper. "I don't suffer fools in the questioning area gladly," Bush says. Then, as if hearing Mother's admonition, he adds, "I'm doing better now."

Yet another message that Bush sends is subliminal. It's the message he can't help but send, the one in which his lineage traps him, the other edge to the sword of privilege. Nothing irks Bush more than the harping about his "preppy" style. He has abandoned button-down collars, half-rimmed glasses, even his striped watchband—something he swore he'd never do—to shed the image. It's all pettiness to him. But there's more going on here. These are totems that remind Americans that Bush is of a world apart. He can preach a renewed American opportunity, equal opportunity, but his life is testament to what can happen when one boy is more equal than others. This doesn't diminish his achievements. God knows there were others who did less with more. Truth is, Bush left the oil business for politics just before oil went gangbusters. He's worth a modest $2 million today, and he occasionally wonders about the fortune left behind.

But in politics, Bush's image must filter through a have-not American knowledge that Bush, for all his empathy, can little understand. So many men have worked for the boss's son, competent or not. So many women have watched men climb the males-only ladder. So many blacks, ethnics, and blue-collar kids have seen competency include social skills acquired not by hard work or brains but by birth, breeding, and education. Why is Bush's ebullient optimism the butt of jokes? Maybe because many people can't share his joy in the American experience.

These aren't *hard* data. They are biases. To be honest, they are my biases. But am I alone? Is it an accident that Americans have elected only one president born to the upper class since Franklin Roosevelt? And that was John Kennedy—a rich kid with the instincts of a rogue Irishman. What I wanted from Bush was an admission, some acknowledgment that on the simplest human level the privileges in his life were unfair. Bush simply doesn't agree with this. Or he can't acknowledge it.

"Any society, any capitalistic society, is gonna have some people who are well-to-do and some who are not doing very well, and who are poor. Abjectly poor. . . . What you do is try to strive hard so that it's as equal as possible. And you gotta recognize that sometimes there are, even in a system as good as ours, certain inequities. . . . In other words, you're looking at the glass half empty, I'm looking at it half full." Of his background, Bush says, "I view it, as you know, with great pride. And no sense of wanting to cooperate by saying, 'Gosh, isn't it awful that my, you know, family were privileged. . . .' So I'm not apologetic. So long as I make a contribution and my kids do."

George Bush is without social guilt, which is probably good for his mental health. He struggled admirably to justify his great privilege—as do many children of successful parents—and in his mind, he has proven his worth beyond all doubt. "You don't think I could have made it, made something of myself?" he asks wearily. There's a plaintiveness to that question, and, frankly, Bush has earned his identity as a member of the deserving rich. But looking at America from the bottom up, doesn't it also seem naive to believe that Bush, if born to a wholly different world, would be vice president today? Hearing Bush preach the American Gospel—no matter how much I like him—is still like listening to a very tall man praise the virtues of being very tall. I think: *Yeah, that's easy for you to say.*

And I think of what John Alsop said of Bush's father. "I always thought Pres did a very good job of mingling with the ordinary guy, but he really didn't understand them very well. He'd just never been one."

They say George Bush is most like himself when he's at Walker's Point. He loves to fish for a while, then roar off with his twin Mer-

cruisers at full throttle, his boat flying into the air over the mountainous swells as he spins the *Fidelity* 180 degrees to a quick stop,
and then fish some more. In the summers, the Bush children visit
Walker's Point with their kids. They're all married, the boys successful businessmen. There has never been a divorce in the Bush
family. The kids work in charities. One son mans a soup line at
Christmas. Bush's son Marvin, thirty, says they are spared the social
guilt so many rich kids suffer because they learned to give something back.

"It's a base for family," George Bush says of Walker's Point. "And
it's the setting that somehow relieves all tensions and frees you up
to think. . . . I love to go out in the sea when it's rough. I like to
stay out on the rocks with my grandchildren. . . . It frees up your
soul. . . . And a lot of it's 'cause it has memories." Walker's Point is
what it's all about for George Bush. The main house was wiped out
in a flood in 1978, and Bush had the place rebuilt. He uses Walker's
Point as his "anchor to windward." So do his children. So will his
grandchildren.

Bush slouches comfortably in a chair on the back deck. It's a
sunny day, the waves crash on the rocks a hundred feet away, and
little George Prescott, now ten, climbs alone on the huge rock boat
between Bush and the sea. Today the rock is a toy; tomorrow it will
be a symbol. The idea is that all this will be passed on. Not just the
house, the educations, the connections, but the values—hard work,
giving something back, the family as rock in a sand-castle world. If
everything goes right, little George Prescott won't feel social guilt,
he'll give something back, he'll be magical, he'll keep the lineage
alive. Because the Bushes are their own kind of American dynasty.
And all these things will be bred in his bones.

SEPTEMBER 28, 1986

JOHN AND SUE WEBSTER
What America's Selling, They're Not Buying

$\mathcal{T}$he Webster family is engaged in a dying ritual.

They are eating dinner together—chicken over white rice, a good, crisp salad with sliced almonds boiled in sugar, steamed broccoli, hot rolls, and, for dessert, layered cream cake that's a few days old or apple pie made this afternoon. Sue and John Webster and their teenage kids, David and Lora, eat like this pretty much every night. They laugh, gripe, brag, replay the day. These are full meals full of meaning. Sue recalls a teacher who once asked her students how many of them still ate dinner with their parents, and out of thirty kids, only two said they sat down to meals as a family. Sue can only shake her head at that and, once again, wonder what this country is coming to. "People make choices," Sue says. "This life is our choice."

The Websters are Main Street USA. John is a Republican, Sue a Democrat. They have degrees from Catawba College in North Carolina, where Sue was Miss Catawba her senior year. Their dog, a collie, is named Lady. Their kids go to public schools. They drive the Lincoln to the Baptist church on Sundays.

Until recently, the Websters were an invisible family living on a street named Hounds Run in the drab, humid southern city of Mobile, Alabama. But the Websters had had enough: They decided that America, just like the family dinner, was going to hell in a hand basket because of an erosion of Christianity. So when they learned of a lawsuit alleging that textbooks in Alabama's public schools violated the First Amendment by giving short shrift to the role religion has played in American history and by promoting an atheistic religion called "secular humanism," John and Sue Webster, and 600 others, signed on.

The urbane and the sophisticated labeled them "fundamentalists," which the Websters are. They believe that the Red Sea parted so Moses could flee Pharaoh, that if the Bible says Joshua stopped the sun, he did, even if it's the earth that does the moving. But a lot goes unsaid in that word *fundamentalist*—images of Bible Belt bumpkins and a damnation-bent Gospel; grainy visions from *Inherit the Wind*, of Clarence Darrow grilling the sad, sweating, slump-shouldered William Jennings Bryan; TV's Lord-oh-Lord, red-faced preachers who, on the evolutionary scale, must rank below the noble chimpanzee; the fear that if these people ever got real power, they would legislate a Puritan morality. These images, these biases, are etched in the national memory.

So the Websters were fit into a tidy, insignificant category: ignorant zealots, book burners, enemies of tolerance, friends of demagogues. Yet it takes a blind arrogance to dismiss the Websters as so much nineteenth-century nostalgia, or as ignorant folk befuddled by the ferocity of change. Because without really knowing it, the Websters are part of a chorus of social critics—from left to right—arguing that Americans have become too self-absorbed and lost in a vain, selfish pursuit of personal "fulfillment" that has left their lives increasingly empty and meaningless while creating a society of people without direction, purpose, or commitment.

The Mobile lawsuit, in which a federal judge ruled in favor of the Websters' side last fall and banned forty-four textbooks from Alabama's schools before his order was stayed by a higher court, will likely go to the Supreme Court. The smart money says the Websters will lose the case. But that won't diminish the importance of the social issues they raise. Good liberals may disdain the Websters' solutions—fair descriptions of Christian morality in the public schools, a national return to Christian values, all of it based on a bedrock belief in Jesus Christ and the literal truth of the Bible. But the Websters are on to something, because they are struggling with the same dilemmas facing all Americans, faithful or faithless. And while they are ridiculed, it is the Websters who have the answer so many modern Americans seek: They know who they are, and they know the "why" of their lives. It is the curious, continuing irony of modern life.

But there's another twist: The unyielding faith that gives their lives meaning is also unsettling, scary, to those who don't share it, because the Websters call up old fears about all True Believers, people convinced that only they know the Truth. The Mobile suit is but a piece of the frame. In *Inherit the Wind*, the famous stage portrayal of the 1925 Scopes "monkey trial," the fictionalized characters based on Clarence Darrow and William Jennings Bryan have this exchange:

Darrow: "Progress has never been a bargain. You've got to pay for it. Sometimes I think there's a man behind a counter who says, 'All right, you can have a telephone, but you'll have to give up privacy, the charm of distance. Madam, you may vote, but at a price; you lose the right to retreat behind a powder puff or a petticoat. Mister, you may conquer the air, but the birds will lose their wonder, and the clouds will smell of gasoline!' Darwin moved us forward to a hilltop, where we could look back and see the way from which we came. But for this view, this insight, this knowledge, we must abandon our faith in the pleasant poetry of Genesis."

Bryan: "We must not abandon faith! Faith is the important thing!"

The debate is unchanged: There is a price for knowledge, a price for fundamental faith.

"I got one!" David Webster announces between forkfuls of rice. "The one where all those women sit around and talk about birth control."

His sister, Lora, laughs. "Every time that commercial comes on, he leaves."

"It's ridiculous!" says David.

The Websters are eating dinner, debating TV's most offensive commercials, and describing what they see as an assault on their values. TV is to them a mass-media hawking not only of products but also of values, seductive values, values they don't share, values that are wrong, even evil, but values that first must be ingrained in Americans if they are to buy the bevy of items foisted upon them by the marketeers. Because before you can go for the gusto, John says, you must first believe the gusto is worth going for—at the expense of, say, family, friends, altruism, and faith in God. The Websters aren't stuffy or self-righteous about this. No, they're having a family belly laugh about it.

John, thirty-nine, pounds the table with one hand and covers his eyes with the other. He often does this when he laughs. Sue, also thirty-nine, throws back her head, musses her short blond-to-gray hair, and releases her staccato laugh, he-he-he-he, flashing a smile that is wide on her lean face. David, sixteen years old, strong and six feet two inches, rolls his eyes and mumbles in his best good-ol'-boy drawl. Lora, thirteen, smiles demurely.

"Talkin' 'bout birth control on TV and why they like it," says David, shaking his head and widening his eyes. "I don't wanna see it."

Says Sue, "There was this pineapple commercial . . ."

Lora groans.

"Oh, maaaan," says David, slapping his forehead.

"I think it was Dole. It was the most sensuous commercial, and there was nothin' to it. I mean it was *sensuous!*"

"She was really eatin' it," says John, sucking his fingers seductively.

"It wasn't selling pineapple!" says Sue, incredulous. "It was selling sex!"

Suddenly, John says, "Douche commercials!"

"*Ohhhh . . .*" Everyone groans at once.

"In my special shape!" says John, mockingly. "It's *so* comfortable!"

"How 'bout the one where they go, 'You can use a thin pad at your worst time of month,'" says David.

Sue's shrieking laugh pierces the room.

"It has wings!" yells David.

Says John, "Sold American!"

If the Websters' table banter sounds tasteless to you, remember that 100 million Americans can watch these ads on TV any given night. Maybe you've seen the feminine deodorant ads or the new commercials showing women in bras, and wondered where it will end. Or maybe you've wondered if TV characters should French kiss before your kids have gone to bed. Or if J.R. or Mr. T or MTV is bad for your son. Or if it's good that Max Headroom was the main character on a prime-time TV show at the same time he was the advertising symbol for Coke at the same time Coke sponsored the Max Headroom show. Maybe you've wondered if you aren't already living twenty minutes into the future, where too much is beyond your control, too much imposed without consent. Perhaps these things sometimes even seem vaguely like moral issues to you, matters of value, of right and wrong.

And sometimes, maybe these thoughts swirl around in your head and, in some vague, unexplainable way, connect with more disturbing realities—teen suicide and pregnancy, the cocaine boom, the Wall Street scandals, Elliott Abrams telling Congress the difference between deception and lying, how you read in the paper that this year's high-school graduates don't aspire to accomplishment or knowledge, but to fame and wealth. Perhaps sometimes, at the dinner table, you, too, stop and worry about what it means to be modern, and what this country is coming to. If so, you aren't unlike the Websters. Except for one difference. The Websters aren't confused; they don't feel helpless. They know the trouble: the loss of fundamental faith in Christ.

A conversation with John and Sue:

"What is wrong with America today?" they are asked.

Sue: "We've got teenage suicide like we've never had before, teenage pregnancy, drug abuse, teenage alcoholism. We've got problems, and what we're doing is not working. It just baffles me that the intellectual elite keeps saying, 'Yes, we've got problems, but what you're saying is too simplistic a view. It's not a viable answer to the complex issues facing us.'

"I think that what threatens the sincere believer is not modernism but the 'expert' view that what we think is the ultimate reality in our lives is not real. It is real! And when the 'experts' start telling our children that our reality is not real, then it's our responsibility to get involved."

John: "It's not another 'mind-set.' It's a faith in a God that's real. As a society we've come a long way, babe, and now we're nowhere. We need foundations people can put a hook into. Pretty soon we're going to take a vote if we have to go to war as a nation. It started with the Vietnam War, it started with Korea. We have moved and shifted, moved and shifted to where many people coming up in the younger generation are saying, 'Who am I, what am I, what do we stand for as a country and as an individual?' Are we contra people, are we noncontra people? Are we pro-Vietnam? What are we?"

He is told, "Well, we're all those things."

John: "I don't think we need to be all things to everybody."

"What else would we be? We are a pluralistic society."

John: "We need to state who we are and be consistent."

"Speak with one solid voice of values and attitudes?"

John: "Maybe not to the extent of limiting thought process, but, yes, I think we need to have a standard, absolutely."

"At what time to do you think we lived like this?"

John: "There was a time that we did have a balance."

He is told, "The good burghers in Europe with the Industrial Revolution had their lives wrenched apart. American farmers were thrown off their farms starting a hundred years ago. The great migrations. The potato famine. The lack of balance that you fear seems to be the history of man."

John: "There was order when we were kids. We knew what to expect. I'm not sure the kids today do. We're always stressing, 'Who am I? Why should I care about my neighbor? Why should I hang in a marriage? Why should I support my kid? Who really cares?' There has to be something in society that says 'Hey, you need to. You need to.'"

"You keep saying that, but how does a 'society' do that?"

John: "A return to basic values, a return to a standard. I'd like to see us take a stronger stand. On abortion."

"The liberal Protestant denominations are some of the strongest supporters of legalized abortion."

John: "Which puzzles us. I mean, that would puzzle anybody. All I can tell you is that the Christians that I know . . ."

"That's because you know conservative Christians . . ."

John: "And the Bible says . . ."

"But there are educated, respected Christians who argue that the Bible does not say what you say it does."

John: "I believe I have an understanding of what the Bible says."

"But so do others."

John, softly: "I can only tell how I feel, what I see. This is where I am with my beliefs: If I can take the Bible and read a passage and interpret it three or four different ways and say, 'Well, I don't know, I can interpret this any way I want,' I'll close that book and say, 'This is nothing more than another novel.' If I could not read the Bible and clearly see, word for word, what it says, then I probably would have to deny my Christianity and my faith."

"The Bible and your faith are accomplishing for you what society can't, which is that it has no ambiguity, everything is clear?"

John: "It's a foundation. It's solid."

"It's a rock?"

John: "It is. Without that, I'm in the pot with everybody else."

John Webster believes he was a different man a decade ago.

In pursuit of promotions in the plastics industry, he had moved his family to seven cities in seven years. He was a decent guy, but he wasn't above bullying Sue, even calling her stupid. If it would help him get ahead, he'd spread a rumor at work. But most important, John judged people in a way that may sound familiar: "What do you do? What's your position?" John went to church, but to look good, and because he figured the kids needed it. He had been raised Episcopalian, was even an altar boy at his family church in New Jersey, but any church would do for John. He was a hypocrite, really, with no commitment to anything—his faith, his employer, his family. John looked out for John.

"Why shouldn't I go for the gusto?" he'd ask. "It's my turn."

Then John did something dumb, miscalculated. He took a job in Mobile as the sales manager of a plastics company, figuring he had finally hit the big time. But it was a bad job, boring and with little future. John—always on the make, always ahead of the eight ball—

had bombed. "What am I doing?" he asked himself. "I'm using the formulas, I'm plugging myself in. I feel lousy, I'm really not pulling my weight at home. For God sakes, I've dropped back five years— and stuck in Mobile, Alabama! Holy mackerel! What a sham I've made of my life."

It was the flash point for John's conversion.

John felt empty—that's the only way he can describe it. He had sensed a vague discomfort for years, as if he were living his life in pieces, watching himself act out life instead of living it. Confused and anxious, he went to Houston on business, where he found himself surrounded by businessmen who were born-again Christians. These were mainstream guys who talked about Jesus like they talked about golf or plastic pipes, describing prayers and sins and miracles. It was weird, and John felt out of place, shallow. When asked, he said, "I go to church," though he knew that wasn't the right answer, not for this crowd and maybe not for him. The next week John was born again.

It happened that fast.

You can remind John that there are secular, psychological reasons for what happened to him. He was closing in on thirty, guilt-ridden about failing his family, learning that the ride to the top isn't guaranteed. Not to mention the social pressure of the Bible Belt, where the language of faith is as important to membership as is the language of cynicism and sophistication in New York. John nods, unimpressed.

"All I know is this: When it happened, my life changed. I became a different person." John's voice is slow and gentle and musical in that southern way, his years in Alabama having smoothed the New Jersey roughness from his words. He is very earnest. "I was so wrapped up in me—and if I was all there was and was able to fail, how sensitive it is. There was hopelessness. I saw other people. I saw their needs. I saw the hurt that I could inflict. I saw it all. I saw where I was headed and what I was becoming. I saw some folks who were happy, with peace in their lives. And I wanted some of that. I had all the ingredients—great family, good-looking wife, nice home. But I just didn't put it all together. With Christ, I put it all together. That was October 1976. And that was the beginning."

Sue Webster was elated.

She had been raised in Asheboro, North Carolina, where the Dogwood Acres Presbyterian Church was the center of her life. Sue was a fundamentalist who didn't realize people could be anything else. It wasn't until her freshman year in college that a religion professor taught Sue that Christ was probably educated by the same Jewish sect that produced the Dead Sea Scrolls, that His teachings weren't unique, that He was not divine. Sue freaked. She told her father, who told Sue's old minister at Dogwood Acres, who said, yes, some historians believe that. The minister didn't seem bothered at all. But sweet Sue, naive and untutored, couldn't reconcile her faith with facts that she believed contradicted the Bible. So she decided not to decide, putting her religion on the shelf. She recalls the next few years as dark and brooding.

Again, you can remind Sue that college is a dark and brooding time for many, and she will shake her head. No, it was her crisis of faith that caused her depression. She knows this because when she returned to Christ—after David was forced to wear leg braces for six months as a toddler—and allowed her faith to imbue her again, when she did this, her depression lifted. "I didn't have the strength to deal with myself, much less what was going on. It broke my heart. Suddenly this real independent little kid couldn't get on his tricycle, couldn't sit on the swing. I went back and said, 'I don't care where Christ was.'" She figured that if He was taught by the sect that wrote the Dead Sea Scrolls, that was fine with her. But soon after that, Sue read in John 7:15: "How is it that this man has learning, when he has never studied?" Sue decided her college professor had been wrong: The Bible said so.

"I interpreted that to be the reality I needed."

A conversation with John and Sue:

"So people who don't have a personal relationship with Christ are doomed?"

John: "That's what the Bible says."

"They go to Hell?"

John: "Yes."

Sue, realizing how harsh this sounds: "Just forget the attitude about the Bible. One of the things we believe is that God is just and that He is good and that He is righteous. Then no matter what happens, it is going to be fair."

John: "I don't believe that there is a difference between you and me, except where I have chosen to go in eternity."

"That's no minor difference."

John: "But I mean that I have no 'better-than' philosophy."

"What about the Zen Buddhist?"

John: "I don't understand why, but the Scripture says that there is only one way, and that's through Christ."

"That won't be reassuring to millions of Americans."
John: "What can I say? There it is."

For those wondering if the Websters are all show and no go on this religion thing, here is how they live. John contributes about 15 percent of his income, before taxes, to his church and to other charities, the Salvation Army, the United Way. Since John left his job and started his own plastics company in 1979, these haven't been paltry amounts. "I write those checks first," he says, "before I pay the bills." John teaches Sunday school at the Cottage Hill Baptist Church, and every Tuesday morning from 5:00 to 6:00 he mans the church's twenty-four-hour prayer phone, taking calls from sick or depressed people asking for prayers for themselves or others. Lora teaches Sunday school to deaf children, and Sue, who doesn't hold a paying job, teaches Sunday school to women. She also meets with several women's prayer groups, support groups really, during the week, visits shut-ins, takes old people to the doctor. Once a week, she takes a six-year-old boy with severe brain damage to swimming therapy.

The Websters are not fringe, holy-roller people. Their kids wear Nikes and jeans and old T-shirts. David has a funky haircut—short in the front, long in the back. He figures it makes his big nose look smaller. He'll probably be a starting linebacker on the varsity next fall. He and his dad go to the Y to lift weights together in the mornings. Lora wears pink polish on her nails. She's captain of the cheerleading squad, president of the student council. They're a clean-cut, joyful crew. Nobody swears much, nobody drinks. They go to movies, dance, watch a few risqué TV shows—"Moonlighting," for instance. But John and Sue are strict with the kids, stricter than any parents David and Lora know. "It's pretty rough having our folks," says David, hiding a smile. "Kinda like livin' in a concentration camp." Everybody at the dinner table laughs.

The Websters make all their own Christmas presents for each other, so homemade lamps and vases and mugs fill the house. But what's most striking about their home is that nearly every item in it—pictures, inspirational sayings (which are everywhere), pillowcases, rugs, everything—is a story. Because most of them are gifts, many in return for favors done by the Websters. The crystal bird is from a neighbor whose daughter Sue baby-sat free of charge for two months after the man's wife died. The tiny wooden house is from the eight teenagers who lived with the Websters for two weeks as part of a church camp. The statue of the old, bent man is from

Ecuador and was given to them by missionary friends. It just goes on and on, and for more than an hour Sue walks through her four-bedroom home, cheerfully telling the stories behind dozens of belongings. Nothing is here because Sue or John thought it would look *just right* with the decor. No, it's a home filled not with good taste but with meaning, decorated from the heart for a family that works.

Sue has no doubt why.

"The life of our family is based on our faith," she says. "It's the only reason we do what we do. I'm not good. I'm not kind. I don't have that in me. I can't do any of that without motivation from God."

A conversation with David, the son:

"How does praying make you feel?"

David: "I feel like kind of a tingling feeling, a light-headedness. I don't know, it sounds kinda hokey, but at church camp every year, that's the time I feel the closest. Like nothing could hurt you, nothing could go wrong. You're in harmony with yourself and everybody around you, and God. It's hard to describe, and it sounds kinda funny."

"Do you ever wonder about your religion?"

David: "I wonder, but I don't honestly doubt. My imagination goes wild, but I don't doubt it."

"Like what?"

David: "Where the Bible things fit in as far as geologic time. Right now, we're working on the geologic rock record. They put all 4.5 million years into a year, and where do Adam and Eve fit in because man didn't come in until ten minutes before midnight of December 31st. And that's Cro-Magnon man! So where does it all fit in? I know it's gotta fit in somewhere."

"Why?"

David: "Because the Bible says so."

"Couldn't the Bible be wrong?"

David: "No, see, that's the thing. It's not. I don't know, it's God's teachings. It's like a road map. This is what we go by—the Gospel truth."

"Men said God told them that. God didn't put a sign up in Times Square or buy space in *USA Today* to say, 'This is my Word.' "

David: "I believe the Bible is 100 percent true. I mean, most of my friends do not. They believe portions of the Bible. They intellectualize things: 'This couldn't be, because of this and that.' "

"What's wrong with thinking about things?"

David: "Nothing is wrong with thinking about things, but that's the truth. And somehow that fits in with everything else."

"What's the truth?"

David: "The Bible. Somewhere Adam and Eve fit in. I'm not too sure where, but I know it does fit in somewhere in that geologic time. Because the Bible says so. We're talkin' a belief in faith. There's only one Holy Bible, and it's right. That's what I've been taught. And I'm not exactly sure why it's all right, but I just know that I've been taught that it's right, and that's what I know."

"Does your faith require that you not think?"

David: "No. Like I said, it's gonna fit in. You can wonder, but somehow it's gonna end up being true. It is really tough to explain. I believe that to go to Heaven, to have life after death, you have to be saved. Jesus has to come into your heart. Somehow I know that the way we believe is right. I mean, without a doubt, somehow I know that that's right."

The Websters first heard about what would become the Mobile "secular humanist" lawsuit at a party. They were told that Mobile's schools couldn't promote Christianity because of recent Supreme Court decisions on maintaining the separation of church and state. And yet the schools were promoting a religion called "secular humanism"—an atheistic philosophy that says man alone is responsible for his fate. Mobile's textbooks were supposedly expounding the values of secular humanism by teaching sociological and psychological theories of moral judgment and human motivation, without complete discussions of religious morality and values. A group of people were going to court to fight these godless teachings, and the Websters joined.

They went to court last fall seeking a ruling that Alabama's public schools, through their history and home economics textbooks, violated the First Amendment separation of church and state by underemphasizing the role of religion in American history and by promoting the values of secular humanism. Tele-preacher/pol Pat Robertson's organization paid a portion of their legal bills. On the other side were the American Civil Liberties Union and People for the American Way. The ACLU portrayed the secular humanism case as nothing more than a smoke screen for fundamentalist zealots trying to get Christianity back in school, and the heavyweight Washington law firm of Hogan & Hartson took the case—to the tune of about $500,000 in pro-bono work so far.

There are two critical legal issues. Can a philosophy that denies the existence of God be considered a religion under the Constitution—especially since secular humanist philosophers sometimes identify their beliefs as the moral equivalent of religion? And if so, do textbooks that discuss secular theories of morality but not religious theories promote a secular religion? From a distance, the whole thing looks like one more assault by the religious crazies, a modern "monkey trial," with social scientific knowledge on the stand instead of evolution. But the ignorance versus enlightenment motif isn't so easily imposed on the Mobile case.

The Websters, for instance, had their first run-in with the schools when their son was only eight years old. He was in a special program for gifted students and came home talking about the "fallout shelter" game. In it, students are asked to imagine that there has been a nuclear war. A group of eight people—including a priest, a doctor, a retarded man, and a pregnant woman—are set to enter a bomb shelter, but there is only room for six. Who will be left to die? The game was part of a teaching program called "values clarification" in which students were supposed to come to understand their own values better by struggling with the intricacies of right and wrong.

The Websters weren't enamored of the intricacies of right and wrong. The Christian answer was simple: You do nothing; only God decides who shall live or die. But John and Sue didn't make a fuss. They borrowed the teacher's study guide and went through it with David, clarifying their own family values. Then they asked that he go into another class while the material was discussed. The school agreed, and the matter ended.

But this kind of debate over the teaching of secular versus religious moral perspectives is at the heart of the suit. Mobile's home economics texts were hit hardest in the court case. Statements such as "Morals are rules made by people" and "What is right and wrong seems to depend more on your own judgment than on what someone tells you" were attacked by the Websters' side as ethical claims conflicting with the religious view that right and wrong are God-given absolutes. The books do contain numerous references to how religious beliefs shaped American history and morality, which the Websters' side conveniently ignored. But the texts also often treat religion as simply another sociological category, akin to age, sex, and race, with religion subsumed under a broader, social-scientific umbrella. Right and wrong are often portrayed as "relative"—changing from person to person, situation to situation.

What upset the Websters most, though, was that in books purporting to teach moral judgment there was virtually no discussion of sin, which is to them a moral reality. "I don't want Christianity taught in school," says Sue. "And I want that shouted from the housetops." What the Websters say they want is religion—and the reality of spiritual belief in millions of people's lives, fundamentalist or not—treated fairly. People for the American Way agrees that books used in Mobile—books used in schools across America—are superficial and intellectually flabby. But bad books, they argue, aren't unconstitutional.

The Websters' concerns can't be sloughed off as the narrow province of fundamentalists. Historian Christopher Lasch caused a sensation with his 1979 book *The Culture of Narcissism*, which argued that secularized, urbanized, bureaucratized twentieth-century America has created a new personality type: The narcissist, self-absorbed and self-indulgent, obsessed with using modern psychology for self-analysis, freed from narrow, traditional roles but often left confused, lonely, and rootless. Lasch's narcissist is the modern, irreligious man the Websters fear and despise.

From the conservative side, University of Chicago philosopher Allan Bloom's *The Closing of the American Mind*, which hit Number 1 on the New York Times best-seller list, attacks the widespread, modern assumption that morality is "culturally relative." The idea, he says, has destroyed our ability to make confident moral choices. Woody Allen's angst-riddled characters—always analyzing themselves analyzing themselves—are Bloom's example of what happens to people who constantly look at themselves as if they were rats in their own experiments. He refers to the modern irony: The dancing family of rabbinic Jews in Allen's movie *Zelig* was probably happier than the oh-so-sophisticated audiences chuckling at Allen's comic portrayal of their quaint beliefs.

But it was Harvard child psychiatrist Dr. Robert Coles, hired originally as an expert witness *against* the Websters, who saw most clearly that the Websters aren't religious freaks but people who have rightly recognized that modern life—from TV ads to birth-control clinics to the dream of wealth and riches to classroom "clarifications" of their values—is an ongoing assault on their traditional lives and beliefs. "Those textbooks are abominable," says Coles, who has for years railed against the arrogance of the "religion" of psychiatry. "They're full of psychological, sociological junk. It isn't what I'd want my kids reading. The so-called intellectuals who leaped to oppose ought to take a look at those books. Let them get outraged about these books, which are crap."

William Bradford, Jr., the Hogan & Hartson lawyer handling the case for People for the American Way, says such cultural criticism is interesting but irrelevant to the Mobile case. To broaden the First Amendment definition of religion to include perspectives that are secular and atheistic, he says, is to go beyond the Constitution's definition of religion and to open the door to fringe religious groups' taking schools to court all across the country. "It's a question of education and culture," he says, "not religion."

A conversation with Lora, the daughter:

Lora: "I have a book right now that says David and Goliath was a myth."

"Did you say anything to the teacher?"

Lora: "The teacher said, 'I don't want to talk about it. I could get fired.' We can't say anything! We're at home and we know what's right, and then we go to school and they have all these 'facts' that say that there's no way the star could have been where it was the night Jesus was born, or whatever." Lora mentions that she has a friend who is a Jehovah's Witness: "I feel like I'm right, but she feels like she's right."

"So what does that mean?"

Lora: "It's confusing that she can believe in something and I can believe in something very strongly. I know what I believe. I know that that's right. It's just weird how many religions there are."

"What do the differences within Christianity mean when we die?"

Lora: "Well, the people who are really Christians, not just say they're Christians—to believe and to have faith and to be able to depend on God for all that you need. It depends on how different they believe if they're going to go to Hell or Heaven."

"What about Jews?"

Lora: "Jews? What do they believe?"

"Christ was a Jew. The Jews have never acknowledged him as the Savior."

Lora: "Okay, I feel like in order—now, I'm only thirteen, you know—in order to be a Christian you need to believe Jesus was the son of God, and if you don't, then you're wrong. That's what I believe. I know what I believe, and nothing can tell me that I'm wrong, because I know that I'm right. I know what I believe and I know what I've been taught. They're just teaching what's in the books. Science is bad about that with evolution and all that stuff. It's weird."

"What do you mean?"

Lora: "They just have so many different ideas of how man came to be. They have to have proven facts. See, that's the thing: Nobody can have faith anymore; everything has to be laid out for 'em. They have to see it to believe it."

"Would it matter to you if you discovered the Christmas star didn't exist?"

Lora: "First of all, the Bible says that that star was there, so it *was* there. And that's what I'm going to believe, so I don't even have to worry about it. The Bible says it was there, it was there."

"That's all there is to the answer?"

Lora: "Right, there's no point in going any further."

Dinner is done, and David rocks anxiously on the back legs of his chair, his Kansas City Royals cap returned to his head. Lora asks to be excused, and she is. David joins her. Sue pours second cups of French vanilla coffee, and John removes his glasses and rubs his eyes. An ink pen is clipped inside the neck of his golf shirt.

"You're tired of it all?"

John sighs. "Well, I don't know if we're tired physically, but mentally. We are not professional lawyers, not professional challengers. We're a family here, please—cameras, mikes, tape recorders, questioning! We're folks here, just trying to survive a day of football and cheerleading."

"We're not afraid of moral absolutes that work for us as a family," says Sue. "We want to guard that."

"But how can you be so sure?"

"I have experienced," Sue says, "the privilege of answered prayer. Oh, God, goodness, every time we see who we're supposed to be on TV, very often read who we're supposed to be in magazines, we can't identify with those people. It's as if it's almost presented in mockery. The reason we agreed to do this is to try to get the truth out. And now that we're in the middle of this, I'm not sure it's possible."

"What do you mean, 'the truth'?"

"What has been printed is that we are a bunch of fundamentalist religious fanatics who are seeking a backdoor way of getting their religious beliefs pushed into the public schools. That we are narrow-minded, that we are shortsighted, that we have no reasonable intelligence, that we are backwoods, that we are emotional, that we just kind of cooked this up to railroad it through the system, that we're book burners. We see things almost completely opposite. We think we are the people who make up America."

"You figure your opinion is just as good as any liberal New Yorker's?"

"Why not?" John says. "We've got a vote."

"There's got to be a point of faith," says Sue, pleading. "The intellect should be added to faith. If it's intelligence before faith, then it isn't faith. And what we have is faith. Does that make any sense?"

"Yes, absolutely." And the last scene from Inherit the Wind comes to mind—Clarence Darrow angrily saying to the flippant, cynical character based on H. L. Mencken: "You smart aleck! You have no more right to spit on his religion than you have a right to spit on my religion! Or my lack of it!" The logic fits here, inspires an empathy for the Websters' predicament. But then, that is a kind of cultural relativism, and the Websters don't like cultural relativism. They don't believe in it. They can't believe in it. Right is right.

"God has set a standard and the standard is His Word," says John. "And it says that separation from God is Hell. Now what that is, we aren't sure. We didn't write the Word. We accept it. And that's part of our belief."

Let's be honest. The Websters have built an enviable life upon their faith. They give back to their community, they aren't divorced, their children aren't druggies or jerks, they enjoy life. They are good people. And faith in God is as real to them as life itself. It shapes their perception and their behavior—the very definition of a moral system. So it hardly seems crazy to expect public-school textbooks to fairly and objectively acknowledge that reality, if they are going to discuss morality and ethics at all.

But why the nagging sense that something scary is going on here, the sense that there are too many questions the Websters can't ask, too many answers that are not possible if Christ's disciples are reduced to dictationists and God to a writer of prose? What if yesterday's fundamentalists had prevailed? Would the earth and man and God still reign at the center of the universe? Would religious fanatics still riot against human vaccinations? What of the miracle, the complexity, the beauty of evolution? Would people who gaze at the world through the Websters' eyes ever have seen a blueprint for the journey of man in the birds and fish and lizards of the Galápagos Islands? And what of the future, when man will act as God, splicing genes and rebuilding DNA to conquer cancer and mental retardation?

The concerns of the Websters, of the Mobile lawsuit, aren't trivial or stupid. Modern life has exacted a woeful human price, and the philosophies that underpin it—from psychology to science to consumerism—should not go unexamined. But will people like the Websters ever ask the questions that might lead them to that frightening hilltop where they can look back and see the way from which they came? Will they ever know the beauty of unfettered knowledge? Will they ever know the exhilaration of unfettered wonder?

A final question: "But do you sacrifice the freedom of curiosity?"

"We believe we are not all-knowing," says Sue. "We are free to investigate, but it has to be in the framework of faith, not dogma. We are not omnipotent. We are seeking the character of God, not the literal details. But belief that is only intellectual is not belief at all."

Since Darrow and Bryan and Scopes, the debate is unchanged: Confusion is the price of knowledge. Fear of knowledge is the price of fundamental faith. Certainty is its reward.

John and Sue, David and Lora Webster have reaped the reward.

John and Sue, David and Lora Webster have paid the price.

JULY 26, 1987

The Websters eventually lost their lawsuit in a higher court.

Photograph courtesy Jack Anderson.

JACK ANDERSON
Fighting His Private War

$\mathcal{T}$he house is empty and the front door is unlocked. The man, an old man now with white hair and a watermelon belly and a grandfather's amble, hesitates a moment, glances around at the overgrown and untended yard where as a boy he watered row upon row of his father's carrots and beans and strawberries. *God, he hated that job!* But he never complained, choosing instead the captive laborer's silent revenge: He refused to enjoy his work. He looks to the east. "See that peak?" he asks, pointing to Utah's Mount Olympus, which towers in the mist only a few miles away. "I've hiked to that peak. I didn't want to. My father did. He won." The man then lets out a kind of chuckle, or perhaps it is a sigh. In the last forty-five years, he has never been inside his boyhood home—a huge, elegant Tudor on several beautifully wooded acres in Salt Lake City's affluent Cottonwood suburb. In the last forty-five years, the only times he has even driven past were when his kids insisted.

Always aggressive, quick to step across the little boundaries that deter other men, the man walks right through the front doorway of what is now someone else's home. The house is being renovated— its wallpaper is stripped, its patched plaster is unsanded, its doors are off their hinges. And for an instant, everything seems wrong. But wait, that crystal chandelier, it was here forty-five years ago. He points to it with a kind of excitement, and it seems that nostalgia might sweep over him, but it passes, and he continues to walk slowly from room to room, commenting in the deadpan tone of a bored tour guide: "These were a couple of bedrooms. This was the kitchen." Then he stops, turns to his right, and looks down a narrow, darkened stairway to the basement. His voice goes hollow and distant . . .

"And this is where *we* lived."

In fine Cottonwood, on these fine manicured grounds, in this fine Tudor home, Jack Anderson—the famed "Washington Merry-Go-Round" columnist, the scourge of the pols, the Pulitzer Prize winner, the pricey speechmaking pundit, the TV celeb—lived in

181

the basement. Jack, his two younger brothers, and his parents all slept in the same room and bathed in the laundry tub. Upstairs, a man who would later become chaplain of the U.S. Senate lived with his family. Only with their rent could Jack's father, on his $200-a-month postal clerk salary, afford this magnificent house. Upstairs, the future chaplain of the Senate had a flush toilet. Outside, Jack's family had an outhouse—over there, Jack points, across the back-yard, where that brown house sits today.

"We had the only crapper in the whole valley," he says, a slight smile finally cracking a granite face. "I would be a little embar-rassed to escort my friends to the crapper. We were the Cinderellas. I think Mother was annoyed with Dad for buying a house we couldn't afford to live in." He thinks of his father, and, once again, his voice goes hollow and distant . . .

"He was a weird guy."

Jack Anderson, one of America's most famous reporters, isn't really a reporter anymore, at least not like he used to be. He doesn't put it exactly that way. As he does with so much in his life, he gives it a grander, nobler face. He describes himself as the "publisher" of the "Merry-Go-Round" column, which is produced by a staff of ten edi-tors, reporters, and interns who are led by the column's coauthor, Dale Van Atta. Anderson consults with the staff, slips them story tips, and writes a few columns a month.

But it has come to this: Jack Anderson has little to do with Jack Anderson's column anymore. There are many reasons, but one stands out starkly: For about the last decade, Jack Anderson has been busy transforming himself from working reporter to working celebrity—too busy to spend long hours reporting, as he once did. Anderson is still busy—giving fifty speeches a year around the coun-try for $250,000, which is his personal income. The $200,000 a year he earns from his other operations—his UPI radio broadcasts, his "Insiders" TV show on the Financial News Network, and his Wash-ington newsletter—is all pumped back into the "Merry-Go-Round." Anderson's support for the column is substantial, but not entirely altruistic. The visibility he gains from the "Merry-Go-Round" helps maintain his popularity on the national speaking circuit.

At sixty-seven, Anderson has been a Washington institution for four decades. He broke some of the biggest stories of his generation—the Sherman Adams scandals of the fifties, the Senator Thomas Dodd scandals of the sixties, and the ITT–Dita Beard scandals of the seventies. He had hundreds of other exposés that, in their season, commanded headlines. He put men in jail, drove one man to suicide. He cajoled and manipulated confessions from some of the most powerful and savvy politicians in the nation. He unmasked the CIA's plans to kill Fidel Castro.

But he also had less grandiose scoops: He revealed that Indiana senator Vance Hartke had bad breath, that Georgia senator Herman Talmadge spat tobacco juice onto the floor of the Senate, and that FBI director J. Edgar Hoover calmed his stomach with Gelusil. Anderson reported such trivialities, he said, to deflate the images and egos of men made arrogant and pompous by power, to prove they were no better than anybody else. That sentiment runs deep in Anderson.

Today he is still feared on Capitol Hill, although his influence has waned. He's not universally respected by his journalistic colleagues, who, despite his thousands of genuine scoops, have often seen his reporting as petulant and petty, holier-than-thou. The number of newspapers carrying his column has dropped from about 1,000 in 1975 to about 650 today. While a smattering of big-city papers, the *Washington Post* among them, carry Anderson's column, it runs mostly in the little towns of heartland America. Again, Anderson gives this a noble face: The "Merry-Go-Round" reaches the real America. Says one respected investigative reporter in Washington: "The guy's outta gas. He's been outta gas for fifteen years."

That is the temptation: to judge Jack Anderson harshly because he has judged so many others harshly. The temptation is to say he's "outta gas," he ain't what he used to be. But the truth is, although Anderson isn't reporting much anymore, he still is what he used to be: layer upon layer of complicated motivations—some so deeply rooted they seem more instinct than motive, more personality than morality. Like so many other American heartlanders drawn to Washington, Jack Anderson eventually achieved power, prominence, and glory. Over the years, he came to see his work as a heroic candle lit against the darkness of political corruption, greed, and arrogance. About this he is undeniably sincere. But deep inside Jack Anderson—in the intimate, painful place where boundless ambition must reside—a little machine also runs constantly, always has, propelling him ahead in private rebellion and indignation.

Les Whitten, Jack's friend and former "Merry-Go-Round" coauthor, recalls a time years ago when Jack asked him this question: "If we didn't have this column, who would we be?"

"Stop here, stop at this bridge," Jack says, as the car crosses a little bridge on narrow Fardown Avenue within sight of his childhood home outside Salt Lake City. "This is a very momentous bridge." He is joking now, enjoying himself, recalling an event that, five decades after the fact, still seems eerily prophetic. Jack's friend, Ray Fritsch, the only man Jack has remained close to from his youth, slows his blue Cadillac but doesn't stop. "Oh, this is *the* bridge," Ray says, with the mocking deference of friends who show affection and respect by never saying a nice word to each other. If the achievements of a lifetime can have an actual beginning, this bridge is where it began for Jack Anderson, Investigative Reporter. When he was twelve, covering local news for the suburban *Murray Eagle* for $7 a week, a car ran a bicycling boy off this bridge, then only a single lane. The boy was badly bruised, and the public outrage that resulted from young Jack's story in the *Eagle* ended with a new, wider, safer bridge.

Jack had changed the world. And it was a taste of real power—used, indisputably, for good. If young Jack was impressed with himself, though, he certainly didn't say so. His father wouldn't have allowed that. Jack doesn't know how it first began, but when Jack was just a boy, his father became convinced that Jack was, well, too big for his britches. Jack was a smart kid. His mother says he knew the alphabet at age one. But Orlando Anderson was wary of Jack's precociousness.

In Orlando—and the Mormon faith he held so deeply—there was a strong vein of egalitarianism that discouraged showiness or flamboyance, getting too far ahead of the pack, which Jack always did, and which he always seemed to relish. The phrase "no one is better than anyone else" was a kind of religious-cultural mantra in Jack's childhood. For the ambitious, confident, and proud, there was always this cut-you-down-to-size question: "Just who do you think you are?"

It started early. Orlando believed Jack's grandparents doted on him while ignoring his two younger brothers. Orlando wouldn't have said it this way in the 1930s, but, looking back, he feared the other boys would get an inferiority complex. His way of handling this was to remind Jack that he was not as smart as his brothers. Orlando, sitting with his wife talking about Jack's childhood on the weekend of his son's visit to the old family home, still seems miffed when he recalls Jack's confident reply: "That doesn't worry me." With an edge in his voice, Orlando says, "He was very much for himself. I thought Jack was a little uppity-up and would rather be in a job, any job, that would give him a boost. He built himself up. I thought he should have been more common."

"He wanted to be tops," says Jack's ninety-year-old mother, Agnes. "He wanted to be in the limelight," retorts Orlando.

Jack's father was a mercurial man, with a quick temper and an opinion about everything. He loved to argue. He loved to be righteously indignant. Jack believes his father even liked being poor. "He had a martyr complex," Jack says, "and it suited him to glory in his poverty." Orlando remembers that the happiest time of his life was when the boys weren't yet teens and he had built them a sandbox and swing set in the backyard, where they all played. Without a hint of emotion, Jack says, "Yes, that's when he could run us."

Orlando Anderson was a stern man who could explode at the most minor provocation. "He would erupt like Vesuvius," says Jack, who tried not to stoke the volcano. But that wasn't always possible. Jack's boyhood friend Darwin Knudsen remembers a time when one of Jack's brothers said something that irritated Orlando, and he reached out and squeezed the boy's nose until tears rolled down his cheeks. Darwin remembers looking at Jack and thinking he was embarrassed by his father.

"He knew what was right," Jack says of his dad. "And even if he was wrong, he was right." Jack doesn't say this with rancor. He says it with a touch of humor, perhaps with a tone of forgiveness. But most of all, he seems to say it with almost no feeling at all. He says, "I understood that Dad's fulminations were meant well."

Over the years, Jack developed a strategy for dealing with his dad: He dealt with him as little as possible. He stayed constantly busy, and out of the house. When his dad barked orders, Jack usually listened intently—and then paid no attention to what his father had said. When his father would sit down with a pencil and paper and figure out to the penny how much money Jack would need for some outing, Jack would take the coins—and then go to his mother, who'd slip him a dollar.

"Don't tell Dad," was her constant refrain.

Agnes Anderson, a serene woman who never lost her composure, played counterpoint to Orlando. With her connivance, Jack maneuvered around the slumbering bear. In personality, he grew to resemble his mom—friendly, well-liked, and gentle. In character, he resembled his dad—self-righteous, certain, opinionated. "I don't think he really enjoyed his childhood," Jack's daughter Laurie Anderson-Bruch says of her father. "He just wanted to get away. My father worked really hard to get away from being raised poor and to show his dad."

Nothing seemed to slow Jack down. His father rode him, and he lived in a basement and wore shabby clothes, but he was president of his junior high and high schools and editor of their newspapers. A lean, handsome, dishwater-blond kid, he got along with everybody. He was an Eagle Scout. When Jack was twelve, Orlando got him a summer job thinning sugar beets. Orlando had thinned sugar beets as a boy. But the job was not for Jack, who hated working on his knees in the dirt, under the hot sun. He quit and got his first job with the *Murray Eagle*. "I think Jack psychologically escaped from his father when he took that job," says Darwin Knudsen, who's known Jack since grade school. "It was obvious that Jack would not kowtow to him." Jack went on to become editor of the Boy Scout page for the *Deseret News* and, while still in high school, the youngest reporter on the *Salt Lake City Tribune*. Yet at the same time, he was runner-up to the class valedictorian. Orlando didn't attend his son's graduation.

"He thought I was getting too many honors," Jack says.

Soon after, while working as a reporter, Jack angered his father like never before—and demonstrated just how far he'd go in pursuit of a story. When Jack discovered that a cousin of his belonged to a polygamist cult, he decided to infiltrate it. Polygamy—condoned by the Mormon Church in the nineteenth century but banned for decades—still flourished secretly in the 1930s, and Jack hoped the *Saturday Evening Post* would buy an exposé. So he went to his cousin—without revealing he was working on a story—and feigned interest in polygamy. The cousin fell for the ruse and got Jack into the select fold. Still without revealing his reporter's intent, Jack began attending the cult's social gatherings.

But he wasn't alone in his curiosity. A detective hired by the Mormon Church to spy on the polygamists took the license number of Jack's car—which was, unfortunately, Orlando's car. Vesuvius exploded. "Steam, fire, brimstone!" says Jack, laughing at the memory. It turned out that Orlando had been called before church officials and questioned about his seeming involvement in the cult. Says Jack, "I don't think he ever forgave me."

Jack reluctantly abandoned the story before heading off to begin his Mormon missionary work in Alabama, leaving the day Pearl Harbor was bombed. Jack would eventually become deeply absorbed in his faith, and Mormonism—with its call for the forces of good to constantly fight the forces of evil—would come to provide a justification for his often ruthless muckraking. But he wasn't particularly religious as a youth—didn't want to go on a mission, didn't want to get off the *Tribune's* career ladder. Still, he went, to make his parents happy, and on his door-to-door visits discovered what every reporter eventually learns: People will tell their deepest secrets to a perfect stranger, if only he strikes a sympathetic pose.

Relentlessly charming and competent, Jack was promoted to a good administrative job in the mission's regional office. At the same time, he reinforced his image as a man apart. "Jack is an abiding psychological enigma," says Darwin Knudsen. "In a way, Jack was estranged. Everybody regarded Jack as a friend, but not a buddy. He was just too self-centered or self-occupied." Darwin was also a Mormon missionary, in a different state, and he recalls a time Jack visited him for a few days. Darwin was living in the house of a poor family with several daughters and one bathroom. But Jack, used to the privy out back and the washtub in the basement, spent forever each morning "primping" in the bathroom, Darwin says, while the girls waited politely for him to finish. "Jack made no apology for this," he says, still amazed. "It was just his nature. He didn't realize this was an imposition."

For years after Jack left Salt Lake City, Darwin and another old friend of Jack's often talked about how they'd write Jack letters and how rarely he wrote back. "It hurt my feelings that he wouldn't write," Darwin says. "Why wouldn't he sit down and scratch out a note? It says to me that he's so self-contained, happy with his menu, that he doesn't need the friendship. Jack is still the loner, standing against the crowd. But, you understand, that's how he was from the beginning. The Bible refers to people being on the Lord's errands. Jack was always on his own errand."

When Jack finished his missionary stint and returned to Salt Lake City, World War II was raging. He avoided the draft legally by joining the Merchant Marines. He had no conscientious objections to war. He simply didn't want to fight for his country in the infantry, didn't want to fight hand-to-hand. "Cowardice," he calls it today. The Merchant Marines made Jack an officer, which angered Orlando, who figured he should have started at the bottom. But the job was short-lived, because after eight months at sea, Jack wangled war correspondent credentials from the *Deseret News*. He quit the Merchant Marines and went to China, where the draft finally caught up with him, and he was assigned to the military newspaper *Stars and Stripes*. It was in China, sitting around with the older, seasoned reporters, that Jack first remembers hearing of the "Washington

Merry-Go-Round" and its feisty, moralistic, crusading, liberal creator, Drew Pearson. That, Jack decided, was the job for him. Soon after his return to Salt Lake City, he headed off to Washington with little more than ambition and an inflated résumé.

As ever, Jack's father was skeptical.

Jack's friend Ray Fritsch will never forget the day he and Orlando dropped Jack off at the bus station when Jack was first heading out for the Merchant Marines. After Jack had ridden off, Orlando turned to him and said angrily, "All these high ambitions he's got. He'll be slapped back, because he's not that smart." Ray's wife, Ella, who was with them that day, could see Ray's ire rising. Ray and Jack, it turned out, shared a mysterious bond. Almost half a century later, Ray still remembers the day clearly: "I was thinking about my own father. Orlando was just like my dad. My dad always told me I'd never amount to anything. He never told me he was proud of me. When I was making more money in a day than he made in a year, you know what he said? He said I was a spoiled brat." That day, Ray blew up. "Why don't you just quit downgrading Jack?" he raged at Orlando. "You have no right to say these things about your own son!"

When Jack hit town in 1947, he was like a character out of Frank Capra's *Mr. Smith Goes to Washington*. Jimmy Stewart does journalism. In 1947, Jack really *believed* his high-school civics lessons: great statesmen struggling in marble halls to serve The People. Well, Jack, from his basement home in Utah, was The People, or about as close to them as you can get. He'd been raised in a strict Mormon home—no drinking or smoking. But perhaps more important, he hadn't shared the birthright of children born to power and privilege: the firsthand knowledge that Great Men really are "just like everybody else." That idea had been pounded into Jack as a philosophy of life, but from the basement, from the bottom of the social ladder, that egalitarian notion was also a kind of populist scream, a little man's cry for self-respect. The absolute truth of the philosophy was a shock.

At twenty-four, Jack was without what novelist John O'Hara called the "unearned cynicism" of the prematurely sophisticated. So he was amazed—at the booze drinking, great volumes of booze drinking! At the skirt-chasing, wrinkled codgers pursuing sweet young things! At the lying, incompetence, nepotism, corruption, laziness, ruthlessness, stupidity, greed, selfishness, pettiness of his Great Men! It was a naiveté that fueled Jack's rebellious indignation, the same kind of naiveté that today fuels the indignation of the "Washington Merry-Go-Round's" young reporters, most of whom hail from average American families in average American places like Montana. It's not that Anderson isn't happy to get an application from some Ivy League genius, but he doesn't get many. Somehow, the "Merry-Go-Round" speaks more to State U grads used to seeing power from the bottom up. Most are like Anderson's current co-columnist, Dale Van Atta, who as a young reporter exposed a police ticketing scam and was called before angry policemen to defend his story. He was terrified, but quickly realized the police were even more terrified. "To have them all in fear of me when I'm usually in fear of them," Van Atta recalls with delight. "It was a great moment."

The tale of how Jack Anderson—despite his father's dire predictions—came to Washington and went on to fame and fortune after landing a job with Drew Pearson is today a piece of journalism folklore. Pearson, who headed the "Merry-Go-Round" from 1932 until he died in 1969, was the most influential muckraker of his day. Sending his message into hamlets all across America, he portrayed Washington as a corrupt place inhabited by pooh-bahs, bigwigs, and brass hats bent on feathering their nests by promoting big business at the expense of the little people. The view fit Jack like his BVDs, and in the next few years he helped Pearson assault and depose Republican senators Joseph McCarthy and Owen Brewster, as well as Defense Secretary James Forrestal.

Jack had one personality trait that made him a great reporter: He could genuinely like a man, but still be hard as nails when reporting about him. He could later look that man in the eye and convince him again that he liked him personally, that unpleasant reporting was simply his job. This wasn't phoniness on Jack's part. It was at the heart of his nature. He had a way of disarming folks, of outmaneuvering them with genuine sincerity. He wasn't troubled by the ethics of this.

He once convinced Connecticut congressman Robert Giaimo that he doubted rumors linking Giaimo to a known gambler, and if Giaimo would only let Jack go through his files, Jack would straighten it out. Giaimo did—and Anderson cited the files as alleged proof of the accusations, although the Justice Department later declined to take any action against Giaimo based on Anderson's information. Anderson once asked Vice President Hubert Humphrey for a letter of introduction when he was going to Iraq. Anderson presented it to the U.S. Embassy there, failed to say he was a reporter, and asked to go through the files. It was days before they asked if he worked for the vice president. "No," Jack said. They turned white. Anderson bluffed California senator George Murphy into confessing that he was on a cash retainer to Technicolor Inc. by saying, after Murphy denied the allegation, "Now, Senator, you and I have been friends for a long time. I don't think you want to be quoted as denying this whole thing. So, because we've been friends, I'll forget what you said before and give you another chance, in fairness." Murphy cracked and confessed. Says Anderson's former co-columnist Les Whitten, "He was just a wonderful con man."

Jack was a curiosity in Washington—a city that breeds, even demands, an arching self-importance and arrogance. In contrast, young Jack was refreshingly unpretentious and open-faced. But as his old friends and his father had sensed, as his hours in the bathroom had hinted, Jack could be pretty self-absorbed, even if his charm hid the trait. Then, as a kind of antidote, Jack met Olivia Farley, one of the more amazing and fortunate discoveries of his life. Libby, as Jack calls her, was from a coal-mining family in West Virginia, and she worked as a clerk at the FBI. If Jack's father was militant in his efforts to keep Jack humble, Libby, also a Mormon, extended that militancy to everyone. Not in Orlando's way, but in her own. She once arrived to meet Jack in President Lyndon Johnson's hotel room—where the Duke and Duchess of Windsor also were guests—wearing slacks and beat-up shoes. "My God, Libby!" Jack moaned. She once took her daughter Cheri with her to buy an evening gown for a night at the Kennedy White House—and they went to Korvettes, where Libby pulled one of about thirty identical gowns off the rack. Her daughter was appalled. "No," Libby said, reassuring her, "I'll be the only one there with this dress."

Over the years, Jack Anderson has made a big thing about how he has refused to be part of the Washington social set because he never wanted to be tainted by friendships with the powerful. "What's wrong is that these reporters adopted the views of the people they're writing about," he once said. "They've become a part of the Establishment they cover." That would never happen to Jack Anderson. A noble view, as always. But it wasn't only Jack's idealism that put the kibosh on the Washington party circuit. It was also Libby's down-home militancy. "A lot of it was my mother," says the Andersons' daughter Cheri Loveless. She says her dad would have gone to parties to help his career, but her mother refused. To Libby—with her plain beauty, a lingering West Virginia twang, and nouns and verbs that don't always match—the Washington soiree scene consisted of people putting on airs and wasting a lot of money doing it.

From their first date, she performed a familiar role: She kept Jack's massive ego in its place. "He was trying to impress me and took me to a French restaurant on Vermont, where they played violins at your table," Libby says. "And then he took me to a nightclub in Baltimore, and Jackie Gleason was playing. He was trying to impress me, but I didn't care about those things. After he stopped trying to be debonair and I brought him back to earth, he was all right."

They had nine kids.

Orlando Anderson was once a hefty, strong man. Now he is thin and frail and fragile, George Burns without the cigar. At ninety-two, Jack's father has the look of a man curling inward upon himself. The less the old curmudgeon complains and gripes about everything and everybody, the less ornery he is, the more people worry about him. Agnes is his reverse image. She never interrupts. She's quiet and sweet and radiant. Ninety years old and using a walker, she still moves gracefully. Orlando pounds out "Rock of Ages" on the piano. She smiles warmly. All this morning, Orlando has insisted, loudly, that Agnes's ninetieth birthday party is tomorrow. No, she says, it's today. When the grandkids finally come to pick them up at the nursing home to take them off to the party this afternoon, Orlando says nothing about his mistake.

"Where should I sit?" he grumbles as he gets to the car.

"Put him in the trunk," says Agnes, sweetly.

Jack is in Salt Lake City for his mother's birthday party. Jack's son Kevin, who lives there and organized the party, has invited dozens of his grandparents' old friends, and it's like a scene from "This Is Your Life." It will turn out to be the last big gathering of friends and family while Agnes is alive, because in only a few weeks she will suffer a fatal stroke. But today at her birthday party, she glows with delight. Orlando, the tough old coot, is overcome. He's so touched by seeing his old friends and family that when people walk up to him in the kitchen, where he is leaning with his left hand on his cane, Orlando looks at them without expression, drops his head, puts his right hand over his eyes, and sobs. People smile, put an arm around his shoulders and say, "Oh, oh, that's okay." Posted at the buffet nearby, Jack watches: "It's the first time I ever saw my father cry."

Orlando is trying. Just the day before, Jack visited his folks, and his father seemed, in his own way, to be struggling to reach out to his son. "We're proud of you, Jack," he said out of the blue. "You know that." Well, yes, Jack knew that, somehow he knew that, but in his entire life he couldn't recall hearing his father ever say it. Just like Ray Fritsch. Not once. Later, Jack chuckled and said wryly, "I guess you get to be ninety and you repent." That same day, Orlando also mentioned Jack's first newspaper job with the *Murray Eagle*. "Remember that, Jack?" he asked proudly. Pleasantly, Jack said, "Yes, I remember you wanted me to thin beets." Orlando said nothing, looked down at his lap. Did he comprehend? Recognize that even now, at the end, his son could not let him off the hook completely?

Orlando: "Jack, did I ever tell you that you were a hard birth?"

Jack, cheerfully: "I heard it all before."

This time, Orlando didn't drop his head. And when Jack left the room, Orlando's voice went hard and angry: "Did you hear what he said? He said, 'I heard it all before!' That's what he said." Yes, Orlando comprehended. He talked of a time when Jack was just a toddler and he got a bladder blockage and was in excruciating pain. Orlando, who didn't own a car, carried Jack all the way to the hospital. "He was so little," Orlando said. "I felt so sorry for him." Later, he said, "He was obedient to me. He was obedient to me. But he didn't like it. I could tell."

At Drew Pearson's death in 1969, the "Washington Merry-Go-Round" seemed destined for the dustbin. But Jack Anderson bought the column from Pearson's widow and worked like a madman, night and day. He eventually hired his own staff of hungry novice reporters who came and went, and he hired a handful of crackerjack investigative reporters. In those days, Jack did half the columns himself, rewrote the others, and oversaw the whole operation. After twenty years in Washington, he had the place wired. By this time, Jack had come to see his journalism as a sword for the little people in their epic struggle against greed and corruption in government. But these heroic motivations aside, at age forty-six, Jack also wanted the recognition that had eluded him in the shadow of Drew Pearson. Les Whitten, who was for years Jack's heir apparent, once asked when he could start sharing Jack's byline on the "Merry-Go-Round." Without hesitation, Jack said, "When I'm as famous as Drew."

That happened almost overnight. In the early seventies, Anderson's flame burned so brightly that it would have taken a waterfall to douse it. President Richard Nixon despised Anderson, who with Pearson had revealed during Nixon's unsuccessful 1960 presidential race that Nixon's brother Donald had received a secret $205,000 loan from billionaire Howard Hughes. Anderson's name adorned

Nixon's infamous "Enemies List." Future Watergate felons and then White House operatives G. Gordon Liddy and Howard Hunt talked of killing him. The CIA gave him a twenty-four-hour-a-day tail. When Anderson discovered his CIA shadow, he dispatched his own nine children—his "Katzenjammer *paparazzi*"—to tail the tailers. It was high, mocking theater, and Anderson won the publicity war hands down. But at the time, there was no guarantee he would win his battles with the Powers That Be, and Anderson showed real nerve, even bravery, in his zealous crusades against the outrages of Nixon and his minions.

For his crowning coup, Anderson revealed that Nixon and national security adviser Henry Kissinger, while denying it in public, were privately tilting toward Pakistan in its 1971 war with India. The exposé won him a 1972 Pulitzer Prize—and the cover of *Time*. In a *Playboy* interview, at the peak of his power, Anderson said: "Too many bureaucrats in Washington have developed an elitist attitude. They are our servants and they want to become our masters. I just want to deflate them a little, remind them of their proper place."

Orlando and Libby must have smiled.

In three years, Jack Anderson had eclipsed the fame of his mentor. But if this tale is mythic, then the hero—made prideful and overly certain by his rise—undid himself. The same year he won the Pulitzer, Anderson reported on one of his radio broadcasts that he had located documented evidence that Missouri senator Thomas Eagleton, the Democratic vice presidential candidate, had been arrested for drunk driving. But Anderson didn't have documented evidence in his hands. He had relied on sources, who then didn't deliver the goods. After days of stubbornly refusing to retract his story, Anderson was forced to admit that he had no proof after all. He had been deflated, reminded of his proper place. And he had done it to himself.

It's hard not to wonder: Did Orlando smile again?

Jack Anderson puts forth this truth in jest: "No matter how favorably you write my story, you will not portray me as nobly as I think I am." He laughs and says that over the years he has noticed that he always seems to remember his own role in events as more heroic than it actually was. He means this as a funny aside, but Jack is on to something. His son Kevin mentions in passing that when he and his dad were picking a nursing home for Jack's parents, Agnes and Orlando, they had to be careful of every legal detail because of his dad's high visibility. No, Jack says, quickly correcting him, they had to be careful of every legal detail because it was the right thing to do. It is his instinct to seize the moral high ground.

That instinct is deeply embedded, perhaps going back to Jack's childhood, when he continued to think highly of himself despite his father's repeated attempts to humble him. But the instinct also is tied to his Mormonism, because as his faith deepened with age Jack came to see himself, his life, and his muckraking as part of the righteous and mystical struggle portrayed in the Book of Mormon.

Members of the Church of Jesus Christ of the Latter-Day Saints, Mormons, believe the Book of Mormon is the third testament of the Bible and that it was divinely revealed to Joseph Smith in Palmyra, New York, in 1823. The book describes a lost tribe of Israel that migrated to this continent in 600 B.C. Mormons believe that mankind is in its last days before the Second Coming of Christ and that America, God's newly chosen land, will keep its special status only if the powers of evil and force don't overtake the powers of good and freedom. The Book of Mormon describes centuries of battles between the Israelite tribe's descendants—the Nephites, who were mostly God-fearing; and the Lamanites, who were mostly wicked. The Nephite-Lamanite wars, Mormon scripture says, finally ended in A.D. 421 with a titanic battle in Upstate New York and the annihilation of the Nephite nation, which by then had lost much of its righteousness—and hence its power. The Mormon truths, inscribed on golden tablets, then lay buried until God revealed them to Joseph Smith.

These Mormon beliefs have created for Jack Anderson a grand and heroic, even mystical, vision of the world and people's role in it. How but for the power of God's providence, asks his daughter Tanya Neider, can you explain the hiring of the unknown and inexperienced Jack by Drew Pearson, the famous Washington muckraker? "The way he talks about it," she says of her father, "he knows it was more than coincidence." Adds Jack's son Randy, "For some purpose or reason he had been elevated into the limelight." The events in the Book of Mormon, its descriptions of the rising tide of evil that preceded the Nephite nation's demise, says Tanya, are akin to the rising evils in modern America. About this, her father agrees: "Some of the things we were warned against in the Book of Mormon are happening in our own society. Mormons don't believe God will punish us, but that if we are unrighteous we will suffer from our own behavior."

The Book of Mormon tells of evil men who made secret compacts and who infiltrated the Nephite society. Does this not sound like the

Mafia? Jack has asked over the years. Does this not sound like the South American drug cartels? he has asked more recently. And some of the evil infiltrators were lawyers! And haven't they hounded Jack Anderson throughout his career? His daughters Tanya Neider and Cheri Loveless say their father's exposing of government corruption helps preserve America's righteousness—and thus helps America avoid the fate of the Nephites. Jack says he has never believed that God determined the events of his life, only that God created opportunities for him to seize. "I've never written a story with the Book of Mormon in mind," he says. "I go after corruption because it's wrong. This is not a religious calling."

Jack's son Randy disagrees. "He feels like his work is a calling," he says of his father. "I don't know if he wants that said, because it's not like God has anointed him. This was something he was called to do, a mission in his life, although he wouldn't put it that way because it can be misconstrued." His children, Jack says, overstate his religious motivations. But, no doubt, Jack Anderson's Mormon beliefs have helped motivate, justify, and sustain his ambition, his muckraking journalism, and his heroic view of himself. He would never say of his work, "Hey, it's a job." Or, "I get a kick out of the power." Or, "It made me rich." Or, "I love the fame."

He says, "The Constitution is a divinely inspired document."

The director of the nursing home where Jack's folks live is bluntly solicitous when the famous investigative reporter visits: "I said, 'We better have this place up to snuff if Jack Anderson's coming.'" So he ordered the staff to clean and scrub and shine the whole place. Jack chuckles, having gotten used to such royal treatment. His son Kevin seems more impressed. He whispers, "They kiss our ass." When Jack arrives at his parents' room, Orlando must be helped out of his chair, but as soon as he's up, he starts complaining that too many of the old people in the home stink of body odor.

"He's feeling fine," says Jack, laughing. "He's more mellow now."

Funny, so is Jack. He was always a great boss, easy to work for, demanding as hell but never harsh or rude. As a father, he was very unlike his own dad. Jack rarely even raised his voice with the kids, almost never disciplined them. He didn't spend much time, say, tossing around the old football, but he was always "available," say his children. He'd always stop whatever he was doing when a child entered his office at home, where he often worked. He once put President Kennedy on hold. Less driven today, Jack sees his two dozen grandkids a lot more than he did his own children. Daughter

Tanya Neider says that three years ago was the first time her dad ever went on a family vacation when he didn't work. She thinks that's great. But this new mellowness—and the implication that at age sixty-seven he's slowing down—isn't something Jack is quick to admit. He says he could yet win another Pulitzer. "No reason I shouldn't," he says grandly. "I've got the sources."

His wife, Libby, knows it's hard for a workaholic like Jack to retire, but she'd at least like him to cut back, sell the big house in Bethesda (it's worth about $1.5 million, she says), and buy a little place in the Virginia countryside. That would mean Jack could afford to do only twenty-five speeches a year instead of fifty. But Jack says he can't retire, that he needs the money, that he has a daughter with a permanent debilitating disease, children with their own kids who occasionally need financial help, huge medical bills from Libby's successful treatment for cancer last year. No, he *can't* retire.

But, never one to abandon the moral high ground for long, he also says the "Merry-Go-Round" is too important, that Drew Pearson's legacy is too historic, that somebody has got to ferret out wrongdoing and defend the little guy, the milkman in Kansas City, that even though he doesn't report much for the "Merry-Go-Round" anymore, his fame is important to its existence. Jack acknowledges that without the "Merry-Go-Round" his demand as a well-paid speaker would diminish, but it's also true that without the money from Jack's radio and TV contracts, the "Merry-Go-Round" couldn't stay afloat. No, he *can't* retire.

Yet there were times in the eighties when Jack considered it. He'd become a kind of folk hero by the mid-1970s, and when TV knocked at his door, he answered. For almost a decade he appeared on "Good Morning America," bringing in up to $550,000 a year. "My folks were finally impressed when I was on television," Jack says. With the huge TV income, all of which Jack poured into the "Merry-Go-Round," the staff burgeoned. But Jack Anderson was less and less a part of the daily operation. He came to think of himself as the column's "publisher." Staffers were less subtle: They called him a "figurehead," a "front," a "public relations man." There was a strong feeling among column staffers that it wasn't only Jack's parents but Jack himself who was impressed with the fame that television brought to him.

"He loved it," says one former staffer who worked with Jack for many years. When somebody walked up on the street and said, "Aren't you Jack Anderson?," the man says, Jack "flared up like a peacock." Even some of Jack's children, his good friends, and his loyal allies lovingly chuckle at what they see as his fascination with fame. "It inevitably went to his head," says Jack's daughter Laurie Anderson-Bruch. "There was a time we had to bring him down. He was just full of himself." For a while, she says, it even seemed to her that getting another TV show was more important to her dad than his Mormon faith. Jack once confided to Les Whitten that when he gets on a plane and is recognized, he hates it because he has to talk to the guy for the whole flight. But, Jack said, if he gets on a plane and nobody recognizes him, he then worries about why nobody has recognized him. When Whitten told Jack he was leaving the column to write novels, Jack asked, "How can you give up this fame?"

"I have a visceral love for the column and Jack," says a reporter who worked for him for several years. "But I'm angry at him. I've been angry at him for years because he betrayed the ideal. It started with 'Good Morning America.' He stopped being a reporter and started being a celebrity. It was a big mistake because he was a great reporter. He had this Everyman quality that was really corrupted by his ego." Says another former staffer, "We always joked on the staff that he'd give up the column for a weekly TV show." Says another, "He craves being on television." Says another, "This is one story where you don't follow the money. You follow the fame." Says still another, "He really wanted to be famous, a household word."

Jack doesn't see it this way. In his mind, his motives were heroic: He could reach tens of millions of people through his column, but he could reach many millions more through TV. It wasn't his name that needed to be a household word, but his message—the message that people must be constantly diligent in policing their public officials. His only interest in fame, he says, was its "market value"— the power it gave him to reach a wider audience. He says that his question to Whitten—"How can you give up this fame?"—was meant only to suggest that Whitten might find it harder to make a living without the public visibility of the "Merry-Go-Round." "Reveling in fame?" he asks. "I'm surprised anyone would say that. It's not true."

Says Whitten, "Fame meant a lot to him."

In the late seventies and early eighties, Jack entered a variety of business deals that brought him the kind of press he was used to giving instead of getting. He held an interest in a bank, for instance, that turned out to have links to the Reverend Sun Myung Moon. Increasingly, questions were raised about his use of poorly paid young reporters to produce his column while he was earning a six-figure income on the speaking circuit. Libby says she and Jack got tired of the criticism and talked about his retiring, maybe teaching at Brigham Young University. But Jack gave up the idea, two of his children say, after experiencing personal religious insights from which he concluded he should continue his work. Says Jack's son Rodney, "He has received guidance from the heavenly father."

Whatever the reason, in the eighties Jack Anderson began putting his fame and credibility behind what he considered to be "good causes." He told his partner, Dale Van Atta, that he was going to be more involved in policy issues than in the past. It was a kind of warning, Van Atta says, because Jack knew his activities would be controversial. Jack asked President Ronald Reagan to support his idea for a Young Astronaut Council to promote interest in math and science in the nation's schools. Jack became its chairman, and Reagan made many public appearances for the group. Jack also became cochairman of Citizens Against Government Waste with corporate executive J. Peter Grace. The group backed controversial proposals for reducing the deficit. Jack also helped his son Randy launch a Hollywood antidrug organization aimed at putting pressure on moviemakers to stop glamorizing drug use. He advised Randy to begin his group in Washington by first winning the backing of key politicians, because that would pressure Hollywood to fall in line. It worked nicely. Nancy Reagan was honored at one of the group's early fund-raisers.

At the column office, they grumbled. The deficit recommendations of Citizens Against Government Waste were off limits, says "Merry-Go-Round" economics reporter Mike Binstein. So was any hint that a tax increase—Reagan's worst bogeyman—might be necessary to fight the federal budget deficit. Jack was plugging the Young Astronauts often, and some staffers believed critical stories on Reagan were increasingly hard to get in print. Other staffers deny this. But Jack's son Randy remembers hearing Van Atta himself once ask, "Who's the sacred cow this week, Jack?" There was much armchair analysis about what had happened to the tough Jack Anderson.

"Jack has a deep need for acceptance," says Joseph Spear, who worked with Jack on the "Merry-Go-Round" for twenty years, but who knows nothing of Jack's childhood. "He was between the devil and the deep blue sea, because there was no way he could write the stories he did and be accepted in this town. It was a fundamental conflict in his personality—the need to be accepted at the same time he did things that kept him from being accepted."

Jack's friend Lee Roderick, a journalist and fellow Mormon, says

Jack was attacked from all sides so often that he got sick of it: Journalists demeaned him, politicians despised him, and even Mormons, with their strain of political conservatism, often criticized him for supposedly tearing down America rather than building it up. "I definitely think he was tired of it," says Roderick, who agrees with those who say Jack was enamored of fame. "Everything about him tells me the guy lives for it, but I think that in recent years what he craves more than fame is acceptance." Says Jack's son Kevin, "He liked Reagan and he liked that Reagan was interested in helping him. It just didn't fit the image I had of Dad from the Watergate days."

Again, Jack sees it differently. "I just decided that at this point in my life, I'd do it, be a good citizen." Drew Pearson had often thrown his public clout behind worthwhile causes, he says, and he decided to do the same.

It is Jack's son Randy who is left to frame his father's heroic role, which he does in the context of his father's religion: The Book of Mormon says that righteous societies can be undermined by evil forces, Randy says, and his father believes that the three greatest threats to America are its eroding educational system, the deficit, and illegal drugs. His dad's three causes—Young Astronauts, Citizens Against Government Waste, and his antidrug work—are all aimed at battling these great threats to the nation. "To put it bluntly, individuals are used to further the work of the Lord, as vessels and instruments," says Randy, who adds that he and his father have talked about this before. "I think he feels there's more to it than just being a journalist." Jack is asked how his recent involvement with these interest groups squares with the remark he made years ago, soon after winning his Pulitzer: "What's wrong," he said then, "is that these reporters adopted the views of the people they're writing about. They've become a part of the Establishment they cover."

Says Jack now, "I believe these are good causes."

Jack is visiting his father for the last time on this trip to Salt Lake City. And given his father's age, Jack can never be sure if it will be the last time he sees him alive, although he believes beyond a doubt that he will see him in Heaven someday. Yet on this Earth, on this trip, it has become clear that the lifelong struggle between the father who tried to humble his son and the son who chafed and rebelled is near its end. The son has won. Strange, how that troubled bond between them set the stage for Jack's remarkable life, as if in trying to restrain his son's ambition Orlando unleashed it a hundredfold.

Jack stands at the door, and his father sits in a chair across the room. Only yesterday Jack saw his father cry for the first time, only the day before he heard him say for the first time that he was proud of his son. Jack is uncomfortable with emotional good-byes, and with a strained cheerfulness, he says, well, gotta go, gotta catch a plane. His father is quiet for a long, awkward moment, until he says, "You're the most generous son a father could have." He then drops his head, covers his eyes, and sobs. Jack hesitates, looks plaintively to his right, shrugs, walks over, and hugs his father, pats him softly on the back. "It's all right," he says quietly. "It's all right." Then Jack falls silent, fighting back his own deep tears.

JUNE 10, 1990

Photograph by Maria Stenzel.

EVAN SHERBROOKE
When Genius Isn't Enough

$\mathcal{E}$van Sherbrooke wants it clear right off: he's no nerd!

Sure, his straight-A average ranks him Number 1 in his senior class of 514 kids at Maryland's Walt Whitman High School. And, yes, he's a National Merit Scholar headed for MIT, captain of Whitman's Latin Bowl team, veteran of the "It's Academic" squad, star of the Whitman math team, and the only kid on this year's county math squad to get the area-of-the-triangle question—1,008 was the answer. But then you have to expect that from a guy with a perfect score on the math SATs. Evan figures he's no nerd because nerdiness to him isn't an IQ score or an A average, but a state of mind— a somber, pretentious, socially stunted state of mind. And Evan, well, he's determined to be about as goofy and naive and hopeful and immature as the next seventeen-year-old. For a boy who counted to nine before he was one year old, achieving this natural teenage condition hasn't been easy.

Evan makes it a point not to talk about school much; that's for nerds. You should hear how they can go on about differential calculus, or an article they read in some math magazine. They drive Evan nuts! He won't read math magazines. He reads *Gross Jokes*, science fiction, and "Peanuts." Even so, Evan can't hide his excitement as he tells how he got 1,008.

It was a question first asked at a New York City math meet in 1955, Evan says, talking faster and faster, standing to assume a schoolmaster's pose, poking the air with a grease pencil, and scribbling numbers and symbols and fractions on the board. Evan is a tall, gangly, fair-faced kid, six feet tall and 125 pounds. The weights he recently began lifting haven't yet taken effect. His long, lean arms and legs and fingers look delicate, which he hates, and his soft, pale skin looks like a child's, which he also hates. It doesn't help with girls. But then girls aren't Evan's only passion. Listen to this mathematical pillow talk, and don't worry about the details. Just remember that it poured out of Evan in a torrent.

"The question was about the medians of a triangle's lengths," he explains of the triangle problem. "The question was, 'What's the area of the triangle?' A very difficult problem." At first, Evan came up blank. So he stared at the page for a while and, boom, it came to him. "I made the lengths of the medians into the sides of a new triangle and found its area. There's a theorem: 'The sum of the squares of the lengths of the medians is equal to 3/4ths the sum of the squares of the sides.' It just connected. You know by geometry that two triangles that have the same angles but have a different length of the sides—if one triangle has a side of length 2 and the corresponding side of the other triangle is length 3—then the ratio of their perimeters will be 2 to 3 and the ratio of their areas will be the square of that, 4 to 9. So because the relationship is sum-of-squares, I figured probably the areas would relate like that too. And it turned out I was right. I still don't know why it worked. It just worked."

When he saw that his answer, 1,008, was correct, it seemed suddenly so clear and simple and pretty to Evan that he couldn't understand why he hadn't seen it immediately. "The intuitive leap," he calls it, explaining the way his mind—and, he supposes, everybody's mind—works, digesting information and making connections ending with, "Ah-ha!"

So is Evan a genius?

"I don't view myself as a genius," he says calmly, mentioning the unimaginable leaps in insight of the nineteenth-century German mathematician Karl Gauss and seventeenth-century French physicist Blaise Pascal, the still unequaled flashes of Leonardo da Vinci and the rare and fresh vision of French impressionist Paul Cézanne. "He could see the world a different way," Evan says of Cézanne, and that is true genius.

Has Evan had flashes that suddenly made him see the world anew? He sits thoughtfully for a long moment, seeming more like a man than a boy. "Yes," he says finally. Coming home from Lynchburg, Virginia, on the bus one night after a Latin Bowl meet he had such a flash of insight. And his life hasn't been the same since. Ah-ha! What a wonderfully mundane place for an intellectual revelation. Evan continues his story, "There was this girl who sat next to me on the bus. . . ." He then goes on to describe his time with a strange girl on a darkened bus after a Latin Bowl meet in Lynchburg. The revelation, if you get the drift, isn't exactly intellectual.

"She fell asleep in my arms," Evan says contemplatively. "That changed my perception of a lot of things."

And suddenly Evan is a boy again.

To be young, smart, and optimistic.

What is it like to be truly gifted, especially now that Evan finally has the playground bullies, pinhead teachers, and macho, single-syllable coaches behind him? He has had the luck of getting through childhood without catching a psychological malady—fear of success or failure, fear of Mommy or Daddy, fear of ambition or anomie, fear of loneliness or freedom or bounded abilities or boundless expectations. He doesn't worry or mull or agonize too much. He takes on faith that the best is yet to come. He is without cynicism.

Like any kid, smart or dumb, Evan's challenge is to sift through the expectations and pressures and demands of friends, family, and adolescence and discover who he is and who he wants to be. Because for all his brains, Evan is still a teenager wrestling with his simultaneous desire to conform and to rebel, to be alike and different at once. His particular anxiety is that others will think him a nerd, an egghead, a pocket-protector type. He has expended a lot of energy proving to himself that this is not the case, just as another boy might be driven to prove that he isn't, say, a dumb jock.

It's a rare, breathless time for everyone, those closing days of high school, but for Evan—a youngster always too smart to be normal and too normal to be happy as anything but normal—it's a time of near exhilaration, of expanding confidence and outright longing for what he imagines is to come at college: "Independence, sheer, unadulterated independence." It makes you smile to think of all the things Evan Sherbrooke is about to learn, about himself and life and others. In so many ways, a boy such as Evan is a national treasure, a great hope for his generation. He's a child with brains and ambition, tempered by charm, humor, and decency.

But just how did Evan get to be Number 1 at Whitman, a school in the heart of the National Institutes of Health brain-trust territory, where whiz kids abound? What secrets did his folks employ? Hypnosis? Silva Mind Control? Infant flash cards?

"Well," says Evan's mother, Rosalie, "it just happened."

Evan is deeply into "senior slump" these days, as are most seniors. Grades were sent off to colleges last semester, and kids have already gotten the good or the bad news. Senior slump is so much a high-school tradition that when the Whitman principal gets on the intercom, Evan, sitting in first-period physics in his University of Michigan sweatshirt, blue jeans, and Docksides, whispers, "I know what he's gonna say: '*Get out of that senior slump!*'" Sure enough, he does.

Says Evan, chuckling, "He says it every spring."

The physics class is filled with smart kids, but Evan stands out. "He's one of Whitman's intellectual giants," says a female classmate with awe. These kids have shared advanced classes together for years, and a relaxed atmosphere prevails. When a boy points out that a graph the teacher put on the board is wrong, the teacher checks it, says thank you, and fixes the graph. Evan doesn't open his notebook. He whispers conspiratorially, giving details of his classmates' personality quirks, pointing out the kids who study long hours, those who can breeze through, those who hate to admit when they're wrong.

Teenagers always put a little self-conscious spin on their images, and Evan's spin is cool and detached. He walks the hallways with the hint of a saunter, his long arms hanging loosely, indifferently. He's cool; studied, but cool. In physics, Evan seems not to be paying attention. But when a question draws silence, he looks up, gives the answer, and returns to gossip. Evan cultivates such effortlessness; only nerds try too hard. The bad news for parents scheming to create genius and an Ivy League diploma for their children is that school has always come easily to Evan. He doesn't study every night, never did. He procrastinates, crams for tests, does the least it takes to get an A. For that, he rarely breaks a sweat.

The boy was doing three-digit multiplication in first grade. His dad is a statistics consultant with a Ph.D. from UCLA. His mother is a librarian with a master's degree in library science. Evan is no up-by-the-bootstraps kid. He had the genes—along with the usual adornments of affluence and education: books around the house, fast and freewheeling debate. It was the kind of house where the teddy bear wore a T-shirt imprinted with James Maxwell's equations of electromagnetic theory. Every night, Evan's father, Craig, read a bedtime story to Evan and his older brother, Andrew. They eventually went through three copies of *Goodnight Moon*. The whole family competed at name-the-capitals and spelling games, and Evan's father, a soft-spoken man with a sharp competitive edge beneath the calm, didn't let the boys win until they could win fair and square.

Evan's mother, a blue-collar girl who grew up worshiping education, was forever running to the unabridged dictionary to check some disputed word, doing crossword puzzles, correcting the grammar in TV commercials—not to mention her kids' grammar. When it became clear that Evan and Andrew could earn A's easily, she came to demand them. "I do get a picture of her being a rather pushy parent," Evan says. "But you get to the point where you push yourself."

In the Sherbrooke house, a nice but not extravagant house in Washington's elite suburb of Potomac, Maryland, knowledge wasn't seen as an avenue to big jobs or incomes. The Potomac neighbors with their gaudy mansions and Mercedes-Benzes were skewered mercilessly by Evan's mom. Earning too much money was suspect. "Do they have a Nobel Prize for arbitrage?" she asks, laughing. Ideas were tossed around casually, politics debated, movies analyzed, all as recreation. Evan's folks valued learning, and that value passed seamlessly.

There were no Gifted and Talented classes at Potomac Elementary when Evan was a boy, and he was lumped with everybody. His folks never had him tested, and even today Evan has no idea what his IQ is. It wasn't until first grade that Evan's folks even realized that Evan and Andrew were awfully smart. School was a breeze. For years, Evan's parents believed Andrew, a year older than Evan, was the bright one. Andrew was gregarious, outwardly precocious; Evan was reserved, quietly determined. The Sherbrookes even worried that Evan would come to feel inferior. Andrew, a National Merit Scholarship finalist, is today a student at the University of Michigan. For a long time, Evan felt a keen competition with Andrew. Then Evan started getting better grades in high school, and even ended up in the same math classes with his older brother.

"I didn't feel competition anymore," says Evan.

In Potomac, plenty of kids excelled in elementary school, and Evan never felt out of place then. He was small and unathletic, and his ineptness on the playground sometimes ended in frustrated crying jags. But other than that quirk, several of Evan's teachers—all of whom recall him as one of the best students they ever taught—remember him as an unusually mature boy with a clever, sophisticated humor and imagination. He'd tell the most elaborate tales of space travel with aliens, while dumbfounded classmates looked on blankly. One teacher remembers telling Evan's class that if they finished an assignment early, they could go home at 2:45 P.M.—otherwise they'd have to stay till quarter-to-three. While the other kids hurriedly did the work, Evan sat smiling and winking. Again and again, teachers were struck by his ironic, almost adult humor. One teacher remembers telling Evan's class she'd just become a grandmother.

"I don't know whether you can be a grandmother," Evan said soberly.

"But why?" she asked.

"Grandmothers are angels," he said, flashing a wry smile.

Even in grade school, some kids were shy and bookish, others gregarious and physical. But Evan seemed to fit neither mold. He was, it is said repeatedly, "a nice boy," well-liked but not a full-fledged member of any one gang. "He wasn't ostracized, but kids didn't play with him a lot," recalls Evan's second-grade teacher, Jerry Perlet. "He was sort of a misfit, because kids couldn't understand what he was talking about." At home, Evan was meticulous and methodical. A Lego building-blocks freak, he'd construct elaborate castles. "Evan isn't a natural at much of anything," says his father, "but he's a plugger. He thinks he can do it and eventually he does."

On weekends, Evan's dad was Evan's live-in playmate. "My father's good at a lot of things," Evan says proudly, "and really good at some." They were always doing something—sailing, basketball, baseball, football, tennis, skiing, building bookshelves or model boats. Sitting around just thinking great thoughts all day wasn't exactly discouraged in the Sherbrooke home, it simply wasn't a choice. There were too many other things to do. "As far back as I can remember," Evan says, "if somebody needed help or wanted to copy something, they would come to me. I don't think there was a time I realized, 'Hey, I'm smart.' It's just something you live with, like missing an eye. You live with it. But I don't think it ever occurred to anybody, 'What a nerd!' I don't think that came across until sixth grade. In sixth grade you began to get the Potomac Princesses."

Evan is still uneasy talking about junior high. He has this way of looking away as he thinks, and he does this, nudges up his wire-rimmed glasses, shakes his head, sighs, and acts as if the subject will go away if he doesn't speak. But then he pushes ahead. "I'll confess," he says finally. "In seventh grade, I fell into the nerds." There, he has said it. Talk to adults who were nerds in school, people who are now respected in their careers, and you'll find it was often years, sometimes decades, before they could honestly talk about their old nerdiness with humor and distance. Evan isn't a reflective kid, but nerdiness he has analyzed to bits. He's a philosopher of nerdiness.

"You know, nerds played chess and they were smart and they had no social life," he says, his words sharp and quick, his tone mocking. "They would sit and play Dungeons & Dragons for a day. That was the salient characteristic. Very serious and studious. They knew they were intelligent and destined for great things and that their fathers had doctorates."

Evan is on a roll, his voice swinging from a William F. Buckley archness to a wild, high-pitched kind of exclamation. Through it all, picture a comedic style that runs more toward understatement than exaggeration, and dramatic pauses accented with a raised brow, a thin, ironic smile, and a bony right hand combing deliberately through thick black hair.

"They were intimidated physically," he continues, his words picking up steam. "They would sooner die than get in a conflict with anybody. Gym is the worst possible time of day. Yet they're always nervous about tests. No matter if they know they're going to do really well, they'll study until the book falls apart. The nerdball is so socially devoid it's like he was raised at IBM. He's a bright kid, but he has no social faculties, no social niceties. I see it as social infancy, complete infancy."

Evan doesn't hide his disgust. He can't. He knows his fascination with nerdiness says something about him, that his opinions are uncharitable, that being unpopular, being different, is painful for anyone, nerd or not, smart or dumb. But even when he tries to empathize, he can't. "I guess I developed an aversion to that kind of character because of the influence it had in my early life," he says. "It never gives you a good feeling when people label you as a geek or a nerd or a doof."

Evan, of course, had his own troubles with nerdiness. In junior high, bigger boys picked on him, especially in gym. There were three thugs who'd swipe his sneakers and toss them around almost daily. Evan got mad and pushed one against a locker, which only upped the ante. It got so bad that his mom—to Evan's eternal mortification—intervened with a principal. At times like that, Evan would find himself thinking: "Okay, he's on top now, but twenty years from now who's gonna have the Ph.D.?" Today, he says, "It is a stupid, unreasonable sentiment you turn to when you don't have anything else."

Young Evan also had a grating habit: He corrected people. His mother and his brother saved him from this great nerd pitfall, Evan says, by telling him how he looked to others: "Like an obnoxious little twerp." So Evan struggled to keep his knowledge—and his piercing wit—to himself. "It was like turning your brain off for the day," he says. At first, it pained him. He couldn't stand mistakes. And besides, he missed being Evan the Answer Man. But over time he learned it was true: Nobody likes a know-it-all. "Appearances matter," he says.

Today, classmates and teachers call Evan self-effacing and unpretentious. Oh, an old girlfriend or a faint-praise acquaintance or two say his modesty is phony: Scratch the finish and he's an "intellectual snob," as Evan jokingly calls himself. Even his mother laughs about Evan's struggle with "hubris" and worries that he can sometimes be arrogant. When Evan talks privately, he is short-tempered with stupidity. But mostly, he keeps it to himself. He has, like a Starman living among us, learned to fit into the world. He has even come to enjoy it: Gym—not French, physics, chemistry, or Latin—is now his favorite class.

For whatever reasons—because his mother is outgoing, friendly, and funny or because his father is droll and accomplished and athletic—Evan couldn't bear thinking that people saw him as a nerd. And in eighth grade when Evan made friends with James Mendelsohn—a smart, athletic, popular boy who called the nerds Evan's "little friends"—Evan bolted from the nerd gang. "You could say James was like an eighth-grade Oral Roberts," says Evan, his humor returning. "James wasn't nerdy." By high school, Evan had abandoned his disheveled appearance for a casual preppy look—pullover sweaters, oxford button-downs, jeans, and deck shoes. He decided not to buy a math team jacket, and he put away his T-shirt imprinted with Maxwell's equations of electromagnetic theory.

This semester, Evan may get the only C he has ever gotten in high school. He almost wants the damned C. He has a class that he hates— hates with the passion of a brash young artist who has outgrown his mentor. The class, Evan says, is a waste of his time. Not because it's too hard, but because it's too easy. Imagine that from your high school days. For Evan, it has come down to answering mindless questions for an A in a class he despises—for the sake of keeping his golden A average—or getting a B or a C in solitary, symbolic protest. In an odd way, that C also would prove to Evan that all nerdiness is finally wrung out of him: Because no nerd would sacrifice a 4.0 on principle, not to save his life. It would be Evan's way of announcing, "This is petty crap," he says. "That would make me feel proud. I'd be ticked off at the C, but not at myself."

Naturally, Evan isn't angry only at this class, but at high school itself. It's the spring of senior year, time to get the hell out of high school. The place is for kids. You bring sick notes from your mommy. They mark you tardy. You take classes whether or not you learn anything. "You're a slave to stupid questions and trivialities," Evan says. Finally, he can see an end to this torture, which somehow didn't seem so bad just last fall. In his mind's eye he sees another place—*college, oh college!*

"In college, you set up your own schedule," Evan says quickly, as if he's spent some time thinking about this. "You don't have to put up with the crap you have to put up with in high school. The sort of closed-mindedness and imprisonment. In college, you're supposed to attend classes but they don't check up on you. Let's say there's a paper due and you have a French class that will last two hours. You just don't go. It's more informal. You just sort of walk around your dorm and if somebody's free, you just go out and play Frisbee or go down to the union or whatever. You don't say a week in advance, 'All right, on Friday night at 7 o'clock, let's do this.' You just sort of walk by and say, 'Hey, anybody wanta come along?' Whitman is hardly a prison in the eyes of most people. It is in mine because I've been here four years. And I don't want to be here much longer."

Gym class has become a nerd's revenge for Evan. He has grown more than a foot in the last few years, and when he went up and spiked the volleyball for the first time this semester, he had another of those profound teenage revelations: His hands were above the net. "I'd never been above the net before," he says. "When I was in ninth grade I was about four feet tall." By the time Evan's feet touched the floor that day, he realized why the playground bullies had enjoyed pushing people around. To be in control physically felt good. He liked it. By the time he hit the floor, Evan also knew exactly what this revelation foreboded for the freshmen across the net, those poor kids so short their feet still don't touch the ground. "It was like, *ah-ha!*" Evan says theatrically. "I looked at this poor little freshman and said, 'Reckoning time has come!'"

Better put, Evan's time had come. He'd sensed it for a while actually. He'd noticed, for instance, that when he walked down the hallway at six feet tall he could see over everybody's heads. He liked the way that made him feel. So he went to his older brother's room and dug out his chin-up bar. Then he moved on to barbells and fist pulls. To be honest, Evan's arms are like spaghetti and he's a million bench presses from Arnold Schwarzenegger. The point is he's so determined to be more than smart. His thoughts on why are once again sublime and juvenile.

"I think I've had enough of the academic stuff," he says, not enough of the physical. "I was so small and not really athletic. I'm glad I got taller. I mean, there are short people who've done very well, look at Napoleon or Alexander the Great. I guess I wouldn't have minded if I were short and strong. It's just that I wasn't. Being tall is an illusory feeling of being more in control, just the feeling that you can count on yourself. Suppose you're walking down the street and this guy comes running out to you and says, 'We need a sixth for our football team.' And so you play a lineman. Just ready for anything."

That has become Evan's motto: just ready for anything. When he looks ahead to MIT, he thinks less of academics and more of getting on a weight-lifting regimen, meeting girls, and joining a volleyball team and a juggling troupe (juggling is his hobby). He'd like to improve his snow skiing too.

"My father taught me there is more to life than being smart," says Evan, who just doesn't worry much about his intelligence anymore. Like an Olympic athlete, he sees his future achievements hinging not on God's gifts, but on concentration, dedication, and motivation. He knows he's got the stuff, unless he loses his drive. "I do think less about the mental identity and more about the social identity," he says. "I take the mental identity for granted."

Evan has had the fleeting fantasy of graduating as MIT's valedictorian, but he figures that's a pipe dream. He knows also that being Number 1 again might not be worth the effort. "It's not a question of intelligence," he says. "There are other things to do with your life. As much as I'd like to graduate summa cum laude. I think that you've got to let your social status graduate summa cum laude also."

Discreetly, Evan then slips into humor and unbridled fantasy. "The ideal situation would be this: I meet this girl at college. She's very good-looking and she's on the volleyball team and we go off together on a ski trip, fall madly in love. And she doesn't oppose premarital sex. That'd be a pretty good situation." He hopes to earn $1 million at age twenty-five, another $1 million at age twenty-six, and $5 million at age twenty-seven, and then retire with a harem. "What do I want to accomplish?" he asks, deadpan. "I'd like to win the Nobel Prize, two or three, one in physics, one in peace, and, oh, what the hell, one in medicine—no, chemistry, I think chemistry. It would be nice to win the Nobel Prize, that'd be cool. I'd get to meet the King of Sweden. Oh, God, what would I like to do? I'd like to have a family, a wife who doesn't talk back and who is outrageously beautiful, probably a brunette. I always seem to be attracted to brunettes."

Evan is asked, "What is success to you?"

"Achieving at what I try," he says, not missing a beat. "I don't know how to say it any better. I'd like to get money doing something I like, that'd be success. I'd like to win the 'It's Academic' tournament this year. We came close last year but we didn't win. I'd like to win the national Latin Bowl, which would be almost impossible. We came in sixth last year.

"I don't know, success is just doing whatever I try."

Friday night pool games in Evan's basement are a tradition, at least since he and his friends skipped school a while back to shoot pool all day. It's a kind of overachievers clubhouse. The guys are all going to good colleges—MIT, Yale, Columbia, Williams, the University of Virginia. They're smart, hardworking kids with stratospheric SAT scores. They're all bored weightless with high school. And just like guys praying to get into a junior college somewhere, they spend much of their time worrying, as Evan says, about doing "strange things to girls' bodies." To Evan's great pride, these guys aren't nerds. None of them wears a backpack stuffed with the collected works of Reinhold Niebuhr, not one would miss a date with a girl to take his Dungeons & Dragons character to Level 5, not one.

Jon Schwarz is a sardonic wit who can keep a roomful of people in stitches. He's the lead in Whitman's spring play, and the big news is that he gets to kiss Rebecca, beautiful Rebecca, onstage. Steve O'Keefe plays basketball and pole-vaults and is an artist with a portfolio. Evan calls him either "the artist-athlete" or "the dumb jock," depending on his humor. Rob Weisberg writes for the Whitman newspaper and is the resident boy Republican. He's a talker with enough teen-angst jokes to fill a Woody Allen movie. And James, the eighth-grade Oral Roberts, well, Evan says James is just the "archetypal yuppie junior exec." "The kind of people you don't meet every day," Evan says, beaming.

Evan does stand out, but not for his brains. His buddies have all started to shave and somehow look older, more worldly, as if they'd already been living in a dorm for a year or two. If Evan were wearing the bulky sweaters he wears to make himself look huskier, it might not be so noticeable, but tonight he wears only a tight, white T-shirt that gives his torso the lean, mean look of a two-by-twelve standing vertically. He looks so young. Except for James, these friends are fairly new to Evan, a finishing touch on his campaign to make himself normal. Judging from the evening, Evan has finally achieved normal male teenage status. "Because I have friends," Evan says, "I don't feel like an outsider anymore." There's no talk of Dungeons & Dragons or math magazines. No, it's red-blooded American stuff, as the guys belt back bottles of chocolate Yoo-hoo and tell Evan Sherbrooke stories.

"Has Evan told you about his weird sexual perversions yet?" asks Jon.

"The Holton-Arms team is in love with me," says Evan extravagantly, referring to the "It's Academic" team from a nearby all-girls prep school.

"They love him because he's so smart and unpretentious," says Steve.

"Yes, that's how I've always thought of Evan," says Jon. "That old Sherbrooke magic. It's some sort of sexual energy."

"Evan, you are scum!" says James, somewhat tangentially.

"It's been a fantastic day," says Rob, also tangentially.

"Sexually *and* scholastically?" asks Evan, clarifying.

"Not yet, but . . . ," says Rob.

"Rob's a Republican," says Evan.

"Evan's a knee-jerk liberal," says Rob.

"It's true," confesses Evan dramatically, "I am a knee-jerker—or a knee-biter." There is a burst of wheezing laughter all around.

"Evan, should I start with Leslie, move on to Bonnie, and conclude with Charlotte?" asks James.

"Let's start with the modern bondage technique," says Rob, again tangentially.

"And love was in the air," says Evan, wistfully.

"Evan asked Leslie to go steady in eighth grade," says James.

"And she said, 'Yes, *oh, yes,*'" says Evan.

"I don't recall her saying that," says James. "I just recall her stalling for three or four days."

"She's too short anyway," says Evan.

"What about your Latin lover off Exit 1?" asks James.

"Exit 5!" roars Evan. "Can't you get anything right?!"

What to say. It goes on like this for hours. And to Evan—now and probably thirty years from now—there has never been a funnier bunch of guys.

Evan intends to complete his transformation to regular guy at MIT, which is some kind of contradiction on its face. The place is the epitome of the nerd school, and Evan knows it. He was accepted at Harvard and thought seriously about going there. He knew that at Harvard he'd get a more rounded education—and that Harvard would have been his ultimate chance to bolt from the nerd gang once and for all. But he chose MIT. It has more math courses, and Evan can still take the Latin and classics courses he wants at Harvard through a special cooperative program. Besides, he's heard that the intramural sports are less competitive at MIT, and he figures he'd have a better chance of playing there. But more important, Evan had a not-so-adolescent insight: He realized that, like it or not, he's an MIT kind of guy. Truth is, Evan now likes himself pretty much the way he is.

So many parents have tried, with no luck, to create in their children the "intuitive leaps" that come so easily to Evan. In him, the gift seems like a miracle, special and rare and wonderful. But Evan insists he can't allow himself to think that way. It sets him apart, makes him different, when he wants to be the same. Evan has seen too many smart kids get too wrapped up in their own intelligence. "They get nerdized," he says, and he then uses this analogy to explain why he refuses to ponder and marvel at his own intelligence: "I figure if my legs and arms operate, that's fine, I'll leave them that way. Why should I dissect them?" He says Wolfgang Amadeus Mozart was compelled to amazingly childish behavior because he couldn't handle his genius, and Vincent van Gogh was driven insane. Finding balance in your life—between work and play, seriousness and silliness, mind and body—isn't just for fun, Evan says, it's a healthy way to live. It's hard to believe this is the same kid who was shooting pool in the basement a while ago. He sounds so wise.

He is asked, "But are you trying to be the person you want to be or the person you believe *others* want you to be?"

"I would say it's a lot of both," Evan says. "Definitely, I want to fit in. It's a natural human feeling. But I don't want to be something I'm not."

"How do you tell the difference?"

"It's hard. I get feedback from myself and feedback from others, but I have a hard time telling. Say a kid becomes a punk, but it isn't really him. That's normal. It's hard to distinguish between your own personal drives and the drives induced in you by others. I'll find my niche. I don't worry about it."

"But if you want to be in the math club, if you plain enjoy it, what the hell do you care what anybody thinks about it?"

"I don't really enjoy it," Evan says bluntly. "I like it when I solve something, but it's the activity I enjoy. I don't like it on the social level."

"No more math club at MIT?"

"No more math club. Oh, boy, I gotta get outta that."

"Looking back, would you be willing to give up some intelligence to have a better social life and greater athletic ability?"

"How much?" Evan asks, quickly moving to costs and benefits.

"B's instead of A's. It means you wouldn't go to MIT. Somebody else in your class would be Evan Sherbrooke. Somebody else would be the one everybody looks up to and says, 'Oh, my God, he's the smartest kid at Whitman.' And you'd be more popular, have more girls, be more athletic. Would you like to have that, or keep what you've got?"

"How can I answer that question?" Evan says. "Obviously, I want to be popular and rich and wonderful and have females thrusting their thighs at me. For high-school happiness you have to go with that, but not in the long run."

"So you'd go with intelligence?"

"I guess. When the chips are down."

MAY 17, 1987

Washington Post photograph.

JESSE JACKSON
All the World's a Stage

*T*he large man with the walkie-talkie smiles broadly but keeps shifting nervously from side to side like a teenage boy at his first dance class. He leans into his walkie-talkie and listens intently, never compromising the smile. Look, pal, he's probably being told, the plane is *loaded*, a jumbo jet 350 passengers strong, loaded and waiting for one guy.

So hustle it up!

Still smiling, the large man from the airline glances toward the problem at hand: Jesse Louis Jackson, relaxed and laughing and chatting on the phone in the British Airways VIP lounge in Boston. You can bet that at the other end of that walkie-talkie, nobody's smiling. More likely, they're saying, *This ain't a private bird, Harold!* or *Howard*, or whatever the big, smiling man's name is. *Who the hell does this guy think he is? The president?* Even here at the lounge, the people with Jackson are milling about, uncomfortable with his insouciance. Although there's the strongest sense Jackson knows exactly what he's doing, his entourage still hangs at the door, coats on, bags in hand, revealing the anxieties of mortal men—this baby's gonna leave without us, and it's not right to keep 350 people waiting, is it?

"Let's go, Reverend."

"Come on, Jesse."

Jesse comes on, all right, with the cool saunter of a man on parade. The jeans, the blue work shirt, the leather vest, all fitting a lot snugger in the wrong places than they did twenty years ago, when Jackson was just emerging as the sexy yet moralistic, threatening yet honey-tongued Baptist preacher-cum-rock-star of a new, more strident civil rights era. It was a time perfectly in tune with Jackson's psyche, a righteous, angry time that Jackson believes he could feel pumping through his veins. It also was a long time ago.

Quickly now, the man with the walkie-talkie tries to lead the way, down the airport hallway, past the escalators, the bar, the restaurant. He could've taken his time. Because every thirty or forty feet he must stop and wait for Jackson, who leisurely signs an autograph, kisses a woman, waves. All the while, Mr. Walkie-Talkie, a white man, keeps smiling. Now that's poetic justice.

"Don't the airlines ever leave him behind?" I ask.

"Not often," replies a Jackson aide. "They're learning."

Jesse Jackson has a job like no other job in America. He's got no boss; he couldn't take that. He's got no board of directors or stockholders fretting over return on equity. The voters, the usual path to leadership in America, can't turn him out or shut him up, either, because Jesse hasn't been elected to anything. Every year he gives scores of speeches, often travels seven days a week, works eighteen hours a day. But if you ask, "Who died and left Jesse boss?" the answer is nobody. Jesse appointed Jesse, and Jesse accepted. Black America confirmed him by acclamation.

Now just past forty-five, Jackson feels very good about himself. Not smug, but certainly self-satisfied. Jesse Jackson: President of Black America. It is a title without portfolio, or salary, or membership in the congressional health club. But it fits Jackson like a tailored suit, because his claim to leadership has always been unofficial, tenuously empowered by the smoke and mirrors of TV and radio and ink. Yet along with Ronald Reagan and the pope, he is among the most respected men in the world, yes, the world! Jackson has spent a lifetime ignoring bitter, angry people who twisted their faces and told him, even as a boy, that he was a prideful, self-deluded phony. Where are they now? Jesse Jackson is President of Black America. Remember that a horde of heavyweight blacks— mayors, congressmen, state legislators—outright opposed Jackson's run for the presidency in 1984. More than a few saw him as an opportunist, a demagogue, a selfish man. So who knows their names? Jesse Jackson is President of Black America. Through a fog of critics, Jackson has always seen his own beam shining, rather brightly. Call it egomania, but the naysayers aren't flying all over the world. They aren't jawing with Mike Wallace on "60 Minutes," or pushing the NFL to hire its first black head coach, or squeezing Revlon to stop wrestling the black cosmetics market away from blacks. And bet on this: When the naysayers walk through the slums of black America, if they do, people don't weep and sing and reach out to touch their garments. The naysayers aren't President of Black America. Jesse Jackson is.

Finally settled into his wide, reclining, first-class seat on British Airways flight 214, Jackson takes off his shoes and slips on the soft, little slippers they give front-of-the-bus flyers. He's on his way to

Mozambique, Africa, a tiny, desperately poor Marxist nation bordering white-ruled South Africa, where Mozambique's president, Samora Machel, has just died in a plane crash. As Jackson is self-appointed to so many things, he's also black America's self-appointed envoy to the black-ruled African states. He leans back in his seat, nibbles at his salmon, takes no dessert, passes on small talk, and begins.

Whites, like you, can understand blacks, but only sensitive whites. . . . Reagan's politics are racist. . . . They said a black couldn't run for president, but I showed 'em. . . . Oh, it's hard for a black man to win respect. . . . But watch out Democrats, we ain't in nobody's pocket. . . . America's on the wrong side of history in South Africa. . . . Morality is the greatest weapon, greater than missiles. . . . The Bible's prophet Nathan, he knew that; Christ and Gandhi and Martin Luther King, they knew it. . . . Yes, speaking metaphorically, I am in the tradition of the prophets.

It's hard, I discover, to carry on a conversation with Jackson—as in he says this, I say that. He talks, I listen—and hear the familiar, lilting, blues-man cadence, the accent on the wrong syllable of words he wants you to recall, the lyrical riffs of phrase. That's the preacher in him. Then, speaking in headlines, his voice changes to flag the quotability of a coming remark. That's the politician. What is most striking about Jackson is his weariness. His eyes are aflame in dark sockets, and he rubs them constantly. It doesn't help that he has grown a bit meaty, with skin that draws over those magnificent cheekbones more loosely than it once did. But he's still handsome and imperial, carrying his head so far back over his shoulders that it seems to be forever catching up with his body, staring at you from the corner of those laser eyes in a way that manages to look cagey and sincere at once.

I'm hardly the first to notice, but Jackson seems always to be "on," always aiming to draw out some response or emotion in you, setting you up, playing off your strengths and weaknesses and ambitions, maneuvering for even small advantage. If there is a Big Question about Jackson, this must be it: Is he sincere? Or tricky? Does he believe his beautiful, compassionate song? Is he a savior, or an operator? No amount of time with Jackson seems to relieve the tension.

After only a few sitdown talks, when I have no strong sense of who he is or isn't, Jackson announces that I am a deeply spiritual person. I laugh and tell him that religion is not my best side; I'm something of an agnostic. No, Jackson says theatrically, not religiously spiritual, but still spiritual, filled with a special empathy found in people only rarely, especially white people. That, he says, is true spirituality.

"I say it," Jackson says, "only because it's true."

Take my word for it, I'm not immune to flattery. But this bit of buttering would be too obvious for even the most vain person to take seriously. Except for one thing: Jackson has inexplicably touched a piece of my identity that I don't believe I've ever talked about with anyone, a self-perception I consciously hide with a jocular cynicism, but which, nonetheless, is an important part of me. I am impressed, and intrigued. Jesse is working me perfectly.

We hit London's Heathrow Airport in the A.M., and at the gate I stand by awkwardly while a British guard searches the briefcases of Jackson and his aide, Kgosie Matthews, a black South African–born man of twenty-nine whose grandfather was a founder of the African National Congress, the black independence organization fighting apartheid in South Africa. Matthews, an intense, volatile man who lived in England much of his life, looks like he is about to explode in anger. Jackson says nothing, and I wonder if he's noticed. After several minutes of walking silently toward the Paris gate, I ask, "Did you notice how they checked your bags, but not mine?"

"Don't ask me," Jackson says, not turning his head. "Don't make me tell you."

Jackson need not explain. He has already told the story of how he was at a glitzy New York hotel, waiting at the elevator just after a meeting with Zimbabwe's prime minister Robert Mugabe, just before he was heading out for dinner at Bill Cosby's house. Jackson was waiting there, undoubtedly in his handsome suit with the gold collar stickpin under the silk tie with the matching handkerchief in the coat pocket, looking, you just know, about as elegant and successful as a man can look, when a finely dressed elderly white woman walked up and said, "I couldn't have made it downstairs without you," and pressed a dollar in his hand. Jackson was confused for an instant, until he realized she had mistaken him for her bellman. The woman's middle-aged daughter was mortified, but Jackson shrugged it off.

"So did you keep it?" I ask.

"Keep what?" Jackson answers.

"The dollar."

"Oh, yeah!"

The story explains a lot about why Jackson's politics, despite his efforts to broaden his base, remain rooted in race. Jackson's Rainbow Coalition aims to bring together America's outcasts—poor and blue-collar whites and blacks, women, farmers, Hispanics, anti-nukers and America's more left-leaning liberals, people at the political and economic fringes—and turn them into a political force. In an effort to be more than the voice of American blacks, Jackson has made recent visits to Japan and Korea, as well as Africa. He has made the national farm crisis one of his major issues, and he talks frequently about how America's slide from world economic superiority hurts blacks *and* whites in America.

Hard-nosed politicos say the Rainbow exists mostly in Jackson's mind. But what's still important is that Jackson unifies his coalition symbolically by talking about something politicians like to forget: social class. That America is divided into layers of opportunity not only by race but also by social class is one American bogeyman usually kept in the closet by politicians. Jackson's zeal for confronting the issue has won him considerable interest among stolid white liberals, the crowd, say, over at the *Nation* magazine. But the more Jackson talks, the clearer it is that the country's black outcasts are, in his scheme, still more equal than other outcasts. This should come as no surprise, since his career is based on obvious race politics and 88 percent of black Democratic primary voters went for him in 1984.

Blacks have not only social class to overcome, Jackson says, but also racial caste. "I'm the guy the woman put a dollar in his hand," he says. Jackson scoffs at the idea that rich blacks in America are any different than poor blacks. "If you don't see, it ain't because it's not there to see," Jackson says of the racism facing even the most successful blacks. "You're just blind. Keep on walkin'. You'll walk into a post. It's just a matter of time."

In Mozambique, the dry season has come, but still it rains for the funeral of President Machel, and on the street, among the hundreds of thousands who gather to mourn him, they are saying that the sky is crying. President Reagan's daughter Maureen is the official American mourner, but Jackson has easily upstaged her. She has arrived the day of the funeral and will leave tonight. He came the day before and walked into the gilded ballroom where Machel's family was in the final moments of mourning before the funeral. As Jackson entered, Machel's wife stood. Jackson visited the home of Machel's bereaved family and, after the funeral, will meet privately with black African leaders. He is treated like an ambassador, and he loves it. Today, the faces of the children lining the narrow road to President Machel's tomb run a dozen rows deep, in eerie, living resemblance to the native African sculptures of faces intertwined like vines in a thicket. Though many of the children are without jackets or shoes, one boy holds a catcher's mitt. Is he some American's mail-order child? I wonder. A long line of women dances slowly through the throng, endlessly repeating a hypnotic Swahili chant, which translates: "*Samora, he takes Mozambique. Samora, he takes Mozambique.*" Some people are wailing, others are proclaiming.

It is a powerfully moving moment and even Jackson—who has methodically tracked down the world press to give interviews, demanded that his car be included in the official procession to the tomb, placed himself at the front of the attending dignitaries—is quiet. As he leaves the tomb and walks through the crowd, through the chants and the wailing and the proclaiming, heads turn, and you can hear the murmurs of *"Jesse Jackson, Jesse Jackson."* Even in Africa, he is a star. Under Portuguese colonial rule, which ended only a decade ago, these people couldn't drive cars, work as maids, even shine shoes. When the Portuguese left after 470 years, fewer than 300 native Mozambicans had college degrees. So you'd be dead or dumb not to feel at this instant some sense of why African and American blacks believe they share a kinship of suffering foreign to whites.

"It's like you're talking to a white man who thinks everything is fine," Jackson says. "And the black man is thinking, 'Can't you see my pain?'" This is why American blacks identify with the Third World, Jackson says; their basic experience of oppression is the same. And it is, he says, a superior experience. "The privileged haven't any story," he says. Black African leaders were imprisoned, tortured, lived in the bush. Black Americans don't care if these nations are called marxist or capitalist, he says, because blacks—African and American—have sought only what every man seeks, freedom.

"That's my mental model for leadership—sacrificial, authentic to the bone," Jackson says of the Africans. "When you think about the role of Political Action Committees and TV in American political leadership and who has the most money and whoever can take the most Hollywoodish picture, over a period of time that will produce a quality of leader that would have absolutely nothin' on his mind, nothin' to say, and nowhere to go. That hangs heavy on my heart."

"But you're so good at these things," I say. "I mean, they helped you."

There is a tinge of anger in Jackson's voice. "What helped me was when the roll was called for my generation to sit in, I sat in. When my generation went to jail, I went to jail. I didn't emerge in 1984. From the time I was a teenager, man, I have never stopped."

We quit walking and stand in the crowd, waiting for a car to take us away. It has gotten cold and windy. Jesse Jackson starts to cry. I can't help wonder: Are these tears real, or for me?

Heading home, the chartered jet carries nine passengers, eight blacks and me, along with two white European stewardesses, gracious and charming. As I walk through the galley alone, a stewardess smiles conspiratorially and whispers, "You're the wrong color for this lot."

The other laughs quietly, and adds, "You'd better stick with us."

When I tell Jackson, he asks, "You surprised?"

You can't help but chuckle at the title they've given Jesse Jackson's speech at the fortieth anniversary lecture of the Harvard Law School Forum: "Moral Choices for an Amoral World." It carries the breadth of *War and Peace*, the depth of Henry Kissinger, and the weight of heavy pancakes, though you have to expect that kind of thing from the hallowed-halls crowd. Still, Jesse's not laughing. "I understand it's a pretty big deal," he says with studied casualness. No, Jesse's not laughing. He's too busy savoring.

Jackson has come a long way, and he knows it, often thinks about it. And it's times like this, when he's getting ready to address 500 of America's future elite, that his achievement is so clear. He used to sit up on those stages during the Democratic primaries, sit with Walter Mondale, Gary Hart, John Glenn, Ernest Hollings, and the rest, and think about what it had taken for each of them to get there, how he'd climbed farther, against greater odds. He believes these men were put on edge by this fact. How could they not be? he reasoned. Here they were, all on that same stage, at the same time—and Jackson younger than any of them! Jesse'd look at Hollings and think about how when Jesse was in college leading sit-ins at whites-only theaters and restaurants, old Hollings was the South Carolina governor defending that abomination. We won, Jesse'd think. We won.

But Jackson himself is a little on edge tonight. At a small, private dinner with a handful of Harvard Law students before his formal speech, Jackson doesn't eat his exotic seafood dish. It turns out he rarely eats the chichi entrees he's offered on these kinds of occasions. "He always says he's not hungry," says a Jackson aide, laughing. Jesse prefers Colonel Sanders biscuits, fried fish, eggs, and grits. As the students eat their chichi entrees, Jackson casually asks if anyone recalls where Ronald Reagan kicked off his 1984 campaign.

A long silence.

"Philadelphia, Mississippi," Jackson finally says. "What is the historical significance of Philadelphia, Mississippi?" Nobody has a clue, though there's a lot of mumbling and fumbling of chairs to cover this up. After dragging out the embarrassment, Jackson explains that it was in dusty, backwater Philadelphia, Mississippi, in 1964, that three civil rights workers were slain by a gang of bigots that included a county deputy. The killings became a symbolic turning point in the civil rights struggle. Reagan's Philadelphia speech, by the way, was about states' rights—once a catchall defense of segregation. "So if the brightest of you don't uncover these signals, who will?" Jackson asks.

Silence again.

On the way to Harvard's famed Ames Courtroom to speak, Jackson whispers, almost to himself, "These kids have hard eyes and intimidating faces."

So it comes out. After all the years, all the accomplishments, all the time onstage with the Mondales and the Harts, haute cuisine and Harvard people still put Jesse Jackson a little on edge, which is no shock. He grew up a poor boy in Greenville, South Carolina, in the days of Jim Crow, gleaning his insights about the larger world by serving dinner to whites, selling them popcorn at football games, shagging their golf balls. Today, maybe only Gloria Vanderbilt's childhood has been more scrutinized than Jackson's: illegitimate son of a seventeen-year-old girl, his father a married neighbor—oh scandal! The good folks at the Baptist church even shunned Jesse's mamma. He stuttered, suffered the whispers of catty adults and the taunts of playmates who'd sing, "Jesse ain't got no dad-dee, Jesse ain't got no dad-dee." Jackson has often described his boyhood as a battle for the respect his illegitimacy denied him. Everything from good grades and sharp clothes to quick wit and athletic excellence became, as he says, "weapons" for winning that respect. One day a vicious neighbor woman called out from her porch that Jesse was nothing but a bastard. He spun on his heels. "Go ahead, call me what you will," he said. "But one day you'll be proud to know this bastard."

Jackson eventually made his struggle for respect—first from blacks and then later from whites—a metaphor for all of black America's struggle to win respect. But it seems that something more is going on here, because Jesse didn't only crave *respect*; he also craved *respectability*, which is different. Respect can be earned; respectability can be an accident of circumstance. Respectability is what the people at the Baptist church had—and what they denied Jesse's mother. Jackson had a kind of love-hate romance with respectability, and the class divisions in black society were a part of this.

The pre–civil rights black middle class, for instance, was sometimes hostile to poor blacks, author Amiri Baraka writes in *Blues People,* because to be respectable then was to be white—if not in skin color, then in attitude, taste, and behavior. Not until civil rights, black power, and black pride were affluent blacks freed of this psychic racism, allowing them to be unashamed, even proud, of having suffered slavery and poverty. Today Jackson is rich—he earned $115,000 in salary and speaking fees in 1983, the last year he publicly reported his income—but he argues that affluent blacks need not lose touch with the compassion and authenticity of being poor and black, at least not since the emergence of an African-American consciousness. Today, Jackson still sees the world, black or white, through a prism of wealth and poverty—and some blacks still see Jackson much as the woman on the porch did thirty years ago.

"He scares me a little," a prominent southern black official told Thomas H. Landess and Richard M. Quinn in *Jesse Jackson and the Politics of Race.* "He represents an element in the black community which needs to be served. But that element will be better served by spokesmen who are a little calmer."

"You're saying that Jesse Jackson is a low-life?" one of the authors asked.

"That's about it," the man said.

Jackson returns this class-conscious sentiment. "These people live in the Twilight Zone," he told Bob Faw and Nancy Skelton in *Thunder in America,* a book on his 1984 presidential campaign. "Too black to be white, too white to be black. . . . They're the equivalent to upper-class whites. They send their kids to Juilliard . . . they didn't have no part of the action back in the sixties, no way."

But still, Jesse's love-hate romance with respectability goes on. He sent his son, Jesse, Jr., to Washington's private St. Albans prep school. "With the Mondales and the Bushes and this and that," he says. For about $12,000 a year. His son wanted to go on to the Ivy League, but then Jackson got nervous about the down side of respectability. He'd seen his son's clothes and style and attitude change in his years at St. Albans.

"Things were comin' right easy for him," Jackson says. "Jesse coulda gone right on to Harvard, Yale, Brown. In four years he'd a been a social misfit. Jesse needed to get a sense of compassion, to be

tolerant of other people who have not had all the breaks. He's visited the pope, visited Syria, visited Africa." Jackson told his son he
needed to go to a school with kids who don't speak well, who don't
wear nice clothes, who have a crooked eye because their parents
couldn't afford to get it fixed—and who still excel. "I said, 'Jesse,
on any given test they gonna be about ten points smarter than you.
You need that. There's no one side of town that's got a monopoly on
genius.'" His son went to North Carolina A&T State University, his
dad's predominantly black alma mater. Jesse, Sr., you see, believes
a man can have it all—the empathy and compassion of the poor; the
money, confidence, and connections of the rich.

I ask, "Do you ever worry that with your success you could become
one of the rich people you despise?"

"I do not despise rich people, that's not true," Jackson says.
"When the Bible says it's as hard for a rich man to get to heaven as it
is for a camel to pass through the eye of a needle, it's talking about
how easy it is for rich people to get insensitive. But one doesn't get
an automatic ride on morality because they're poor. Nor is a man
condemned because he's rich. It comes down to the character of a
person. Many people who are blinded by racism and wealth cannot
see their essential kinship with poor people. It is that I despise."

Back at Harvard, Jackson gives a hell of a speech—for intellectuals, anyway. It's full of facts and stats, election returns, poverty
figures, the maldistribution of wealth in America, the drop in black
admissions at universities, including Harvard. He talks less race,
more Rainbow, and appeals to social guilt and youthful idealism.
His slang recedes, except when he cornpones it up, telling them
that in his old neighborhood folks didn't use fancy Harvard words—
a not-so-subtle reminder of just how far Jesse has come. Jackson
thinks America's privileged, down deep, believe that anyone who
rises to the top from the bottom—the classic self-made man—is better than they are. He sees this as the dirty little secret of the rich, and
he likes to tweak them about it. Now, imagine Jackson's voice as
you've heard it on TV, the rising and falling of pitch, the resonating
rhythm of his sentences, the erratic halts in delivery, the feeling that
he is not giving a speech, but appealing to a friend. Imagine this,
because Jackson's words without Jackson are like Bob Dylan's lyrics
without Bob Dylan.

"What difference does it make if the wagon is pulled by an elephant or a donkey, if both are chauffeur-driven?" Jackson asks, his
lyrical vibrato crying, condemning, and cajoling all at once. "Most
poor people are not on welfare, most poor people are not black,

most poor people work every day. Who are these poor people? They drive cabs. They are robbed, threatened, and harassed; they keep on workin'. Who are these poor people? They sweep streets. They catch the early bus in the morning. They're the ones whose sons are the first to die in war, last to reap the benefits in peace. It's time for another way, it's a new day. There is no world market for *yuppies*. There is no world market for *buppies*. Your generation can wipe out malnutrition; your generation can do justice in America and bring peace in the world. It's your challenge. It's your chance. It's your choice."

From the Harvard kids, those he wanted to keep his son away from, those with the hard eyes and intimidating faces, comes a raucous standing ovation. Afterward, Jackson wonders if something he said tonight might affect some kid the way he was affected when he heard Bobby Kennedy say in the early sixties that segregation was not only illegal, but *immoral*. He'd never heard a white man say that, and it opened such possibilities.

"I'm planting seeds," Jackson says.

I ask, "What did you mean, 'These kids have hard eyes and intimidating faces'?"

Jackson is curt, instinctively closing a small window of vulnerability: "Oh, I was just *talkin'*!"

The next morning's hotel curb-call is for 5:00 A.M. and Jackson, as usual, is late. So I sit in the lobby with Melvin Reynolds, a thirty-four-year-old black man who worked in Jackson's campaign and helped organize his Harvard visit. Reynolds was born poor in Mississippi, but was plucked away by minority recruiters and packed off to an elite Eastern boarding school. He went on to Yale and a Rhodes scholarship at Oxford. Along the way he fell in love with a daughter of one of America's great, white, rich, liberal families. But when the couple got serious, the great, white, rich, liberal family went nuts. The woman was so naive, Reynolds says, smiling. "You know," she once told him, "they never let me meet any poor people, not even poor *white* people." The couple never married, of course, and I look at Mel Reynolds—dapper, sophisticated, urbane, affluent—and I think of Jesse Jackson's words.

"Keep on walkin'," he had said. "You'll walk into a post. It's just a matter of time."

"You know who you are?" Jesse Jackson asks, as we drive into Savannah from the airport. "You're the centurion. That's who you are."

"The who?"

"The centurion. The Roman soldier sent to spy on Jesus. That's what you are, you're a spy. You're the centurion."

I nod warily.

"You know what happened to the centurion?"

"No."

"They said, 'What did you find out?' And he said, 'I've never heard a man speak like this. What manner of man is this?' That's you, you're the centurion."

This odd exchange isn't as odd as it seems. Jackson knows by now that as a person I'm sympathetic to his liberal politics, but he also knows that journalists aren't free agents, that they work for editors, that they are pathologically sensitive to being called anybody's patsy. He has mentioned that when reporters covering his campaign became too sympathetic to him—those who after a few nights of sleeping in poor people's homes with him began to show a sense of urgency about poverty—they were seen back at the office as going soft. They'd be reminded, he says, that they weren't Jackson flacks, but newsmen, damn it, so get tough! Most journalists, he says, buckle.

So Jesse has given me a way out of this fix—the centurion. I can be a visionary with, yes, that special insight that the Romans—and my editors, colleagues, and most white people—are supposed to lack. All I must do, like the centurion, is suspend my cynicism, resist my professional values, go with my emotions. Jesse never stops maneuvering, even for small advantage.

Onstage at the Savannah Civic Center, behind the podium, before a thousand black Baptist preachers and their wives, Jackson starts out slowly. Still, a smattering of "amens" is already rising from the crowd. There's a buzz in the air because Jackson appearing before black southern Baptist preachers is like Harry Houdini performing before a convention of master magicians. Ain't no easy tricks with this crowd, not like when Jesse stood before millions of white Americans on TV during the Democratic National Convention and made New York governor Mario Cuomo's impassioned keynote address sound like he'd just read a fund-raising letter from the Episcopal bishop.

As Jesse speaks, I marvel at his power, and I think of Willie Stark, the populist southern governor in Robert Penn Warren's novel *All the King's Men*, the way Willie started out slow and then seemed to cross some invisible line and become a medium, when his words stopped coming from his head and instead seemed simply to pass through on their way from someplace else, grabbing people's emotions like "a cold hand in a cold rubber glove." Jesse's got that hand, that glove.

His southern dialect is thick today, his speech laden with God and Christ and Goliath and crossing the River Jordan. He moves from whispers to shouts to bellows, and the preachers chant back with humor and appreciation, "Preach some, Jesse!" There's an ominousness in this Willie Stark power, this ability to stir the emotions of the dispossessed. But these people aren't frightened; they understand the music. And as Jackson preaches, the aisles fill, people go to their feet, hands rise toward the sky. Jesse is sweating, his shoulders are twitching, his feet are stomping, his voice wavering. Harvard this isn't.

"We ain't just Negroes or colored people or niggers," he says, with an ironic inflection on that last word. "We were not brought here by masters to be their slaves. We were sent here by God to save the human race. We have this awesome burden of being prophetic. I'm God's barometer measuring the weight and worth of your soul. Our strongest weapon is that we're right. If you're right, God will fight your battle! If you are right!"

There came a time when the leaders of the civil rights movement abandoned this style and strategy of moral activism and took hold of what the political scientists call "legitimate" power, becoming businessmen or bureaucrats or politicians. Jackson never did. "The movement's me," he once said. "I can't decide the struggle is over, because the struggle is my life." So Jackson draws on the symbolism of the prophets, and their supposed moral authority beyond that which man can bestow—that of Christ, Gandhi, and Martin Luther King.

"Politicians ask, 'Will it work?'" Jackson tells the preachers. "Prophets ask, 'Is it right?'" He clings to the idea that he is more prophet than politician. The strategy is no secret. The great power of social protest is the way it holds up a nation's stated moral values as a yardstick to measure its true accomplishments. Comparing the American belief in equality with the oppression of blacks before civil rights, for instance, revealed a gap that shamed a nation. The tactic is in any social movement's text or any radical community organization's handbook. Morality—rightness and wrongness—is a "weapon" for the powerless to win respect and power, much as achievement and wit and charm were weapons for the young Jackson to win respect and power.

But it's a tough act, and perhaps it is at the root of the uneasiness about Jesse Jackson's sincerity. A small story illustrates. Jackson recently visited South Carolina's Citadel military college, where a black cadet had just quit after white classmates in white robes had burned a paper cross in his room. As Jackson stood on campus talking with black cadets about the incident, a Citadel official walked up and told him he couldn't speak there. Jackson describes a comical scene in which Jesse then asked if that meant he couldn't speak *loudly*. Or softly. Or could he perhaps pray out loud? Well, yes, the official said, he could pray. Quickly, Jackson grabbed the man's hand and began to lead the group in impromptu prayer. Now, a Jackson prayer can be more incendiary than another man's call-to-arms, and the official soon yanked his hand away in frustration, realizing he'd been had. Jackson had taken prayer—a deep and sincerely felt event for most people—and transformed it into a weapon.

"Theater is what it's all about," he says.

Perhaps, but will the man at The Citadel ever again be moved by the prayerful image of Jesse Jackson? For any aspiring prophet, such worldly victories have a price because they reveal his political pragmatism and earthly manipulation, forcing at least the skeptical to wonder whether his beliefs are deeply held or a cynical means to an end. And even if his ends are noble, the prophet suddenly looks suspiciously like a politician.

Today in Savannah, though, Jackson is talking to the converted. "I'm gonna tell ya truth if I have to run!" he roars. "I'm gonna tell ya if it hurts! I choose prophecy over politics." These Baptist preachers don't need convincing. They seem to envelop Jackson, imbue him with strength; and it's suddenly as if he is not taking them somewhere, but as if they are taking him.

The place is bedlam.

Jesse Jackson has come home to Greenville, South Carolina, to help jog his memory for his autobiography, for which he has received a hefty $350,000 advance from Simon and Schuster. He conducts a guided tour of bygone indignities. The swimming pool the city turned into a flower garden to keep blacks out. The hardware store where blacks came on Saturday nights to sit outside the display window and watch the TVs they couldn't afford. The city park blacks couldn't use, the ball field where they couldn't play, the zoo they couldn't visit, the neighborhoods they couldn't walk through, the jobs—cop, fireman, bus driver—they couldn't hold, the schools they couldn't attend, the places they couldn't eat or drink or live.

"You learn to yearn," Jackson says, "learn to wish you could do

that, that you could sit where other people sit, that you could do
what others do."

Young Jesse was marked for glory—quarterback of the all-black
Sterling High School football team, a top student, a class leader. He
was a popular, devilishly outgoing kid, often leading his classmates
in benignly disruptive antics, playfully testing authority. Even then,
he angled for attention, always making sure his teachers saw that
he'd taken a stack of books with him on football road trips. He was
diligent, though, never missing an assignment. He also had a rep in
those days for coming up with reasons whites weren't as good as
blacks—whites wouldn't play blacks in football because whites
were afraid, wouldn't go to school with blacks because whites were
poor students, wouldn't debate blacks because whites had those
whiny, nasal voices, always talking through their noses. It was
whites—not blacks, not Jesse—who had a problem.

Jackson still believes this today. He talks about how the Mondales
and the Bidens and the Harts can't feel comfortable before the wide
range of people he can relax with, because their backgrounds are,
well, deficient. Maybe they can be U.S. senators, but they can't do
Jesse Jackson's job. He can go from Harvard kids to black preachers
to white farmers to derelicts and be at ease, he says, and in many
ways he can.

Yet Jackson's critics, black and white, are harsh and plentiful.
After Martin Luther King's death, press reports incorrectly claimed
that King had died in Jackson's arms, and civil rights leaders present at the assassination believed Jackson had fostered this misap-
prehension to leap over other movement leaders in line for King's
mantle. Although Jackson has denied that he did this, to his critics
the affair became a grave example of Jackson's blind ambition.

Moreover, Jackson isn't exactly the model of Christian forgiveness, piety, and poverty that you might expect in a prophet, or even
a preacher. He has angrily denounced blacks who criticize him. He
once assailed as racist the remarks of a white woman who criticized
his judgment after having worked tirelessly for his election. He has
said insensitive things about Jews. And despite his references to the
life of Christ, Jackson lives elegantly, and his pride is legendary. It is
this gap between Jackson's proclaimed high morality and his own
foibles that led black journalist Barbara Reynolds to title her Jackson
biography, *Jesse Jackson: America's David.* Jackson, she says, is like
David in the Bible—the flawed vehicle of an inspired message.

So is Jackson a savior, or an operator?

Maybe he's both. Maybe that's why he has done so well.

On Greenville's Green Avenue, where Jesse hung out when he was young, they're still hanging out today, in the rain, when Jackson drives up to the bar, the pool hall, the liquor store, with bricks still gray and the sidewalk cracking and buckling. Standing around are a dozen guys, some Jackson's age who look much older, some younger who still look much older. This corner, then and now, isn't a place of boundless possibility. But it's about to give Jesse Jackson the boundless affirmation he needs to ignore his critics.

"How y'all doin'?" Jesse cries, as the gang crowds 'round, everyone wearing a hat and smoking a cigarette, everyone talking at once. "There's that damned Wilbur Ross!"

"Hey, Jesse!" Wilbur says.

At the center of the crowd is a thirty-two-year-old man, Joe Nathan. He looks so old it's startling. He has been drinking, and his voice drowns out the rest. "How many people!?" Joe shouts. "How many people in the White House, how many in the public, how many people do this like you do!?"

"Nobody!" cries the gang.

"How many would do it?" Joe roars.

"Nobody but him!"

"When a man walk with a president," Joe says, starting to sob, "and come on Green Avenue, you *are* some*body*!" he bellows to Jackson, who by now has quietly, almost shyly, succumbed to being upstaged. "You are some*body*! You are somebody for us! You come from a poor community and see a person like that, it makes people feel so good! I'm talkin' about how you *feel* it, how you *feel* it, man! I *feel* it! It's good. Things move when I see him. He's my king. I'm not sayin' he'll sit in the president's seat. I'm sayin' one of these days, I'm gonna see a black president. I'm gonna see one. I want to see one."

"Yeah!" cries the gang.

Jackson drives away from Green Avenue without saying a word, and he tools through the old neighborhood, past rows of little houses, many nothing more than shacks. "How many generations do you think it will be before America outgrows this disparity?" I ask. Jackson doesn't answer; he's not thinking social justice right now. He's lost in nostalgia. "Clark's Flower Shop," he says absently, as we drive past an empty lot. "That was big business." He stops to see Mabel Perkins, who raised eleven kids, all of whom went to college. She still lives in her little house with the oil-burning stove in the living room.

"Where did they all live?" I ask.

"On top of each other," Jackson says, laughing. He jumps and lands heavily on the living room floor, laughs again as the TV picture flickers wildly. "That was the remote channel changer when we were kids!" Everyone laughs. Then Mabel Perkins cuts a homemade yellow cake, and we stand in the kitchen eating it with our fingers.

"Ma Perkins went back to adult education," Jesse says.

She adds proudly, "And I finished grammar school, too!"

"People who are poor are strong on details," Jackson says later. "Ma Mabel? She said, 'And I finished grammar school, too!' She didn't say nothin' about the Indian-China conflict. 'I finished grammar school, too!' You have a different measuring rod comin' from the bottom up."

Jesse Jackson says a lot of things you can't take at face value, so many balls does he keep in the air. But one thing he says so many times, so many ways that I believe he believes it, plain and simple: Life at the bottom is a fuller, richer life than life at the top. Here is where race and class finally meet in Jackson's mind. He says poor people—from before the time of Christ, black or white—have always been the voice of conscience. Their vantage is superior. It's why the Christmas angel visited shepherds, not kings. It is the rich who lack insight. It's *their* deficit, *their* problem. It was their problem when Jackson was a boy; it is their problem today. As he said, "The privileged haven't any story." It is a kind of chauvinism from below, but it makes Jesse go. It has made him President of Black America.

JANUARY 25, 1987

Washington Post photograph by John McDonnell.

DAVID CARMEN
The High Price of a Washington Education

> *"Them that's going, get in the goddamn wagon. Them that ain't, get out of the goddamn way."*
> David Carmen's favorite quote,
> from "The Bear" by William Faulkner

*D*avid Carmen is a young man who came to Washington, D.C., six years ago to get married, make a living, and grow up. He is seated at his desk in front of huge glass windows that converge in the corner behind him at Seventeenth and K streets in downtown Washington. He is thirty years old, short, with a slight but constant slump in his shoulders. His voice is like gravel; his hair is a memory. His suit is European, dark blue with a subtle purple stripe, expensive. His tie is Armani. Camel filters are his cigarette, and the smoke rises off his ashtray and seems to disappear into its own reflection in the glass atop his desk, which is appropriate because the slippage and similarity between image and reality is David's business—political public relations.

His firm is Carmen, Carmen & Hugel. Last year, it billed $1.5 million. Not bad for a novice. David laughs an ingratiating, relaxing laugh. He's a good talker, David, and today—for many days, really—he has sat and talked about himself and about the mysterious ways of Washington.

He's describing the education of David Carmen—how one smart young man got ahead in the nation's capital using everything from brains and hustle, to friendships and favors, to competence and connections. Oh, maybe David is self-aggrandizing, sees himself writ large in the scenes of his life, but then who doesn't? David isn't a big Washington dealmaker; he's still a young and aspiring dealmaker. But he has done better than most in his journey from simple to sophisticated knowledge of Washington. For those who admire people like David, his journey is a primer. For those who despise people like David, it is a warning.

This is David's Principle: Washington is about results.

Nobody in this town cares how hard you work or how smart or how nice you are. This is no family. People care about results. In Washington, you are in the wagon or you are out of the wagon, out of the way. You make things happen or things will happen to you. These are shallow aphorisms for the young and the hungry, but they can't be ignored. Always remember Harry Truman's remark, "If you want a friend in Washington, buy a dog." David laughs. He really doesn't believe Truman, not yet, anyway. He must still remind himself to be that cynical, impersonal, purposeful. He still shakes his head and wonders at the very idea of it.

But, he says cheerfully, "You have to play to stay."

The speaker phone in David's office is behind him, and because he faces forward at his desk when he talks to it, there's a weird sense that he's talking to a ghost or maybe God. But no, he's talking to Sidney Blumenthal, a reporter for the *Washington Post*'s Style section. It amuses David that Blumenthal is a liberal while David is a right-wing conservative whose PR firm handles press for T. Boone Pickens, Jr., Jack Kemp, Jeane Kirkpatrick. But ideology matters not here; results matter. Years ago, David convinced Blumenthal, then a reporter for the *New Republic*, to write a profile of David's boss. It was the first big story that young press agent David Carmen ever placed. Blumenthal went on to become an expert on conservative politics and eventually moved to the *Post*. "All of a sudden," David says gleefully, "I had a buddy at the *Washington Post*." David genuinely likes Blumenthal. But he is also a good man to know.

"Sid," says David, in that exaggerated way speaker phones make people talk.

"David," says Blumenthal, who also genuinely likes David.

"I think I have a really hot one, but it's really sensitive, and it can't ever come from me. Like, go to jail for me."

David and Blumenthal are speaking in the arcane language of source and reporter, and they both laugh. David's style smacks of a joyful irony about the crisscrossing nature of enemies and allies in Washington. He isn't mean or slimy, but relaxed and droll. He has a gentle, likable, intimate way of putting people at ease, inspiring trust. It's the psychological equivalent of draping an arm around a person's shoulder, leaning into him, whispering in that conspiratorial way. This all comes naturally and sincerely to David, but in Washington it's also his best weapon in a game that's all about making people recognize that it is in their interests to do what you want them to do.

David tells Blumenthal his tip, which is juicy—about the faltering marriage of one of Washington's most powerful men. The tip never makes it into the paper, but that won't bother David. He's just being friendly, keeping his line to Blumenthal open.

Says David, "The whole town does it."

David moved to Washington because he got scared—scared at his youthful discovery that people's lives don't always follow desire's script. His father, as fathers do, had tried to tell David this for years, wanted him to be a lawyer. David had other ideas. He saw himself as a rebel. At the elite Phillips Exeter Academy prep school, David was part of the counterculture gang. Some teachers feared he was part of the campus marijuana drug culture. David smiles and says candidly: "I engaged in all the tenets of the youth culture."

David's father, Gerald, was a self-made man who had become wealthy as the owner of tire stores in Manchester, New Hampshire. But Gerald Carmen never lost his Jewish working-man's style— even as he rose from tire store owner, to state Republican chairman and architect of Ronald Reagan's 1980 primary victory in New Hampshire, to head of the General Services Administration. David's father was a Republican's Republican, and without much thought David had worked the streets for conservative Republicans since he was a boy.

So it was wildly ironic to David that at Exeter—filled with kids from America's richest families—everybody seemed liberal. He hung with the intellectual crowd, wrote a novel, acted in campus plays. David was not so much a conservative then as an iconoclast. He delighted in making fun of classmates for, say, wearing $300 boots to an anti-Nixon rally. Exeter had a coat-and-tie dress code, and David mocked it by wearing coats and ties that clashed.

"David was always an operator," says Myra Donnelley, a friend and former Exeter classmate. "He was a bad boy, very charismatic. He delighted in exploring the rules of the game, the boundaries at Exeter." But David always had a charm that let him get away with it. A lot of his Exeter friends were eventually kicked out, but not David. He was a hybrid: a rebel who skirted the rules, but who was still named dorm proctor by the faculty. When Harvard, Yale, and Stanford all rejected him, though, David became convinced that his rebelliousness at Exeter had led to bad faculty evaluations that had kept him out. It was a cost this rebel didn't want to pay—and David suddenly wished he had studied more, rebelled less.

David finally took his dad's advice and went into prelaw at the

University of Chicago. But he hated it and soon rebelled again. He transferred to Sarah Lawrence College in New York to study theater. His father went nuts. How will you get a job with a degree in, what, theater? After graduation in 1980, David moved to Boston, where he worked as a stagehand, directed little theater, and finally wrote and produced his own play, *Bobby Brown: Brass Tacks for Spring Chickens*, a sci-fi adventure in which a blind kid invents a machine that makes him see and then gets kidnapped by evil German scientists. On opening night, David was behind the audience watching the last scene—Bobby Brown being blown up by the military-industrial complex—when a winch operating a stage elevator gave out. David's girlfriend, Alexandra, reflexively reached out to stop it and got the tip of her left index finger cut off, blood everywhere.

She took the accident in stride, but David fell into a funk, had nightmares. It wasn't Vietnam or a death in the family, David knew that, but the accident was still a dose of cold reality in his fortunate life. Here he was, twenty-five, too poor to pay the lousy heating bill, no health insurance! And David liked money, always had, lots of it. He enjoyed buying Alexandra extravagant gifts. He wanted to marry. David told himself: Broadway actors make $30,000 a year—and that's Broadway! It was another cost this rebel didn't want to pay. You might say David was scared straight.

He'd never wanted to enter politics. That was his dad's thing. But he called Dad, then head of GSA, and asked if he could get him a job. Dad did, at the Republican National Committee. This was David's plan: He and Alexandra would move to Washington, get married, save some money—and then head for life in the theater. In the eternal struggle between father and son, David felt horribly defeated. But his father, who had fumed at his son's offbeat interests for years, didn't feel victorious. No, he felt oddly saddened that David had traded in his youthful dreams for an $18,000-a-year job.

"Page!" David suddenly hollers into the next office.

An old college friend of David's is looking for a job as a TV producer, and when Page Lee, David's assistant, hustles in, David asks her to call Hal Bruno, John Ellis, and Marty Plissner, political news honchos at ABC, NBC and CBS, and ask them to set up interviews for David's friend. Only a few years ago, David would never have sought such favors. "I would die before I asked someone to do something for me," he says. David did favors, all right, as many as he could, whenever he could, whether or not he thought a favor would be returned. He had been nurtured in politics, had a sixth sense for its back-scratching dimension, knew that doing favors in politics was like doing good works in the Bible: They will be returned manyfold. But David believed that asking for favors was different—asking for favors was a sign of weakness.

He was wrong.

David explains: People mistakenly think favors are like toothpaste in a tube—the more favors you use, the fewer favors you have left. Not so. The more favors you request and the more favors you do, the more potential favors are created. See, when you ask for a favor, you're making it easier for someone to ask you for a favor—and you want people to seek favors because then they'll do favors for you, in an ever-expanding circle. The modern word for this is *networking*, a technocratic term conveniently devoid of the ethical ambiguities of people feathering one another's nests.

"I just take networking for granted," says David. "It's the vehicle by which everything happens in Washington. I don't know anyone who has ever gotten a job who didn't know somebody. It's like a secret little racetrack, and only some people have a key. It's a big network. That's how I got my jobs."

But no luck this time. David's friend got two interviews, no job.

David moved to Washington in 1982 and went straight to Sy Syms discount designer clothes. On his mother's advice, he bought two $99 suits—one dark blue, one dark blue pinstripe. Then he bought "the uniform"—blue blazer and tan slacks. (His father tells this story: Once, when David's mom and dad were invited to sit in the presidential box at the Kennedy Center, they arrived to discover that all eight male guests, including David's father, were wearing blue blazers and tan slacks.) David bought rep ties for $10, black tie-shoes—the big, plain, shiny kind—and a half-dozen 100 percent cotton, Oxford button-down white shirts for $12.95 each. His father had them monogrammed, just like his own shirts.

David's big mistake was that he bought a brown suit, a nice suit, one he really liked. But everybody gave him grief. "A *brown* suit?" they'd ask. "Ronald Reagan wears brown suits," David would say. It was no use. David, who had once mocked the dress code at Phillips Exeter, relented and put away the brown suit. But he did get one big sartorial break: His mom ran across a Polish knockoff of a Burberry overcoat at a little place in Georgetown, $99. David had never even heard of a Burberry overcoat, but other people sure had. The first time he wore it to the Republican National Committee, where—to David's amazement—everyone dressed exactly as his mother had dressed him, he was assaulted with comments: "A Burberry?" or "Hey, a Burberry!" David marveled. The remarks came not from women, but from men.

The RNC turned out to be everything David had feared—a huge, depersonalized maze. His office was in a storage closet, with the protective padding still on the walls. David, whose job it was to create a computerized data bank of quotes from potential Democratic presidential candidates, was flabbergasted to learn he was expected to write memos under his superiors' names—as if they had written them! Ideas were weapons. Even the quotes David selected for his data bank led to arguments among RNC experts vying to decide which quotes would go or stay. Ideas, David learned, often rose or fell on the names of the people suggesting them. "Whose idea was that?" he'd joke. "We'll decide if it's good after we know whose idea it was."

With amazement, David told his old friend Myra Donnelley that everyone in Washington seemed to have "an angle"—and that gossip seemed to be the glue that held the city together. In Washington, David said, he couldn't even go out with people after work for a few beers, because he was afraid he'd get relaxed and say something that would later come back to haunt him. Donnelley was shocked: This was the same David who used to yell to the waiters, "More champagne!"

For all the petty maneuvering, it seemed to young David—brash, confident, impatient—that nothing ever *happened* at the Republican National Committee, that ideas floated around for months and then disappeared into the ether. Philip Kawior, in charge of RNC research then, says David's political instincts were sometimes frighteningly brilliant. But David—trying so hard to dress and act the role of a good bureaucrat—was still too much the iconoclast to really fit in. Then he made the mistake of asking his boss, William Greener, for a raise.

"We have our raise reviews in November," Greener said.

"But do you think I *deserve* a raise?" asked David, pressing.

"Yes, but we have our processes." David's job just wasn't *worth* more than the $22,000 he was then earning, Greener said, no matter how well he did it. If David wanted more money, he'd have to get a new job or wait for a promotion.

Now, this conversation comes as no shock to anyone who has worked in an organization with "processes," but David was confused. He figured he was being shown the door. All of a sudden, David found himself back in the job market—and once again, his father played the angel. His dad told Marc Holtzman, then executive director of a new group forming to plug Reagan's conservative agenda, that David was looking for a job. The group, Citizens for America, was the brainchild of Jack Hume, a California millionaire and one of Reagan's most trusted personal advisers. Lewis Lehrman, the former president of Rite-Aid drugstores and an unsuccessful Republican candidate for governor in New York, was its head. David met Holtzman and Lehrman and was offered a job at $30,000 a year. David stood tough for $33,000—and he got the money. David was elated: Standing tough was risky, but it paid off.

Today, a more seasoned David Carmen smiles and says, "What I didn't understand was that Lew Lehrman had presidential ambitions." For him, it was smart to have the son of New Hampshire's Gerald Carmen on his payroll—just in case Lehrman ever made it to the 1988 New Hampshire presidential primary.

Maybe he should have asked for $38,000.

David calls Christine Dolan, political director for CNN.

"Hi, I've got a story for 'Inside Politics.'"

Today's tip: The rumor is that a staffer for Republican presidential candidate Robert Dole messed up and got lousy film footage from Dole's campaign announcement. Dolan appreciates the tip, but knows it's too insignificant to use.

She asks, "What else is going on around town?"

David is a trusted source for Dolan. He doesn't waste her time, any reporter's time, with bad tips. And unlike many right-wing politicos, Dolan says, David understands that reporters aren't out to "get" conservatives, that reporters just want a good story, that they'll deal with the devil to get it. Sure, David's self-serving, out to help his clients—in this case Republican presidential hopeful Jack Kemp. But he isn't misleading. And that's the way to a reporter's heart. "David has a seductive, charming personality and is straight with you," says Dolan, who has since left her job at CNN. "In Washington, these people aren't a dime a dozen." Minutes after David's conversation with Dolan, David's secretary comes on the intercom: "A friend of Christine Dolan's on 3."

"A friend?" asks David, perplexed.

Dolan's friend—a social friend, not a journalism colleague—wants, well, a favor. Does David have any idea how she can get vacation accommodations on short notice at St. Barthélemy? Since David became well-to-do, he likes to vacation on the island in the French West Indies and often talks about its beauty. St. Barth is expensive, but it has little poverty, so David isn't racked with what he calls the "poverty guilt" he feels vacationing in, say, Jamaica. But David has no inside track to hotels on St. Barth.

Sorry, this is a favor he can't do. He would if he could.

Without ever being told, David got the point: as press secretary for Citizens for America, his job was to sell the Reagan agenda—and Lew Lehrman. With its million-dollar budget, CFA launched local chapters in congressional districts in 1983 in an effort to set a more conservative tone to public debate on everything from Reagan's budget cuts to the landing of U.S. troops in Grenada. David was by now a confirmed conservative, and he relished his job at CFA. But David also attended to his other job: He made sure local TV stations had camera-ready slides of Lew Lehrman. Eventually, David compiled a computerized list of 12,000 journalists across the country.

He told Alexandra, who had become his wife, "I'm thirty feet over my head." Alexandra enjoyed the new life, found it exciting to meet people she'd only read about. But she didn't enjoy the layers of intrigue at every party, the phone ringing late into the night. "We're getting further and further from theater," she once told David. "We'll never go back."

But David loved it. Every morning, he felt as if he were being strapped into a linear accelerator—and rocketed through the day. With Lehrman, the living definition of a Type A personality, there was never a down minute. Car rides to the airport were used for interviews with local reporters. The few minutes before takeoff were used to make three or four phone calls from the terminal. David used to lose his wallet a lot, show up late for appointments. There was no time for such indulgences now. David learned the hard way. One day, he and Lehrman were at New York's La Guardia Airport on their way to Chicago to unveil new CFA television commercials backing a Reagan plan to rejuvenate the cities. When the plane door closed behind them, David realized he had left the TV tapes in the terminal.

"Lew, Lew, I forgot the tapes!" he said, and he could see the little vein on Lehrman's temple begin to pulse. "Open this door!" David said sternly to the plane's attendant.

"No."

David thought fast. He lied. "I'm with the networks. I have live feed for the news tonight from Chicago."

"No."

David looked at Lehrman and saw that vein pumping. He thought fast again. "The truth is we're on a mission for the White House."

"Take your seat, sir."

David did, despondent. Almost too calmly, Lehrman said, "Dave, I'm sure this is the beginning of a long relationship, but the fact that we've spent $40,000 on this project and the films are not going to Chicago with us is not good." David could not speak. The tale did have a happy ending, though. The tapes came on the next flight, and David offered an airport cabbie $50 if he got David and the tapes to the press conference in downtown Chicago in seventeen minutes. The guy flew like a madman, his left wheels riding on the median strip, nineteen minutes! David tipped him $70—and the show went on.

It struck David that political operators are a lot like stage directors. Hundreds of details swirl about seemingly out of control, the unexpected always happens, microphones or lights fail, people get sick or quit, relatives die at the wrong times. But in the end, nobody wants to hear it.

David realized: "Only the show matters."

David rings up Frank Lavin, the Number 2 political affairs guy in the White House. Lavin is thirty years old and a friend of David's. They had talked a while back when Lavin called to ask David to set up a meeting between Lavin's White House boss, Frank Donatelli, and David's client Jeane Kirkpatrick. Yes, Lavin could have called Kirkpatrick directly, but he did David the favor of putting him in the middle, making David a player.

"Hi, Frank, a couple of things . . ."

David has read in the paper this morning that Jon Breen, the man in charge of the microphone at the famous 1980 Republican debate in Nashua, New Hampshire, is about to retire. That was the debate in which Reagan got Breen's name wrong but still stole the show with, "I paid for this microphone, Mr. Green." Wouldn't it be great publicity for Reagan to call and wish Breen good luck?

"Will you put that out over there?" David asks.

Lavin does, but Reagan never makes the call.

Nothing works like the personal touch.

So everyone David met—everyone who had or could someday have anything to do with CFA—received a note afterward. "It was so nice to meet you last night . . ." At receptions, David slipped into the hallway and wrote names on matchbooks. Every name, along with a phone number, went into what a friend of David's called the "nuclear Rolodex." David even had perks of his own to hand out. When CFA needed TV ads done, for instance, he steered the contract to Mike Murphy, a young campaign consultant David had met through Craig Shirley, a young campaign consultant David had met at the RNC.

David was frenetic. Every reporter, big-time or small-time, got a note after meeting David. He discovered that reporters—even the stars—often answer their own phones. And he discovered that reporters—even the stars—respond to "the personal touch." If David mentioned a detail from a reporter's recent article or column, he noticed that the reporter usually perked up. David might clip a reporter's article, jot a note in the margin, and send it to him out of the blue. He once did this with *Washington Post* White House reporter Lou Cannon, circling a passage and scribbling, "You got it right." David couldn't believe how easy it was to move from the storage closet at the RNC to meeting America's leading journalists— George Will, David Broder, Jack Germond.

If David had by now learned that only results matter in Washington, he also was learning that only people make results. His father and the RNC's Greener had taught him the first rule of dealing with the press: NEVER LIE—refuse to answer, admit you don't know, say you can't answer, but NEVER LIE. During the 1984 Republican convention, David saw the power of telling the truth. CBS correspondent Lesley Stahl called David before CFA's planned "spontaneous" demonstration during Jeane Kirkpatrick's speech to the Republican convention. As ever, the idea was to promote, this time through Kirkpatrick's hawkish image, conservatism—and Lew Lehrman. Stahl told David that the "CBS Evening News" was going to report that Kirkpatrick would switch from Democrat to Republican during her speech. David suspected that the White House had leaked the tip to pressure Kirkpatrick into doing this. He told Stahl that Kirkpatrick would not switch. CBS got it right, and Stahl thanked David.

Later that night, Stahl interviewed Lehrman on national TV. She recalls this as a coincidence—Lehrman must have been standing on the floor in the sector she was assigned to cover. But David considered it a coup—especially since Stahl asked Lehrman the Big Question: Was he running for president in 1988? Lehrman graciously brushed off the inquiry. But for Lehrman and David, the interview had gone according to script. Says David, "Lew wanted to be asked that question."

The lessons kept coming fast and furious.

* While on vacation, David was tracked down by a reporter. David was angry that his trip was interrupted, and when the reporter charged that CFA was a front for Ronald Reagan, David lost his temper. "Reagan doesn't use us so much as we use him," he was quoted as saying. Not smart.

Lesson: In Washington, you are never on vacation.

* David jumped at the chance to help Sidney Blumenthal do the *New Republic* profile of Lehrman. But the story was not uncritical. It described the conservative big-money network that had helped create Ronald Reagan, and it explained how that network planned to keep conservatism alive after Reagan was gone. Yet the article still shot Lehrman to national prominence. CFA distributed 500 copies.

Lesson: A story with "good stuff" and "bad stuff" is better than a puff piece—the bad stuff makes the good stuff credible.

* David was in a bar in Dallas late one night with Ward Sloane, then assistant political news director at CBS. Sloane looked at David and said, "You know, the amazing thing is that you get to be friends with people and then comes the day you have to do them in." Says David, "He wasn't talking about me, but even an idiot would have seen that he *meant* me."

Lesson: In Washington, you have no permanent friends, only permanent interests.

Finally, David learned that even allies have conflicting interests. He was at a large, private CFA reception where President Reagan was speaking. David happened to be looking at Ed Meese when Reagan mentioned that as many as 1,000 terrorists, many of them Iranians, were assembled in Lebanon readying for suicide-bombing missions—and Meese's face dropped. David was sure Reagan's remark was "news." He also was sure that Reagan hadn't meant to go public. Yet for David—an employee of an organization that ardently backed Reagan—the slip-of-the-tongue presented a tempting opportunity. David had been looking for a hot news tip to ingratiate himself with the *Washington Post*'s Lou Cannon.

This was David's dilemma: To do his job promoting Reagan's cause, he needed good press contacts. But to get good contacts, he needed to help the press do its job, too. So David did it. He called Cannon and told him what Reagan had said. He also told him he had seen people tape-recording the speech. Cannon confirmed David's tip with several sources and listened to portions of Reagan's taped remarks. The next day, David picked up the paper to find a front-page, above-the-fold story by Cannon: "Reagan Says 1,000 Readied As Mideast Suicide-Bombers."

"I had two thoughts," David says now. " 'There's only 365 headlines a year, and I got one.' The other was, 'Am I a leaker?' " An aide to Meese soon called David and charged that someone at CFA had tape-recorded Reagan's speech. David denied the accusation. Fortunately for David, the aide asked no more questions. Says David, "He didn't ask if I leaked it."

That quick, David had become a player.

The intercom crackles again: "Max on 6."

Max is Max Hugel, a former covert operations chief for the CIA under William Casey, a Republican high-muck-a-muck in New Hampshire, and, with David and his father, a partner in Carmen, Carmen & Hugel. David wants Max to do him a favor today, but David can't exactly ask Max to do it. David is an unpaid consultant to Jack Kemp's presidential campaign, and he wants the *Manchester Union Leader* to publish an op-ed article by Kemp about his opposition to an oil import fee—a hot issue in New Hampshire, where the fee would raise heating bills. This morning, David called Kemp's press secretary, John Buckley, and offered to call and ask *Union Leader* publisher Nackey Loeb, whom David knows, to run the article.

No, Buckley said, he thought David should wait; Kemp had enclosed a note to Loeb. The conversation was tense, the two men fencing politely over turf. Finally, David promised Buckley he wouldn't call Loeb, and he won't. But the ethics get murky if, let's say, Max Hugel were to call Loeb. David won't out-and-out ask Max to call—that would break his word to Buckley. But David tells Max about their talk, hoping he will think to call.

Max doesn't bite.

David was soon out of work again.

He lost his job at CFA in 1985 after his patron, Marc Holtzman, quit as CFA's executive director to run for Congress. Holtzman lost despite the support of Jeane Kirkpatrick, who helped raise $135,000 for the young man whose former organization had helped raise her political stock. In short order, CFA's new director forced David out. Lew Lehrman—a combination rabbi and professor to David—let the new man do it. Nothing personal. Lehrman just didn't believe David was ready for the top job yet. David was angry then, but today he says, "In Washington, a new Number 1 gets his own Number 2. I should have known that."

David got a kind of sweet revenge, though. A few months later, Lehrman fired much of his new staff. When the *Washington Times* ran a story quoting sources blaming the shake-up on Lehrman's "unstable" behavior, David, still loyal to Lehrman, was furious. He complained to a *Washington Times* editor that the story was one-sided, but the paper stood by the article. So David called his old *New Republic* contact Sidney Blumenthal, who was by now his new *Washington Post* contact. Blumenthal checked the story with other sources and wrote an article reporting that Lehrman had acted after discovering "lavish spending" and financial mismanagement.

David moved on—with his father again as his angel.

"Well, here's your law degree," his dad said as he handed David a $25,000 check to start his own public relations business. Lehrman hired David as a CFA consultant and Jeane Kirkpatrick signed on for press consultation. Holtzman persuaded a friend, a Philadelphia lawyer, to hire David, too. Mike Murphy, to whom David had steered the CFA television ad contract, gave David free office space while he looked for offices.

By now, David knew that in Washington image is often reality. Wasn't politics a lot like theater? David decided, what the hell, he'd rent digs on K Street, Washington's Lobby Inc.—at $5,000 a month, up to $22,000 a month today. Then he did something else gutsy: He had the plain wooden door to his new offices ripped out and spent $7,200 of his $25,000 installing glass double doors. Inside those doors, visible from the hallway, he hung a life-size photo of Ronald Reagan waving from the steps of his helicopter. David then hung historic, nonpartisan photos on the walls—Franklin Roosevelt, Frederick Douglass, a photo from John Kennedy's funeral, a picture of a young Ronald Reagan at a Harry Truman rally. But the picture that leaped out at people—the crustiest conservatives always move quickly away from it and on to the next photo—was that of several dozen kids, filthy and exhausted, in a turn-of-the-century sweatshop.

It was a subtle message: David was fashioning himself as a new conservative, unembarrassed by America's past, proud that these children—and their children's children—eventually entered the American mainstream.

David opened his business in May 1985.

By July, he was $100 from bankruptcy.

Today, his time will cost you $250 an hour.

Working for conservative causes, David's firm took off. He paid back his dad the first year, and when Hugel and his father joined the firm, its success was assured. For his clients, David staged press conferences, orchestrated letter-writing campaigns, wrote and filmed TV commercials. He handled press for Republican Joyce Hampers in her losing campaign for Massachusetts treasurer. She had hired David over far more experienced press consultants because when she called him one day, he flew up and was at her doorstep the next. He did controversial TV ads for the National Right to Work Committee that showed a gorilla—representing the power of organized labor—speaking before Congress. David landed an account with corporate raider T. Boone Pickens's United Shareholders Association, a Washington-based group aimed at offsetting the power of management in American corporations. And as the New Hampshire primary approached, David, so well connected through his father, handled press for the brief presidential campaign of Republican Paul Laxalt. Then he went with Kemp.

David worked constantly. He wanted a racy Datsun Z, but bought a black Oldsmobile 98—getting a good deal through his uncle's auto dealership. He needed a car that made him look older, more serious, a car he could use to pick up clients. He hired a driver because if he drove and parked himself, he couldn't always make it to three receptions a night. He got a car phone. He often scheduled two business breakfasts—at 7:30 and 8:30—at the Hay-Adams Hotel. He learned that if he didn't want to meet with someone, he could propose a 7:00 A.M. breakfast—almost nobody agrees to a 7:00 A.M. breakfast. He still dressed dull as ever, trying not to offend. And he discovered that Exeter was a surprise bonus. Jack Hume, CFA's founding father and Reagan's friend, was an Exeter man, and he always mentioned it when they met. "It was a badge," says David, and only a select few wore it.

David's three years in PR on his own have been three more years in the linear accelerator, and he has loved it. He's thirty years old, and he's a player—a supporting player but still a player. Today, he comes away from most of his Washington encounters having seen a lot—or imagining that he has seen a lot. He analyzes everything into infinity. He'll analyze a person's clothes—is he too dapper or not dapper enough? He'll analyze a person's drinking—does he drink at lunch because he's confident of himself or because he can't stop himself? Right or wrong, David has become very confident of his perceptions.

He organized what has come to be called the Loeb Dinner, at which Vice President Bush honored deceased *Manchester Union*

Leader publisher William Loeb, who had mercilessly attacked Bush in his newspaper for years. Getting Bush to agree to honor his old enemy was a coup. David tells of a dramatic meeting between himself and Bush strategists Lee Atwater, Ron Kaufman, and Robert Teeter. Atwater tried to muscle David into promising that Loeb's widow, Nackey, would say nice things about Bush in return for Bush's appearance. David felt intimidated as hell, but he made no promises. "Lee," he said, "I don't work for the vice president, you do." The Bush people don't remember the meeting this way at all. They say they can hardly even remember it, but certainly there was no effort to intimidate or exact promises. But, they say, it was a big meeting—perhaps it loomed larger in young David's mind.

David laughs hard and cynically at that.

David also tells of the time Robert Dilenschneider, chairman of the huge New York public relations firm Hill & Knowlton, called and asked to meet him. When they met at the Four Seasons Hotel bar in Georgetown, Dilenschneider said David's father had told him about the great work David was doing. Dilenschneider said he'd like to bring David on board at Hill & Knowlton, which represents many of America's largest corporations. In passing, he asked how David's work with Boone Pickens's anti-corporate-management group was going. David later went to New York to talk again, and Dilenschneider asked David to be sure to take copies of the literature in the outer office. On the plane, David read the material— almost all of it anti-corporate-takeover literature. In short, anti-Boone Pickens literature. At the time, David thought he was being paranoid, but today he's sure Dilenschneider was either trying to take him out of the game or to gather reconnaissance on Pickens's operation.

"He should relax," Dilenschneider says. "I didn't even think of that."

David laughs hard at that, too. His education has been too good to relax.

The intercom again: "Marc is on 1."

"Hello, Marc."

"David, good morning. How was the ski ball?"

"It was fine. I went home early."

Washington's ski ball is an annual yuppie charity event for the U.S. Ski Team. David went the other night, but he went alone. He and Alexandra separated last spring, and David is still adjusting. "She

thought David had compromised too much on his artistic dream,"
says David's old friend Myra Donnelley. David says only that the
breakup of his marriage was more complicated than that and that it
is private. But when the marriage ended, David did ask himself,
"What have I done with my life?" He worked all the time, even
Sunday mornings. He'd even become close friends with other young
political operators in town. David had come to Washington to get
his feet on the ground, and now they were implanted. He got ulcers.
But David still loved Washington. He had come full circle. "I never
used to understand my father," he says, "and now I do."

David's new confidence has changed him. He goes only to important receptions, finding it more efficient to meet people in their
offices. He limits his power lunches to a quick fifty minutes. He
even gave his father the black Olds 98 and bought a red Porsche 911
convertible—used, but still $25,000. He began wearing European
suits, double-breasted with wide, fashionable lapels, suits made of
subtle but unusual weaves. He switched to Armani ties—they have
that new wavy feel, weird but arrived, Establishment artsy. And
when he recently noticed that his black, knee-high stretch socks
were wearing out, he decided to go all the way, buy socks with color
patterns in them. David was tired of blending in, never standing
out, never offending—he wanted to rebel again. He still won't wear
that brown suit he liked, but he says, "Now, if people don't take me
seriously for driving a Porsche, that's their problem."

David has found a place, Washington, where it seems that he and
people like him can have it all. They can sincerely believe in something—liberalism, conservatism, whatever. They can be important,
have real power, make a difference—and they can be rich, too. All
these things motivate David, perhaps they always did, back when
he decided it wasn't worth being a rebel if it meant he couldn't go to
Harvard or Stanford, back when he decided theater wasn't worth it
if it meant living on $30,000 a year. Today, David says, "Just because
you have a six-figure income, drive a Porsche, and wear nice clothes
doesn't mean you've sold out." The price? Well, there is a price.

"It can be a rootless existence," David says. "You aren't even your
job. You're your next job. You're who you are about to be—somebody on their way out or somebody on their way in." In Washington,
David says, real players can't stay in any job for more than a few
years. If they do, they disappear, become irrelevant—the worst fate.
You move or you cease to exist. In Washington, the eternal verities
are upside-down: Motion is substance, change is stability.

"There's a tendency to run from people when they're down,"

David says. "So many people are dependent on being connected with people who are up. Your boss isn't the only person who's going to affect your future. It's your next boss. To be secure, you have to read the wind, and the players are constantly changing. And your next boss may not like your old boss." Washington, David says, is a town full of "new friends"—people who won't be there when the wind changes. "To stay permanently," he says, "you have to be willing to adapt."

David handles only conservative candidates and causes now, but who knows? Someday, maybe he'll take a Democrat into the firm, a retired congressman whose job it would be to lobby Democrats on the Hill or in a Democratic White House. To stay, you must adapt. "I think he's more resigned to paying the piper," says Myra Donnelley. "He's very pragmatic now. Some things you do to get things done. It was disappointing to David."

When David was growing up in politics in New Hampshire, it was the Washington types he despised—the guys with the assertive manner, the fancy suits, the quick and certain talkers, the obsessive achievers. David hasn't missed the irony. "I have criticized this in an earlier life," he says, "said these people are empty. But, really, that is laziness talking, that's just not right. Why put down people who are more organized than you are?"

But still, David doesn't *only* want to be a Washington type. He can't imagine anything worse than a Bob and Liddy Dole marriage, a Washington power-couple marriage. He cringes at the thought of marrying a woman who has only known him since he became what he is today. When he and his wife split, David began dating old girlfriends from his theater days, began spending more time in New York with people who, as they say, knew him when. A woman friend once visited him in Washington, and later a Washington woman said, "You know, David, she just doesn't fit in." David liked hearing that.

He's even become obsessed with getting back to theater. He's working on a play he plans to produce and direct off-Broadway next fall, a big-idea play about man's insatiable search for self-knowledge, an avant-garde play with Amelia Earhart and Sir Isaac Newton as the main characters. He has spent $15,000 working with a playwright on the script, commissioning the rock-jazz music that will go with it. He insists that he has never regretted coming to Washington, that making a lot of money has opened doors for him in theater. But David's close friend Mark Barasch, a New York guitar player whom David knew in his other life, says that over the years

David has often said he is sorry he left theater, that he envied and respected Barasch for not giving up. But David isn't leaving town.

No, politics is like theater, theater is like politics.

He'll stay.

A final scene . . .

Bob Gray is a legendary public relations man in Washington, and David is in Gray's magnificent Georgetown office overlooking the Potomac, plugging a friend who is looking for a job. Suddenly, Gray reaches into his desk drawer and pulls out a draft copy of President Reagan's upcoming 1988 State of the Union Address. Gray is working on a section of the speech, which is about as close to the heartbeat of Washington as any PR man could ever hope to get.

"We're working on this thing on line-item veto," Gray says.

He's searching for sexy instances of pork-barrel projects in the federal budget that Reagan can cite to prove that Congress should give the president line-item veto authority to reduce the deficit. Well, says David, by chance he's working on that exact question for his very first client, CFA. He'll send over a dozen examples this afternoon. Now, the chance to help Bob Gray write the State of the Union Address doesn't come along every day, and David gets his office right on it. And from the list he supplies, President Reagan actually uses two examples—federal funds for cranberry and wildflower research. After the speech, there's a holy furor, with Democrats whose districts get the cranberry and wildflower money attacking Reagan and defending the projects. But that is to be expected. This is a David coup.

David Carmen and those like him are always in motion, always making a call, doing a favor, dropping a tip. Most of it never pays off. But then—because you were there, because you were ready, because you were in motion—it just happens: you are two lines in the State of the Union Address. And suddenly, euphorically, you are a player. You are in the wagon.

Suddenly, you exist.

FEBRUARY 28, 1988

LEN HARRINGTON
My Father, My Son, Myself

*M*y father's guitar has his name, Len, printed immodestly in three-inch iridescent letters on its body, and they glisten as he tunes up to play for my son. His lyrics, scrawled into homemade booklets, are spread out on the floor, the kitchen sink, the music stand. As ever, my father takes his hootenannies and himself seriously. He has always had this gooselike way of craning his neck as he reads, and, silhouetted against a single lamp, he does this as he peers through silver reading glasses that are oddly over-sized for his head. Knowing what a skinflint my father is, I figure he got a deal on them a long time ago and they've been falling off into his soup ever since.

At sixty-seven, my dad still looks as I remember him, hair full and brown, body trim, face tanned, eyes sharp. What's different, what I can't get used to, is his gentleness and his patience. I remember neither as a boy, and I wonder which of us has changed. My son is four, and as my dad thumbs through his children's songs, Matthew bounces on the couch, furtively strums the guitar he's not supposed to touch, and talks incessantly.

"You know 'Give Me a Home Where the Buffalo Roam'?" my father asks in the high-pitched, teasing voice he reserves for kids and, on occasion, my mother.

"No," says Matthew. "We gotta find some I know, right, Grandpa?"

"How 'bout 'I Been Workin' on the Railroad'?"

"Yeah! I know that one. You know why? One time I heard my daddy sing it. So I know it too." Then with a fierce pride that shoots through me unexpectedly, Matthew adds, "My *daddy* taught it to me!"

I think to myself: *And so it begins.*

How I once despised that benign old man.

I don't recall why I despised him, only that I did—and that I made sure he knew it. All the classic stuff, the painful yet gleeful realization that he didn't know everything, the shouting matches, the

257

strange friends and clothes and beliefs—it all seems surreal today. But I still recall vividly my two great revelations about my dad. The first came sometime in my late teens when I suddenly realized that I was *not* my father, and that I could stop trying to prove that I wasn't. The second came about age thirty when I realized, in contradiction to my first revelation, that I *was* my father, like it or not. By then, I'd come to like it. What this says about my Freudian profile, who knows? These things came down between my father and me, and that is that.

There's so much talk these days about the New Fatherhood. Freed from being the sole paycheck, fathers no longer carry the pride or the burden of being the family giant-killer who goes off to battle the world every day. They baby-sit, wash laundry, mix formula. Fathers today are able to do what fathers of the last generation couldn't do for their sons: They hug them and kiss them and tell them they love them. These changes have liberated fathers from an isolation they once suffered within their own families. But even knowing these things, a friend of mine once lamented the passing of the old bonds between father and son—the hunting trips, the tinkering with the old jalopy, the undisputed authority of Father, the unrelenting masculinity of his model. "What's left for a father to teach his son?" my friend asked.

I've thought about that a lot lately, which is predictable after having had a son, and I now see my father with what seems a remarkable clarity. And instead of finding my father in myself, I now find myself in my father. I don't have my father's voice; we share a voice. I don't have my father's humor; we share a humor. I don't have my father's stubbornness; we share a stubbornness. I didn't always see these similarities as desirable. But I've grown into them. My father, for instance, has this way of answering the phone. "*Hellll-o*," he says, putting a heavy accent on the first syllable and snapping the *o* short. I picked this up as a boy and dropped it along the way. But call me today and you'll hear, "*Hellll-o*," just like the old man. Every time I hear myself say it, I feel good. I've grown into it.

On the way to the hardware store recently, my boy asked, "Sons can grow up to be their daddies, right, Dad?" This was no small struggling for insight, and I was careful in my response. No, I said, sons can't grow up to be their daddies. They can grow up to do the same work or to be like their daddies in some ways, but they can't *be* their daddies. They must be themselves. My son would hear nothing of these subtleties. He insisted that his friend Justin would grow up to be his daddy and that he would grow up to be me.

"Sons *can* grow up to be their daddies!" he said defiantly. "They can."

I didn't argue. It made me feel good.

My dad wasn't around much when I was a boy. He worked seven days a week and built our house in his spare time. But I've got plenty of warm memories—my father and me on the couch watching TV, riding the tractor, walking the gravel road at dusk, riding home at night in a darkened car singing "Red River Valley." Wedges of time inserted between miles of distance.

He was a good man, my father, and I knew it then. He laughed easily and was the life of a party, playing the guitar, singing, organizing the games. He also was a rugged teaser, and it was during his teasing that I always sensed his great, unspoken love. When I was older I would learn that this is how men show affection without acknowledging vulnerability. I'm sure there was a time when I yearned to be with my father more. But the day came very early when I also dreaded his presence. He was stern, with a quick temper. Even when at work he was the taskmaster in absentia. Infractions were added up, and at night my father dispensed punishment. This rarely went beyond a threatening voice and a scolding finger, and never beyond spanking, but in time my father's masculine warmth paled next to his feared judgment. When he was around, life seemed harder. I was in trouble more, there was less laughter and silliness, more attention to correct behavior. It was as if my father was trying to cram a lifetime of teaching into the little time we had together.

But there are things a boy cannot understand. I didn't understand, for instance, that my parents were a short step from poor. I didn't understand that my father had worked in the steel mill for eighty-five cents an hour before I was born and that he was fired when he refused to work nights, refused to leave my mother and my sister at home alone. I didn't understand that we lived from paycheck to paycheck and that he got up at 3:30 every morning to deliver milk because he had no choice. I just knew that he was a stranger in our house. He appeared occasionally, announced decisions, passed judgment. It was the way fatherhood went in those days. Like so many others of that era, my sisters, mother, and I fell into a pact to maneuver around the slumbering bear. "That's your father," my mother would say with pleasant resignation.

When he was home, my father was the boss, no question. But when he was gone, which was most of the time, rules were less stringent, conversation and feelings more free. My mother became the emotional fulcrum. It seemed that I could tell her anything, while I could tell him nothing. At least nothing that counted, nothing of the heart or the soul. If I was angry at my father, I told my mother, knowing she'd pass it on. If my father was sorry he'd yelled at me, my mother would relay his apology. "Dad didn't mean it," she'd say. "He's just tired tonight." None of this seemed odd. And not until I was a father myself did I discover that my father wasn't only the perpetrator, but also the victim, of this little dynamic.

But I never doubted my father's love, which was our lifeline through some pretty rough times. Always, he had this way of smiling at me, this way of tossing a backhanded compliment that let me know he was proud and watchful of my achievements. He was no insecure bully. I teased him plenty, and I imitated his way of saying "I love you" by telling him his nose was too big or his ties too ugly. But even today I can't recall a time my father hugged me or kissed me or said he loved me. I remember sleeping next to him on Sunday mornings. I remember the strong, warm feeling of him holding me as I dozed off in his arms. But men, even little men, did not kiss or hug, they shook hands. There were times much later, times when I would be going back to college, with the car packed and my parents and me standing on the driveway in those final few seconds, times when I wanted so badly to hug my father. But the muscles wouldn't move with the emotion. I hugged my mother. My dad and I shook hands.

"It's not what a man says, but what he *does* that counts," my father would say. Words and emotions were suspect. He went to work every day, he protected me, he taught me right from wrong, he made me tough in mind and spirit.

It was our bond. It was our barrier.

Matthew and I, visiting my parents in Arizona, are out for a walk. We see my folks rarely, and the chance to spend an entire week with his grandfather is a treat for my son, who seems especially bent right now on comprehending his place in time and family and gender. We leave the grandparents back at their winter trailer to rest from Matthew's frenetic energy.

"When I'm grown up," Matthew says, "I'll be walking here with my boy, right? You'll be back at the trailer with Mommy, right? You'll be old."

No matter how often I hear my son make these kinds of connections, I am amazed. They seem to blare from a loudspeaker, making me stop and turn my head in an involuntary pause. It's as if history is breaking before my eyes. Yes, that's right, I tell him, you will be walking here with your son, and your mother and I will be back at the trailer and Grandma and Grandpa will be dead. I wait for his reaction. There is none.

Matthew is at a nice age for fathers. It's all glory. A neighbor, who is six feet five inches tall, recalls that when his son was about Matthew's age, the boy believed he had the tallest dad in the world. My neighbor was deeply saddened when his boy met a man who was taller. It just can't last. Here is how another friend describes his son's transformation from adoring boy to resentful teen: "When he was six, he'd ask me a question and I'd answer it. He'd say, 'Dad knows everything!' When he was fourteen, I'd answer a question and he'd say, 'Dad *thinks* he knows everything!' It could have been the same question."

Like so many so-called New Fathers, I've tried not to repeat what I saw as my father's mistakes. I've refused to be the enforcer, expecting my wife to take an equal role, because I know what that did to my father and me. Matthew and I talk about emotions. We touch and cuddle and kiss good-bye. I try never to be embarrassed about this, though I suspect he senses my occasional uneasiness. This is the new masculinity, and it's as common today as the old masculinity was in my father's day. But, honestly, I'm not one who believes this will in the end save Matthew and me from what novelist Larry L. King called the "mutual thirst to prevail" between father and son. All I hope is that we build some repository of unconscious joy so that it will remain a lifeline between us through some pretty rough times. Because being a father simply isn't that new.

I remember once coming home from college and sitting at the dinner table lecturing my father about something. On and on I went. Now, my father loves a good argument, but as I talked that night he ate passively, occasionally glancing up, giving me that smile. Finally, I asked insistently, "Well, what do you think?" Without interrupting the arc of his fork from plate to mouth, my father looked into my eyes and said slowly and quietly, "Yep, you're still the same old knucklehead." I can't tell you how many times I've laughed at that memory because some things really never do change.

If there is a universal complaint from men about their fathers, it's that their dads lacked patience. I've thought of my own father's impatience a great deal in the last few years: as I painted my house and Matthew insisted he help, as I remodeled my second floor and Matthew insisted he help, as I sawed down dead trees in the backyard and Matthew insisted he help. At these times, and plenty more, memories of my father's impatience came clearly to mind. Because no matter the task, I never seemed to get it done right or get it done fast enough for him. It seemed that as soon as I'd started, my father would intervene: "Here, let me finish that up for you." God, I hated that.

So am I better with my own son? Well, I always start out with that in mind. I feign patience, give him a brush or a hammer, play along for a while. But in the end, I explain that these chores must be done, that they are dangerous, and that he'll have to find something else to do because I can't work and watch out for him at the same time. I sometimes say this patiently, sometimes less so, considerably less so. But no matter how I say it, there's a scene. I suspect that one of these encounters will live engraved on my son's mind as the life-long example of the old man's ill temper.

At least it was that way for me. I remember a lousy, dark, and rainy day when I was about six and my father was putting a new roof on his mother's house. I, of course, wanted to help. When my father said no, I made a scene and got the only spanking that I can recall. My father has chuckled at that memory many times over the years, but I never really saw the humor. It had happened decades earlier, but I still saw it through the eyes of a six-year-old boy. Only now that I've struggled to find patience in myself with my own son am I able to see that day through my father's eyes. I mean, climbing around on a roof is dangerous enough when it's dry, much less wet. Besides, the man had the shingles torn off and the rain was pouring into my grandmother's house. He was cold and wet and, to use a modern term, under stress. You see, I've put a new roof on in the pouring rain since that day. It's a miserable job—and the concerns of a little boy look mighty insubstantial in comparison. Who'd have guessed I'd be angry about that day for thirty years, until I could relive it with my own son, who, I suppose, is angry at me about it now.

This empathy for my father finally led me to a startling insight: If I am still resolving my feelings about my father, then when I was a boy my father was still resolving his feelings about his father. He raised me as a result of and a reaction to his own dad, which links my son not only to me and my father, but to my father's father and, I suspect, any number of Harrington fathers before. That realized, I suddenly imagined that if the phone had rung as the first Harrington stepped off the boat, he'd have answered by saying, "Hellll-o."

When I am with my father and my son, it is sometimes as if I don't exist, as if I am only a bridge separating and uniting these two people. For instance, I have this way of negotiating with Matthew about daily matters. "Do we have a deal?" I ask. "Yeah," he responds, "we have a deal." Then one day, I seem to disappear when I hear my father ask Matthew, "Well, do we have a deal?" These reprises go on constantly, most of them more subtle than words. I am, for example, proud of my son's curiosity, a quality I've always liked in myself. But as my father and Matthew and I drive back to Arizona from California, where we had visited my sister, it is again as if I've disappeared.

"Wanta stop?" my father asks enthusiastically as we pass someplace called Bible Land, where an old sculptor has spent his entire life crafting sandstone Bible scenes in an open field. Nobody but Matthew says yes, but my dad's driving, so we stop. In California's rich Imperial Valley we hear all about gravity irrigation systems and stop to see Old King Solomon, the first date tree imported to California. I ask how long it takes an orange grove to bear fruit after planting. "I don't know," my dad says. "I'll have to find that out." We learn the names of countless cacti and grasses, that hornets don't fly at night, which is nice to know, and that ants don't eat fish. We learn the price of gasoline at every station we pass. We stop in the desert to admire the dunes. "Look over there," my father says suddenly, pointing to an endless horizon of sand. "Look at that lonesome mountain back there." There's a silence until he says, "Everything's beautiful if you just look at it right."

I disappear. It is a sentence I have said to my own son.

There is a time in every son's life when he is angered by the echoes reminding him that, for all his vaunted individuality, he is his father's son. But there should also come a time when these echoes call out only a profound repose, neither nostalgic nor exhilarating, and the understanding that the generations have melded and blurred without threat. I am not my father. We still disagree on just about everything to do with politics and society, and, plagued with more education, I'm far less confident that the world as I see it is necessarily as it is. I can't bait a fishhook, repair an engine, or stalk a pheasant. John Wayne is not my idol.

Yet these matters aren't of consequence. And looking back, I sometimes think my father's generation was right: "It's not what a man says, but what he does that counts." Because if I ever learned anything from my dad's lectures, I don't recall it. I hold him responsible and I love him not for what he said, but for what he did or didn't do. Because what good fathers have always taught their sons, more or less unconsciously, isn't a checklist of hunting and fishing skills, but what it means to be a man, some seedling sense of how to be strong but not destructive, self-reliant but not invulnerable, of what self-mastery means in a world we must pretend to control when we can't.

I once believed that manhood required that I stand up to my father, even if it meant fists. Then this happened: Some friends and I buried our high school's parking-lot barriers under the woodpile for the annual Homecoming bonfire. We hated the things because they kept us from leaving school in our cars until after the buses had left. I thought the prank was pretty funny, and I mentioned it to my dad. He didn't think it was funny, and he ordered me to go with him to dig them out of the pile. Can you imagine anything more humiliating at age sixteen? I refused, and we stood toe-to-toe. My father was in a rage, and I thought for an instant that the test had come. But then he shook his head and calmly walked away. The next day, my friends told me they'd seen him at the bonfire celebration that night, that he'd climbed into the woodpile before hundreds of kids, pulled out the barriers, and left. He never mentioned it to me. He still hasn't.

For reasons too profound and too petty to tell, there was a time years ago when my father and I didn't speak or see each other. I finally gave up my stubbornness and visited unexpectedly. For two days we talked of cars and work, politics and old friends, of everything and nothing. Neither mentioned that we hadn't seen each other in several years. During a Sunday snowstorm, I left as depressed as I've ever been, knowing that reconciliation was impossible. Two days later I got the only letter my dad ever sent me. I'm the writer, he's the milkman? Ha! The letter's tone and cadence, its emotion and simplicity might have been mine.

"I know that if I had it to do over again," my father wrote, "I would somehow find more time to spend with you. It seems we never realize this until it's too late." It turned out that as he had watched me walk out that door—at the very instant I was thinking that we were hopelessly lost to each other—he was telling himself to stop me, to sit down and talk, that if we didn't, he would never see me again. "But I just let you go," he wrote. The muscles wouldn't move with the emotion, which is all I ever really needed to know.

All morning I am anxious.

Matthew and I leave Arizona today for home, and I am determined to do something I have never done. I am determined to tell my father that I love him. I fret over the timing, knowing that there will be little left to say after that unheard-of declaration. Not surprisingly, I opt for the easy route, the last minute before Matthew and I walk through the gate and onto the plane. "Dad, I want you to know that I love you. That I always have." There is a bag in my left hand, and I lean over and hug my father with my right arm. He is impassive. I suppose he's in shock.

"Yeah, yeah sure," he says awkwardly. "No problem."

Then we are gone. It wouldn't surprise me if my father then turned to my mother, shook his head, and said, "Yep, he's still the same old knucklehead." But now, after my own voyage, it also wouldn't surprise me if he cried. Knowing that, I hope, will someday make it easier for me, and for my son.

JANUARY 11, 1987

AFTERWORD
On Profile Writing

*M*ostly, it's no mystery.

Like all good journalism, good profile writing grows from an accumulation of knowledge and experience, a mastering of method, and a dedication to hard work and accuracy.

But then there's that smidgen of magic . . . Some people say it's flair or style, maybe a touch of moxie that lets a journalist experiment just a little more, take a calculated chance of falling flat. As baseball player Crash Davis said in the movie *Bull Durham*: "You gotta play this game with fear and arrogance." All these things are true. But at the risk of sounding oddly metaphysical, I think it also has to do with a journalist's willingness or need to wrestle the piles of conflicting and seemingly disconnected information into a shape that's not only true and accurate but also makes interpretive sense. It has to do with your willingness or need to transform that research pile, that life, into YOUR STORY. Without that drive to impose sense on it all, you will not find the threads, the themes, the theories that will do it. And here is where the smidgen of magic comes in . . . Because you can't do this without taking a breath, closing your eyes and relaxing, letting that pile of research sweep over you, seep into your dreams at night and into your daytime mullings. You can't do it without *feeling* your subject. The tough-guy journalists will hate this: You must use your intuition.

But first, you gotta get your mind right.

I was once a young journalist serving time at a little paper in Harrisburg, Pennsylvania, telling myself that nothing ever happened in this one-horse town that would let me show editors the great work I could do. What I needed was a great IDEA, but great ideas didn't exist in Harrisburg. They were in New York, Washington, Los Angeles. Then I picked up *Esquire* magazine, where a man named Arthur Bell had written a profile called "The Wife of the Accused." Location: Harrisburg, Pennsylvania. Oh, sure, I'd read about the wild case of the father-and-son team charged with burglarizing and terrorizing suburban housewives. They were on

267

trial, and dozens of reporters were covering it. What could I write that wasn't going to be written? Well, Arthur Bell answered my question. The wife of the accused was a strange, self-absorbed woman who wore too much makeup, giggled, and smiled during the trial that was to determine if, while she slept or cleaned the house, her husband and son were out breaking into other women's homes.

I got the point: If there are no bad stories, only bad storytellers, the same is true for ideas. William Faulkner won a Nobel Prize writing about a fictional county in backwater Mississippi. Herman Melville's greatest work was about a crazy man chasing a whale. Sociologist Elliott Liebow's classic *Tally's Corner* was about the lives of men who hung out on one street corner. James Agee's *Let Us Now Praise Famous Men* immortalized southern tenant farmers. Theodore Rosengarten's *All God's Dangers* was the life story of one old sharecropper. Michael Lesy's *Wisconsin Death Trip* captured the chilling quality of life in one nineteenth-century rural American town. Philosopher John Berger and Jean Mohr's *A Fortunate Man* told the story of one English country doctor. Photographer W. Eugene Smith's photo essays in *Life* portrayed the life of a country doctor, as well as the lives of rural villagers in Spain and Japan.

So look around you. The Journalism of Everyday Life is infinite: a farmer as winter comes to the farm, a country priest, three men who have for years met every Saturday morning to play basketball, a week in the life of a suburban housewife, the annual deer-hunting expedition, a high-school football quarterback, a welfare mother, a pool shark, an aspiring jazz musician, an old man and an old woman who fall in love in a nursing home. Not to mention several of the profiles that appear in this book: a high-school genius, a family that has lost a son to suicide, a fundamentalist family, a retarded man. These stories could have been done in any town in America, including Harrisburg.

Never think of such pieces as cute feature stories. Think of them as, well, journalistic anthropology. Read Georges Bernanos's 1937 novel *The Diary of a Country Priest*—and think about how if you spent hour after hour, day after day with a *real* country priest, made his rounds with him, prayed with him, went to weddings and funerals and christenings with him, helped set up the folding tables for Friday bingo, talked to his parishioners in their homes about what he has done for them in times of tragedy or joy, about those qualities they admire and those they don't, how if you talked to his parents and his childhood friends, and then talked with him again and again about what he *feels* when the communion host is miraculously transformed into the body and blood of Christ . . . Think about how if you did these things—and more—with a *real* priest, you'd have a hell of a story: A real-life version of Bernanos's *Diary of a Country Priest*.

Naturally, you'd want to know the names and symbolic meaning of the garments he wears for Mass. You'd want to know where each of the paintings, posters, and statues in his house came from. You'd want to know the complete story of his life, beginning with, "So how did your parents meet?" You'd want to have him draw the floor plan of his childhood home, because it would jog his memory about his siblings, mother, and father. You'd want to take notes on the texture of his skin, the number and depth of the wrinkles in his brow, the curve of his hairline, the timbre of his voice and when it changes, the manner and trajectory of his gestures, the length of his gait, the angle of his walk. You'd want to note if the paint on his house is peeling, if he stacks several days of dirty dishes or does them after every meal. You'd want to note what books are on his shelf, what poetry he reads. You'd want to read those books, that poetry, talk with him about it, about lines and paragraphs. You'd want to note the way the sunlight plays through the rose window in his church. You'd want to know the masonry bond style of his church's brickwork. You'd want to know exactly what he thinks when he elevates the host and says "for this is my body."

You'd want to know all these things and more, because they would be the authenticating detail—the "color," journalists would call it—that would, as novelist Nelson Algren said, allow you to write "from the poise of mind which lets us see that things are exactly what they seem." Around this documentary detail you would wrap the real point of your investigation into this one priest's life: What does his faith mean to him? And by intimation, what can deep faith mean to anyone in so modern a world? But you cannot find this only by collecting details. This you must find through interviews with those who know the man and through conversations with him—long, rambling conversations. You must have done enough reading and interviewing of theologians to raise the important issues facing Catholicism today. You must know enough about why men join and leave the priesthood to ask searching questions. You must ask if he has ever doubted his faith. But remember, you are neither shrink nor interrogator. You are, for this time, more like a friend.

At least that's what I would do, or *try* to do. I'm convinced that unless you first *envision, imagine* your profiles in such a grand fashion, you'll never do memorable work. You must maintain a simultaneous attention to detail and larger meaning, and you must be constantly thinking about how the two intertwine. Unfortunately, you can't know which of the thousands of details will later come to carry some emblematic meaning as the themes of your story emerge. So you must get it all. To help organize the job, I try to keep a counter running in my head that reminds me to observe details through *all* of my senses. Seeing is the easiest, of course, and you must resist the temptation to record only what you see.

I stop myself and ask: What is the *smell* of his room? What do I *hear* as he walks across the gravel drive? What is the *feel* of his priest's collar? What is the *taste* of the spaghetti sauce he is sipping at the stove? You won't know what of this blur of detail you'll use until you're actually writing, but if you don't collect it, you won't have it. You must be methodical. I read somewhere that *New Yorker* writer John McPhee was once asked how he could know the exact temperature of the river in which he was canoeing at an exact point in his text. The answer: McPhee had dangled a thermometer over the side of the canoe, and every once in a while he had pulled it up and recorded the water's temperature in his notes. It is this attention to the *technique* of collecting detail that every stylistic journalist must master.

It can get pretty arcane. When I was in Carl Bernstein's New York apartment, for instance, I didn't at first realize that the many batches of drooping cut flowers decorating the place would in any way symbolize a new, mellower Bernstein, but I dutifully noted their locations and colors and asked Bernstein where they came from. He gave me the name and phone number of the man who delivered them. Later, after I recognized their symbolism, I had to call the man to collect specific flower names. They included an oncidium orchid and French lilacs, but the man was uncertain of the name of the roses. So I called the florist, who knew them by several names. So I found a rose expert and we settled on Vivaldi roses. I suppose I spent two or three hours tracking down those few details.

I also didn't know when I was wandering through Jack Anderson's boyhood home that I would use that scene to begin my story. I sensed only a sudden edgy quiet in Anderson. I knew little about his stormy relationship with his father then. Only later did I realize what had gone on during our tour of his old home. Fortunately, the details and the mood of the moment had been recorded. The same was true for my use of Lynda Johnson Robb's hair as a symbol of her discomfort with being on display. She kept talking about her hair, and I kept noting her talking about it. But only after an old friend of hers told me about how Lynda had fussed over her hair in the dressing room before her husband's inauguration as governor of Virginia did the significance of what I had seen earlier click. Later, in my notes, I found a forgotten reference to seeing Lynda in the foyer of the women's room, at the mirror, again working on her hair.

And certainly, when Kelly McGillis walked on stage the first day of rehearsal with her face dolled up in heavy makeup, I took note of it, but had no idea that it meant something about her deep and raging insecurities. Fortunately, when I realized its significance, my notes included a description of her appearance and attire that first morning a month earlier. This constant collecting and sifting through seemingly disparate information is also what led me to read Rainer Maria Rilke's 1929 *Letters to a Young Poet*, which Kelly had mentioned as one of her favorite books. Only after I had seen Kelly fight off her great fear and ace her performance as Viola did the words of Rilke come back to echo in my mind: "Perhaps all the dragons of our lives are princesses who are only waiting to see us once beautiful and brave. Perhaps everything terrible is in its deepest being something helpless that wants help from us." Suddenly, it was clear why Kelly had loved this book. In short, you can't know what matters until you know what matters. So relax, cast the widest net, and see what rises up to intertwine in meaning. With the strictest attention to technique, dogged work, and a patient cast of mind, your story will emerge.

But remember always that journalism is a child of fact. Yes, I know we can debate all day what *is* or *is not* fact. But like art and pornography, we know what it is when we see it. Journalism isn't a philosophical pursuit; it's a commonsense, real-world pursuit. In journalism, a fact is something that ten people in a room will always agree upon—blue is blue, words spoken are words spoken, the temperature is 72 degrees Fahrenheit, sunlight is casting through the foliage of that oak tree. Facts are the body of perceptions we agree to agree upon.

In journalism, even the stylistic type, there's no room for messing with facts. But the *meaning*, the interpretation or elaboration of those facts, is a different matter. The sky is blue. But ten people who agree about that *fact* will certainly disagree if you say, "The sky is so blue it looks as if it is about to disappear into itself." No, somebody will say, "It's not *that* blue." Or, "What the hell does that mean?" Or, "Only gray skies look as if they are about to disappear into themselves." But these differences of opinion don't make our elaboration about the *nature* of the blue sky inaccurate, because our commonsense notion of accuracy allows for differences in the eye of the beholder, as long as we are working from a shared premise, the *fact* of blue. The stylistic journalist must take full advantage of this interpretive opportunity to breathe life and texture and poetry into stories, as well as using it to help set an interpretive mood. It's one of the ways a pile of facts becomes *your* story.

Unfortunately, all *facts* aren't so easy for people to agree upon. In profile writing, where you are often trying to reveal the internal landscape—the mindscape—of your subject, it's especially tricky because profiles are most dramatic and engrossing if, in line with Algren's notion, they're written as if the action is happening before the reader's eyes. The use of the techniques and tone of naturalistic fiction is today so ingrained in the assumptions of stylistic journalism that it's hard to believe that when Tom Wolfe, Truman Capote, and Gay Talese were writing their New Journalism in the 1960s, it was controversial. I'm not going to recap that debate or the methods that emerged, but any journalist aspiring to write intimate profiles should know the history of the approach. If you don't, read Wolfe's several essays in his 1973 anthology with E. W. Johnson, *The New Journalism*, where you'll find Wolfe's style of "saturation" reporting explained. Also, read two books edited by Norman Sims, *The Literary Journalists* (1984) and *Literary Journalism in the Twentieth Century* (1990). They'll suggest dozens of other readings. I'll say only that journalists who argue that style, interpretation, and fact don't mix are dinosaurs who just don't know their stuff.

It's hard work turning human emotions, feelings, and attitudes into *facts*, but, as Jesse Jackson once said about his grueling schedule, "It ain't as hard as pickin' cotton." It can be done by comparing and contrasting the recollections and writings of your subjects and human sources, as well as documentary sources such as old newspapers, memoirs, and court records. If you can use these sources to know what a person was thinking, say, the morning of September 2, 1950, then you have created a "fact" by the traditional standards of journalism that treat a double-sourced piece of information out of, say, the Pentagon as a fact. Reading Bob Woodward and Carl Bernstein's 1976 book *The Final Days*, about the fall of President Richard Nixon, was for me, as a young journalist, like turning on a light in the dark. *The Final Days* proved that reporting about feelings, emotions, and impressions could work successfully on even the hardest-edged story based on interviews with the most savvy and manipulative of sources—White House staffers.

With confirmations from documents and sources and often the subject, I have no qualms about treating emotional facts exactly as I would the fact that the sky is blue. But since we aren't novelists, if the subject disputes a source's recollections, then drama must take a backseat and an elaboration or denial from the subject is required. My Carl Bernstein profile includes an example. A trusted source told me Bernstein had once said he was deeply hurt when he wasn't invited to *Washington Post* board chairman Katharine Graham's seventieth birthday party, but Bernstein denied this vehemently. I returned to my source repeatedly for more details and was personally convinced the source's version was correct. But because Bernstein continued to deny the recollection, I described the incident this way: "Bernstein says he found the snub rude, but amusing. A friend says he was hurt and angry." If Bernstein had confirmed the story, I would have written without attribution that he had been deeply hurt by the snub. If my source had waffled under Bernstein's denial, I wouldn't have used the anecdote at all.

So a great deal of profile reporting goes into "sourcing"—not documentary facts and money trails, as in investigative and public affairs reporting, but emotions, feelings, and attitudes. As I said in the Introduction to this collection, intimate profile writing tries to understand a subject from the inside out. But getting at these non-traditional kinds of facts is done through traditional journalistic methods. For instance, one of the first lessons of reporting about public officials is to remember to constantly compare "promise versus performance." What did they *say* they would do in office? What have they actually done? The fit or slippage is your story. Investigating character borrows a variation on the same approach. In the introduction to her book *Character*, a collection of profiles about the presidential primary candidates of 1988, journalist Gail Sheehy wrote that she always tries to compare her subject's "personal myth" with her own reportorial assessment of the subject's life.

In full-blown profiles on public figures (as opposed to more narrow slice-of-life profiles), I do much the same thing. I try to interview the subject uncritically about his or her life. I try not to even think of this as interviewing, but rather as conversations with the subject. I see this as *their* version of reality—what Sheehy calls their "personal myth." In short, I let people talk and talk. Then I begin what I think of as "continuity interviewing" of friends, family, and enemies from every important period of a subject's life. In George Bush's case, I found people from his preteen years, his years at prep school, his years in the war, his years at Yale, his early and later years in the Texas oil business, his years in Texas politics, and his years in Congress. I look for diverse and multiple sources from each important period, and I treat each period as a whole that must be understood in and of itself. I collect what I think of as parallel versions of the subject's life, and I lay them all out next to one another to see where the versions meet and diverge. (It was only during this comparison that I realized several sources had independently mentioned that people had repeatedly said the young George Bush would be president someday.) It's quite likely that you'll need to go back to sources again to confirm, disprove, or flesh out important anecdotes, maybe more than once. What you're looking for are continuities or discontinuities—patterns or breaks in those patterns—in a subject's behavior.

In doing profile interviewing, I don't ask sources their opinions of the subject's motives or psychological makeup until the end, and I almost never tell them what I'm thinking about the subject, unless this is necessary to induce a source's recollection. For one, you shouldn't have *any* firm opinions about the subject yet; you just began. For another, you should always remember that many of your sources are reporting back to your subject what you have asked and how you've asked it. In fact, it's possible to send your subject a message about your sense of fairness and balance by the way you handle interviews with his acquaintances. What I want from profile sources are anecdotes, memories, stories about what a subject actually *did* or *said*. I want sources to walk me through their recollections of the subject, as if we were turning the pages of an old scrapbook. (In fact, sometimes I get them to pull out their old scrapbooks and do just that.) At this point, I have no idea what I'm looking for; I'm simply casting that wide net. I often begin with, "So how far do you and George go back anyway?" I almost never have a list of questions. I want a free-flowing, annotated, fact-filled narrative of the source's relationship with the subject.

Over the years, I've found that, contrary to journalistic lore, it is a person's friends and loved ones who are the best sources. You must interview enemies, yes, and you'll get good stuff. But ask yourself, "Who knows me at my best and my worst?" Is it that boss or professor who despises you? Or is it your mother, father, and siblings? Your oldest and best friends? Your husband or wife of twenty years?

If a subject is famous, it's likely that sources will have been interviewed many times about their acquaintanceship. So they're likely to have a story line they'll slip into like a train on its tracks. It's important to intervene in this reverie by interrupting them frequently with seemingly silly questions: "By the way, what was George wearing that first day you met him?" Or, "Was it sunny or rainy that afternoon?" Or, "What color was that Studebaker he was driving then?" This interrupts the worn version and also hints at the depth of detail you want them to recall.

Direct your questioning toward your subjects' human qualities: Do they have a lot of friends or a few? A good family? Do they easily show emotion and affection? Do they treat people politely or rudely? Are they vindictive or forgiving? Do they have a sense of humor? Do they laugh at themselves and allow others to laugh with them? Do they treat subordinates as equals or servants? Do they demand that people adore them? Are they different people in different settings? Do their enemies respect them? Are they considerate? Do they remember birthdays? Do their old friends last? Who do they look to for personal affirmation and respect? Are they risk takers? Do they listen when people talk? Do they take advice respectfully? How have they dealt with failure? With success? Are they prone to rebel against authority? Or do they accept it willingly? Of course, you can't phrase your questions so bluntly, but these are the kinds of questions you need answered, especially if your subject is seeking political or other public power.

You should know that this "fame thing" skews the whole process of intimate profile reporting. I've never enjoyed profiling famous people as much as ordinary Joes. Famous people—defined as anyone in the public eye—are trouble because they're so experienced and cynical about the press that it's hard to pierce their facade or win their trust. They've been burned too many times. Their experience has taught them, as Lynda Robb's mother taught her, to imagine how every word will look "on the front page of the New York Times." They have numerous and complicated agendas for agreeing to cooperate with an in-depth profile, and your writing as authentic, unvarnished, and truthful a story as possible rarely has anything to do with it. In the end, you'll probably have to settle for structured time with your subject. Your conversations will be relatively short and formal, and you'll never be able to establish a sense of intimacy. You'll be forced to rely heavily on dozens of interviews with sources. None of this, however, frees you from the responsibility to capture the human truth about your subject. If your subject gets in your way, you must work harder.

It's now that experience writing about ordinary people is helpful. You must reach back and remember what it was that interested you in, say, the country priest. Profiles of ordinary Joes will rise on your ability to find the extraordinary in the ordinary, mystery in the mundane. Profiles of the famous will rise on your ability to find the ordinary in the extraordinary, to demystify the majestic. But famous people can be intimidating. For one, they're usually charming. If you have royalist leanings, you'll want to please them, want their status to rub off on you. If you're of a populist bent, perhaps you'll want to gut them. Instead, you must recall all you wanted to know about the country priest—the intricacies of his thinking, the documentary reality of his world—and you must seek the same. You must reach back and remember the mood and tone of your inquiry into ordinary lives and try to find that mood and tone in your inquiry of extraordinary lives. Now is when you need to remember most that your goal as a writer of intimate profiles is not to judge whether a person has been a good or bad president, police chief or county commissioner. Your goal is to understand them as they understand themselves—at night when they say their prayers.

I have no secret formula for winning the cooperation of famous subjects. I suggest being honest about the depth you are seeking and the time it will take. When I first met with George Bush to try and win his cooperation, he angrily said that the *Washington Post* had treated him badly, so why should he trust me. On the hot seat, I told him that I could certainly help my career immensely by writing the profile that hammered the last nail in his political coffin. I said one colleague had even suggested that I write a story that would "ream George Bush a new asshole." Bush nearly jumped out of his chair. His press secretary, Marlin Fitzwater, who wanted Bush to do the profile, grabbed a pillow from the couch, covered his face, and groaned. Then I told Bush that after the smart-ass remark I had refused the assignment, saying, "Find yourself another boy," unless I was promised the time to do the profile my way. Now, the "ream George Bush" remark had been only cynical newsroom humor, and I had perhaps heightened the drama of the encounter. But on the spur of the moment, blunt honesty was all I could come up with. It seemed to work. "You really said that?" Bush asked, calming down, and our arrangement was soon set.

In seeking famous subjects' cooperation, I have played one psychological game with myself: I have convinced myself that if I ever tell a subject I will begin my profile with an open mind and then do not do so, I will lose my power to write that profile. ("Magical thinking," one journalist sniffed.) I know it sounds like Samson and his hair, but I believe it. Whatever qualities a person has that make other people trust him with the stories of their lives are somehow signaled in a thousand unconscious ways. If a profile writer lacks these qualities or is insincere in claiming them, I believe he will fail.

None of the facts or the interpretations in your final profile should surprise your subjects, because one of the last steps in profiling is to discuss them with your subjects. He or she is going to read the profile anyway, and in every case you'll find that any elaboration or explanation, denial or confirmation will only make your profile better. More often than not, if you've done your reporting, your subject will agree with your interpretations, even if grudgingly. When he or she does not, listen carefully. In the most serious mistake of my career, I ignored a county commissioner who looked me in the eye and said, "If you print that, you'll be wrong." Well, I printed it and I was wrong. Actually, the privileged public records where I'd gotten my information were wrong, but wrong is wrong. I should have listened more closely—for his sake and for mine.

Usually, it helps to begin testing your ideas on your subject while reporting. In profiling actress Kelly McGillis, I would ask her every few days to tell me what she was thinking and feeling when she was onstage acting at her best. It was impossible to describe, she said. But over the weeks, she'd find a word or two of description or I'd suggest something and she would say yes or no and explain. All of these tiny emotional gleanings went into the profile's final scene, wrapped around a speech that Kelly had told me was her finest moment that night: *Kelly's not thinking of where her arm is resting or if a prop is in place . . . Her emotional frenzy has freed her of self-consciousness . . . She hears not only her own voice but that of her character . . . She's not thinking of the audience or other people's expectations . . . For this instant, no one else is in control of Kelly McGillis . . . She doesn't care what the critics will say . . . She believes every word of written dialogue that she is saying . . . She has, for this moment, become Shakespeare's Viola.*

None of this is hyperbole or poetic license on my part. The reader learns it all in one fell swoop—as if seeing it happen. But if I had waited until after that final scene and tried to understand the moment in one fell swoop, Kelly would have said she couldn't describe what she had been feeling, that it was impossible to describe. Only by pulling it out of her one detail at a time during the weeks of reporting could I describe accurately the full sense of the brief moment.

Now comes the hardest part: *Writing.*

Over the last fifteen years, I think I've tried about every approach known to modern man. Unfortunately, what works best for me finally is the artless, laborious, rock-breaking method. I sit down in a quiet room with my boxes and file drawers of well-organized material and I read it all one more time and take notes. Atop a separate page, I write: Possible Themes. As they come to me, I jot them down. When I'm done, I'll have from several to many legal pads that include everything important from my records. Then I put the boxes and file drawers aside, stack up the pads before me, read them all one more time, turn to my keyboard, put my feet up on my desk, close my eyes, try to let it all sink in, think of my subject, and see what comes to mind. And this is where the smidgen of magic comes in, because four out of five times what I see in that instant is my lead: Jack Anderson wandering emotionless through his childhood home, Rob Thate staring at the FBI composite taped next to his door, Kelly McGillis in all that makeup, my own father playing his guitar, Gary Poe sitting beneath that single light, Carl Bernstein in his tuxedo, George Bush in his speedboat, Anton LaVey at his iridescent organ. After all the work, these images flashed. So I figured they were, in some way, the distillation of everything I had learned and felt.

When nothing comes to mind, or when no single strong image comes to mind, I close my eyes and think in sentences. That's when I wrote, "She is her daddy's daughter" about Lynda Robb. And "Ruth and Bucky Jenkins are suspended somewhere between despair and redemption." And "He was never a great preacher" about Jerry Falwell. Don't get me wrong, I've got to play with these scenes and sentences for hours, sometimes days. But I figure these ideas and images are me talking to me, and I try to listen. Maybe I enjoyed my Kelly McGillis profile so much because the way she gets in touch with her characters is a lot like the way a profile writer must get in touch with his subjects.

For instance, I once wrote companion profiles about a corporate mogul and a Catholic bishop locked in a struggle over the future of three city hospitals. The mogul was dead and the bishop wouldn't talk to me. I did dozens of interviews with people who knew them, but it wasn't until I had a dream one night that I felt comfortable portraying them. In my dream, I was interviewing the men together, and they were answering, arguing, cajoling. The mogul kept jumping up, striding around the room, gesturing forcefully. The bishop sat Buddha-like, quietly and firmly having his say. My dream made these men real to me. At the risk of sounding oddly metaphysical, I believe that's the depth of emotion a profile writer should try to reach. At least it is the level of obsession that works for me. In fact, when I start dreaming about my subjects, I know it's time to write.

In simple terms, write what you find. It's dishonest to write a story tougher than your research warrants because an editor prefers it, or because you're afraid your journalism colleagues will think you are too "soft," or because you think the truth might hurt your career. I had some anxious days after my profile of Rob Thate appeared, because although the FBI had formally stated that Rob was *not* a suspect in the disappearance of his son, I knew off-the-record that he was still under suspicion informally. To have written a sympathetic article and then have Rob arrested for the crime would have been a humiliating and, quite likely, a career-shortening experience. But I'd done my legwork, spent hours and hours talking with Rob and his wife, and I believed I knew more about him than the FBI did. His memory was too precise, the details too sharp, too much in line with his wife's independent account for Rob to be lying. You do your best and say the hell with it. To have treated Rob's guilt as a possibility would have ruined the story, not reflected my findings, and, ultimately, been wrong.

Yet there are times for pulling your punches, because profiling ordinary people is more complicated ethically than profiling public figures. For one, ordinary people will often tell you the most intimate details of their lives without thinking about how those details might look in print. Often they're in emotional crises and they quickly come to think of you as a friend and counselor. I know many journalists don't like to hear it, but I believe it's your responsibility to look after these people. My first responsibility is to tell readers a story that's honest in what it says and what it doesn't say. With that done, I can watch out for my subject too. For instance, I had originally planned to tell the story of how the entire Jenkins family had reacted to the suicide in their midst. But I came to believe I couldn't do this without revealing details about the surviving children that were potentially damaging to them emotionally. I thought I would have to leave too much out or sugarcoat some of the siblings' stories, and this would be dishonest to readers. But I believed that the parents, Ruth and Bucky, were so committed to telling their story so other families could avoid their tragedy that nothing I knew about them would be too painful for them to see in print. So I changed the focus of my story to concentrate only on their reaction, more or less leaving out the children.

If you aren't learning intimate details about your ordinary subjects that you believe are too personal for print, you're probably doing a poor job of reporting. If you don't often struggle with the ethics of what you will include in your profiles of ordinary people, you're either a schmuck or not really facing the ethical dilemmas.

Writing is always the hardest. I hate it. I rant and rave. I tell my editors I don't think this one is going to work. But you must have this ultimate confidence: If you stare at the blank page long enough, something good will eventually come out. I vouch for this commandment. Naturally, full-blown profiles need to be written differently from slice-of-life profiles. But as a general rule, it seems best to create a narrative that moves through time from when the subject isn't revealed to the reader—and sometimes not even to himself—to a time when the subject is revealed. I try to follow the dictum of short-story writing that says the main character's self-awareness should in some way change during the course of the story. This is accomplished by describing the grand sweep of changes in a person's life, as well as the changes that occur in the midst of the story itself: Bucky Jenkins finally vented his anger at his dead son; Rob Thate discovered his deep faith; Evan Sherbrooke discovered he liked himself the way he was; Jack Anderson finally faced his father.

Besides the time frame of the subject's entire life that almost always runs through a profile, a time frame of events happening while you are with the subject often runs parallel. For Kelly McGillis, it was the making of a play. For Jack Anderson, it was a visit with his parents. Sometimes the contemporaneous time frame is created by a series of unrelated but unifying scenes or anecdotes, as when the Carl Bernstein profile moves from scene to disconnected scene, separated by sections on his earlier life, moving to today when the contemporaneous scenes and his larger life meet in a final scene at the Andy Warhol Ballroom. That kind of sequencing technique is used in most of the pieces in *American Profiles*. All in all, some kind of movement through time seems necessary to give a profile a storylike quality, with questions that emerge at the beginning being answered at the end. But always remember that real life isn't a "story." Real life is unpredictable and its lessons are contradictory, not neat. Yet we all start out at one point in time and are changed by how we interpret the meaning of our experiences as we pass through. In that way, every life is a narrative.

A final word . . . Journalists are wise to be skeptics, doubters who forever demand proof, who want to put their hands in the wounds of any would-be savior. But the field is also heavy with those who have what John O'Hara called "unearned cynicism"—skepticism gone over the edge. If you wish to understand people, to appreciate their personal journeys, to win their trust and to deserve it, you cannot let this happen to you. Don't be naive, but don't wear dark glasses either. To borrow the insight of novelist Amy Tan, you must learn "to lose your innocence but not your hope."

It is good advice. Try to take it.

SUGGESTED READINGS
A Personal List

Just about any journalism professor could give you a more exhaustive list of readings for learning to write stylistic profiles. But these are books that have mattered to me.

In journalism, David Halberstam's *The Best and the Brightest* (1972), about America's Vietnam policy planners, was a wake-up call leading me to the realization that personality, character, and public policy can never be separated. Robert Caro's *The Power Broker* (1974), about New York public works planning czar Robert Moses, strongly reinforces that notion. Bob Woodward and Carl Bernstein's *The Final Days* (1976) sends the same message, as does Neil Sheehan's *A Bright Shining Lie* (1988). Although I was never much for his manic style, Tom Wolfe's work, particularly *The Right Stuff* (1979), greatly expanded my own and a whole generation's thinking about stylistic methods. John McPhee's steady and staid writing always tempted me to turn on a ball game, but he has no equal in turning fact into literature, as exemplified in *The John McPhee Reader* (1976).

Gay Talese's collection of articles, *Fame and Obscurity* (1981), particularly his Frank Sinatra profile, is a classic in creative form and reporting. Michael Herr's *Dispatches* (1977) is the peak of stylized reporting from the Vietnam War. Also essential to read are the famous works of "faction"—Truman Capote's *In Cold Blood* (1965) and Norman Mailer's *The Executioner's Song* (1979). I've already mentioned E. W. Johnson and Tom Wolfe's *The New Journalism* (1973) and two books edited by Norman Sims, *The Literary Journalists* (1984) and *Literary Journalism in the Twentieth Century* (1990). All three are must-reads—*The New Journalism* because it includes Wolfe's essays on stylistic methods, and the Sims books because they are a true overview of what he calls "literary journalism."

The nonfiction collection by Harry Crews, *Blood and Grits* (1979), taught me the creative possibilities in profile writing. (I'll never forget reading a Crews article about an old man who raised fighting cocks that made me appreciate the beauty and complexity of the man's bloody expertise.) A book by Douglas Bauer, *Prairie City, Iowa* (1979), about life in a tiny midwestern town, reminded me that anything—I mean anything—can be a good story. Howard Kohn's book *The Last Farmer* (1988) did the same, as did Tracy Kidder's *Soul of a New Machine* (1981), *House* (1985), and *Among Schoolchildren* (1989). For the same reason, I loved the *Essays of E. B. White* (1977) and White's *The Second Tree from the Corner* (1965).

Two other realms of nonfiction writing have been important to me: nature and travel writing. Both forms are particularly good at capturing the inter-play between detail and meaning, by finding metaphor in the intricacies of nature and the seemingly trivial experiences of travel. First on my list of travel literature is Peter Matthiessen's *The Snow Leopard* (1978). Next is William Least Heat Moon's *Blue Highways* (1982), V. S. Naipaul's *Among the Believers* (1981), Alan Cheuse's *Fall Out of Heaven* (1987), and Bruce Chatwin's *In Patagonia* (1977). From the world of nature writing, Edward Abbey's *Desert Solitaire* (1968), Aldo Leopold's *A Sand County Almanac* (1949), and William W. Warner's *Beautiful Swimmers* (1976) all embarrassed me into trying harder. Several of Wendell Berry's pieces in *Recollected Essays: 1965– 1980* (1981) are unforgettable examples of the blending of nature, everyday life, and literature into nonfiction, particularly "The Rise," "The Long-Legged House," and "Nick and Aunt Georgie."

The area of "oral history" is also a rich vein for stylistic-profile journalists, because it shows how good interviewing—*good conversation* and *good listen-ing*—can capture people's lives from the inside out. Studs Terkel's *Working* (1974) and *Good War* (1985) do the job. For a remarkable experience at feeling people's lives through their words, read anthropologist John Langston Gwalt-ney's *Drylongso* (1980), a collection in which ordinary African-Americans talk about their lives.

On the other end of the social-class spectrum, psychiatrist Dr. Robert Coles's *Privileged Ones* (1977), about how the children of well-to-do Americans see themselves and their insular worlds, illustrates how good listening can capture the interior sense of even children's lives. Pete Earley's *The Hot House* (1992) is a lesson in journalistic good listening as it reveals the bizarre minds of a hand-ful of unredeemed criminals in a federal prison. I've already mentioned James Agee's *Let Us Now Praise Famous Men* (1941), a classic blending of documen-tary and literary intent; *A Fortunate Man* (1981), John Berger and Jean Mohr's inquiry into the meaning an English country doctor finds in his life; Theodore Rosengarten's *All God's Dangers* (1974), the autobiography of a sharecropper; and Michael Lesy's chilling study of life in a rural midwestern town in the nineteenth century, *Wisconsin Death Trip* (1973).

From literature, it's silly to make a list. Reading any naturalistic fiction, novels or short stories, will help make you a better profile writer. So will read-ing books on the methods of biography such as *Telling Lives: The Biographer's Art* (1979) with essays by Leon Edel and others. So will taking courses in fic-tion and autobiographical writing. So will taking courses in the methods and assumptions of oral and documentary history, qualitative sociology, and an-thropology, all of which aim to understand people and their worlds in their own terms.

As for myself, every few years I reread Robert Penn Warren's *All the King's Men* (1946), the finest "profile" ever written.